Embassies in Armed Conflict

About the Series

Key Studies in Diplomacy is an innovative series of books on the procedures and processes of diplomacy, focusing on the interaction between states through their accredited representatives, that is, diplomats.

Thus its volumes focus on factors affecting foreign policy, and the ways in which it is implemented, through the apparatus of diplomacy – the diplomatic system – in both bilateral and multilateral contexts. But they also examine the how diplomats are sometimes able to shape not just the presentation but even the substance of their states' foreign policies.

Given that the diplomatic system is worldwide, all the series' volumes, whatever their individual focuses, contribute to an understanding of the nature of diplomacy. They do so authoritatively – in that they are written by scholars specializing in diplomacy and by former diplomats – and comprehensibly. They emphasize the actual practice of diplomacy, and analyze that practice in a clear and accessible manner, hence making them essential primary reading for both beginning practitioners and advanced level university students.

Embassies in Armed Conflict

G. R. Berridge

Key Studies in Diplomacy
Lorna Lloyd, Series Editor
Kai Bruns, Executive Assistant

2012

The Continuum International Publishing Group Inc
80 Maiden Lane, New York, NY 10038
The Tower Building, 11 York Road, London SE1 7NX

www.continuumbooks.com

ISBN 978-1-4411-8007-0 (PB)
978-1-4411-0462-5 (HB)

Library of Congress Cataloging-in-Publication Data
Berridge, Geoff.
Embassies in armed conflict / G. R. Berridge.
p. cm. -- (Key studies in diplomacy)
Includes bibliographical references and index.
ISBN-13: 978-1-4411-0462-5 (hardcover : alk. paper)
ISBN-10: 1-4411-0462-3 (hardcover : alk. paper)
ISBN-13: 978-1-4411-8007-0 (pbk. : alk. paper)
ISBN-10: 1-4411-8007-9 (pbk. : alk. paper) 1. Diplomatic and consular service. 2. Diplomatic and consular service, British. 3. Diplomatic and consular service, American. I. Title.
JZ1405.B48 2012
327.2--dc23
2011035217

Typeset by Fakenham Prepress Solutions, Fakenham, Norfolk

In memory of my grandfather, Pte. W. T. Jones, 1/5th Battalion, The Lincolnshire Regiment (1914–18)

Also by G. R. Berridge

BRITISH DIPLOMACY IN TURKEY, 1583 TO THE PRESENT: A study in the evolution of the resident embassy
THE COUNTER-REVOLUTION IN DIPLOMACY AND OTHER ESSAYS
A DICTIONARY OF DIPLOMACY (*with Alan James*) (*second edition*)
DIPLOMACY AT THE UN (*co-editor with A. Jennings*)
DIPLOMACY: Theory and practice, Fourth Edition
DIPLOMATIC CLASSIC: Selected texts from Commynes to Vattel
DIPLOMATIC THEORY FROM MACHIAVELLI TO KISSINGER (*with Maurice Keens-Soper and T. G. Otte*)
ECONOMIC POWER IN ANGLO-SOUTH AFRICAN DIPLOMACY: Simonstown, Sharpeville and after
GERALD FITZMAURICE (1865–1939), CHIEF DRAGOMAN OF THE BRITISH EMBASSY IN TURKEY
INTERNATIONAL POLITICS: States, power and conflict since 1945 (*third edition*)
AN INTRODUCTION TO INTERNATIONAL RELATIONS (*with D. Heater*)
THE POLITICS OF THE SOUTH AFRICA RUN: European shipping and Pretoria
RETURN TO THE UN: UN diplomacy in regional conflicts
SOUTH AFRICA, THE COLONIAL POWERS AND 'AFRICAN DEFENCE': The rise and fall of the white entente, 1948–60
TALKING TO THE ENEMY: How States without 'Diplomatic Relations' Communicate

Contents

Preface

I formed the plan to write this book after reviewing *Diplomats at War: British and Commonwealth Diplomacy in Wartime* (2008), a collection of essays edited by Christopher Baxter and Andrew Stewart. I thought they had come up with a good idea and gathered in some valuable work, and that the subject now merited pursuing further. In particular, I felt that it needed a more thematic treatment over a time period coming up to the present, and a focus broadened to include embassies in all forms of international armed conflict. I was able to proceed from the foothold already established in the subject by virtue of the chapter I had written on the Second World War experience of the British embassy at Ankara in my *British Diplomacy in Turkey* (2009).

For advice on particular points, I wish to express my warm thanks to Brian Barder, Ken Brown, Lorna Lloyd, Larry Pope, Antony Best, Kishan Rana, Keith Hamilton and John W. Young; and, for general support for the project, to Marie-Claire Antoine of Continuum and Margery Thompson of ADST.

G. R.B., Leicester, June 2011

List of abbreviations used in text and citations

BDOHP	British Diplomatic Oral History Programme
BIS	British Information Services
BSC	British Security Co-ordination [SIS station in New York in World War II]
CAC Cam.	Churchill Archives Centre, University of Cambridge
CentCom	US Central Command
CIA	Central Intelligence Agency [US]
CPA	Coalition Provisional Authority [in Iraq]
DCM	Deputy Chief of Mission
DfID	Department for International Development [British]
DGFP	*Documents on German Foreign Policy*
DIA	Defense Intelligence Agency [US]
DoD	*A Dictionary of Diplomacy [Berridge and James]*
DS List	*Diplomatic Service List [British]*
FAC	Foreign Affairs Committee [British House of Commons]
FAM	Foreign Affairs Manual [US Department of State]
FCO	Foreign and Commonwealth Office
FO	Foreign Office [British]
FRY	Federal Republic of Yugoslavia
FRUS	*Foreign Relations of the United States*
GPO	Government Printing Office [US]
HCPP	House of Commons Parliamentary Papers

ICRC	International Committee of the Red Cross
ILC	International Law Commission
IRD	Information Research Department
ISAF	International Security Assistance Force [in Afghanistan]
MACV	Military Assistance Command Vietnam
MoD	Ministry of Defence [British]
OSS	Office of Strategic Services
PCO	Passport Control Officer [British]
POWs	Prisoners of War
PRT	Provincial Reconstruction Team
SIS	Secret Intelligence Service/MI6
SOE	Special Operations Executive
SoS	Secretary of State
TNA	The National Archives [British]
UNSCR	United Nations Security Council Resolution
USFAOHC	*U.S. Foreign Affairs Oral History Collection* on CD-ROM (Arlington, VA: ADST, 2000)
VCCR	Vienna Convention on Consular Relations, 1963
VCDR	Vienna Convention on Diplomatic Relations, 1961

Introduction

In the long history of diplomacy, some embassies have been caught up in armed conflict in the most catastrophic fashion. For example, between 16 and 18 September 1963, at the outset of 'Confrontation' between Britain and Indonesia, the newly-built British embassy in Djakarta, as it was then known, was attacked by a large mob which looted its contents, terrorized its staff and then put it to the torch; the diplomats moved into temporary accommodation, where they remained for the duration of the conflict. In a different kind of situation, on 7 May 1999, in the course of the NATO air campaign against Yugoslavia during the Kosovo War, the Chinese embassy in Belgrade was struck by bombs launched from a US stealth bomber. This caused major damage and three deaths, and a dangerous dip in Sino–American relations.

The chief focus of this book, however, is not on the details of incidents such as those just described, but instead on the issue of how embassies come to find themselves in the sort of situations which can lead to them. Are the embassies of newly belligerent states, finding themselves within states suddenly turned enemies, not supposed to close their doors and depart in anticipation of fighting, and certainly once it has started? Is it really prudent for the embassies of any state to loiter in a war zone, especially if they are located cheek by jowl with military targets? If, in both such cases, they actually hang around, what are they up to? And how do they manage to stay in business? What, in addition, are the typical strategies of belligerent embassies more safely ensconced in neutral states, and those established with more or less security – depending on the style and fortunes of the conflict – in the states of frontline allies? In short, what do embassies which are alike in that they all find themselves touched in some way by armed conflict but different in their relations with their hosts, actually do – and how do they cope?

Why embassies in armed conflict and not embassies in war? This is because the term 'war' is still sometimes interpreted narrowly to signify only an armed conflict which has been formally declared, while this book deals with embassies in international armed conflict whether declared or not. It is important that it should do so because 'declaring war' went out of fashion in the twentieth century, with greatly gathering speed after the Second World War.[1] This seems to have occurred for three main reasons. First, war other than in self-defence was outlawed by the UN Charter. Second, revolutionary or protracted warfare, in which irregular forces are employed, became much more common than traditional military strategy; and the new form of warfare was neither controlled politically nor led in the field by men schooled in the old traditions and codes of honour. Third, declaring war forfeited the advantage of surprise, which was more important than ever in an era when science and engineering had so extended the power and reach of conventional military establishments.

If this book is to focus on what embassies do in international armed conflicts, it is as well to begin with a detailed look at their military component. This is not by any means to suggest that the embassy's other sections always become less important once the fighting starts. In some circumstances, any one of its political, commercial, consular and propaganda departments may have the decisive role. Nevertheless, except in the case of the belligerent embassy in a frontline ally (for reasons which will be noted in Chapter 5), all major embassies significantly affected by an armed conflict usually gain an enlarged military component. With enlargement inevitably comes greater influence; and, as a result, the military component, broadly defined, is often the leading actor in the play.

[1] As early as 1904, at the start of the Russo–Japanese War, Japan attacked Russia's naval forces outside Port Arthur before declaring war, although after breaking diplomatic relations, Piggott, *Broken Thread*, p. 24.

1 The Military Component

Chapter Overview

In the general wars of the twentieth century, the embassies of the major belligerents developed economic warfare sections and propaganda arms. However, the most distinctive feature of embassies touched by armed conflict, then and since, is a greatly strengthened military component. This consists of the service attachés in what is now usually called the 'defence section' or, in the US Foreign Service, the 'defense attaché's office'. For some embassies, notably those of belligerents in neutral states, this is usually the extent of their military component. In other embassies, however, particularly those of powerful belligerents in allied or otherwise closely related states, the defence section is merely the inner core of this component. In these situations, there are other service personnel more loosely associated with the embassy, who may in fact not only be far more numerous, but also senior to those in the defence section.

When the military component of the embassy is better funded than its diplomatic counterpart as well as numerically dominant, there is a real risk that the embassy will have a military outlook and style; in short, that it will be militarized. This will be even more likely if the embassy is apprehensive of attack, whether deliberate or accidental, because in these circumstances states may even go so far as to make their embassy buildings into fortresses. The militarization of embassies in armed conflict – which reached its apogee in the American concept of embassies as 'command posts' in the 'War on Terror' following the attacks on the World Trade Centre in New York and the Pentagon in Washington on 11 September 2001 – may well be unavoidable but it comes at a heavy political price. The full implications of this development are discussed in Chapter 5 because militarization is most likely to occur in embassies to front-line allies. For the moment, what does the military component look like and what does it do? What, too, of those intelligence officers in the embassy who are not service personnel but work closely with the military component? They also tend to multiply in times of armed conflict and can create problems for ambassadors asked to give them diplomatic cover.

The defence section

The defence section of an embassy contains its armed forces or service attachés, who are officers in the armed forces (air force, army or navy) temporarily attached to it.[1] Persons resembling service attachés had begun to appear in embassies in early modern Europe, but it was not until the second half of the nineteenth century that the appointing of recognizably modern ones began to be an entrenched habit of the major states.[2] Even in the first half of the twentieth century service attachés were not abundant in peacetime, and diplomatic missions at lesser capitals usually had to make do with an occasional visit from one based elsewhere. This applied even to American embassies,

[1] The term 'defence attaché' is also sometimes used for this group as a whole although the British, French, Americans, and no doubt others now usually reserve this title for the *senior* service attaché at a diplomatic mission. For other variations in terminology, see *DoD*.

[2] Hamilton and Langhorne, *The Practice of Diplomacy*, p. 125; Cecil, *The German Diplomatic Service*, pp. 124–5.

which had a surprisingly large number of service attachés in the inter-war period. Air attachés, who were often permitted to keep a light aircraft for their personal use, had the rapid mobility which suited them particularly well to side accreditations.[3] In 1931, Britain had a worldwide total of only 30 service attachés, and all but seven had responsibilities at other posts. For example, Wing Commander Ernest Johnston, one of five air attachés, was based in Buenos Aires but was also side accredited to Rio de Janeiro, Santiago and Montevideo. Only the British embassy in Washington had an air attaché with no responsibilities beyond the capital at which he was based.[4] At the beginning of the same year, half of all US service attachés also had side accreditations, some of them extensive. The air attaché, Major George Reinburg, for example, was based in Berlin, but was also accredited to six other posts.[5] Generally small in absolute terms in peacetime, as a rule embassy defence sections were also small relative to the diplomatic staff in the chancery or political section.

The minimum duties of service attachés have always included technical advice to the embassy on military matters and, above all, obtaining intelligence on the armed forces of the country or countries to which they are accredited: their numbers, equipment, training, geographical disposition, tactical and strategic doctrines, defensive fortifications, morale and so on. Among other skills they need for this are the ability to take photographs without attracting attention.[6] When relations are close, service attachés may well also be directly involved in organizing military collaboration – joint

[3] Side accreditations are convenient for sending states, but receiving ones given only a small proportion of the attention of an officer based elsewhere can sometimes regard this as demeaning, McLachlan, *Room 39*, p. 186.

[4] *FO List 1931*, p. 28.

[5] These were Berne, Copenhagen, Prague, Stockholm, The Hague and Vienna. It was not, however, only air attachés who were sometimes so itinerant. The US naval attaché, Lt. Eliot Bryant, was also accredited to seven different posts: Berlin, London, Paris, Rome, The Hague, Stockholm and Copenhagen, *Register of the Department of State*, 1 January 1931 (GPO: Washington, 1931).

[6] In the early 1970s, a week's training in this was thought by the British to be sufficient for a new military attaché going to a friendly country, but was

training exercises, officer exchanges, harmonization of weapons systems, defence sales and after-sales services and training, naval ship visits, visits in both directions by senior and other officers and units and so on. However, when relations with their hosts are tense, service attachés tend to find their functions restricted chiefly to intelligence gathering, which, in the circumstances, becomes both more important and more difficult. In neutral and unfriendly states, their known intelligence functions are also likely to lead to their harassment by the authorities, and – from time to time – to their expulsion.[7]

Franz von Papen, whose exploits as military attaché at the German embassy in Washington in the First World War are legendary and led, in December 1915, to his own expulsion (together with that of his naval colleague), observed in his memoirs that in wartime the duties of service attachés become 'much more onerous and complex'.[8] There is no doubt about this. In addition to their normal duties, they might be asked to take a lead in defending an embassy from attack, reassure and thereby discourage the premature flight of an edgy expatriate community, assist in the planning and carrying out of an emergency evacuation, and even organize the blowing up of a facility with military significance in a belligerent neighbouring the state to which they are accredited.[9] Naval attachés might be required to supervise the

considerably longer for an officer going to a hostile one, Raschen, *Diplomatic Dan*, pp. 15–16, 99–100.

[7] It is because of the sensitive nature of the work of service attachés that their appointment by Germany was completely banned under the terms of the 1919 Treaty of Versailles; this ban was not lifted until 1932, Hamilton and Langhorne, *The Practice of Diplomacy*, p. 192. For the same reason, the VCDR stipulates that, apart from the head of mission (for whom *agrément* is mandatory), the service attaché is the only member of the staff of a diplomatic mission whose name may, if the receiving state so requires, need to be submitted for approval prior to appointment and, in practice, this is something on which receiving states invariably insist.

[8] Papen, *Memoirs*, p. 30.

[9] Papen, *Memoirs*, ch. 3; Munro, *An Embassy at War*, p. 109; McNamara, *Escape with Honor*, pp. 86, 119–21; Bernstorff, *My Three Years in Germany*, pp. 91–2, 168–74.

security of shipping in a port;[10] and air attachés of a belligerent may be expected to negotiate an agreement on overflying rights with a neutral.[11] They might also be required to serve as a channel of communications to a potential ally through the network of service attachés at the post to which they are accredited, for these 'comrades in arms' tend to form a well-organized and often convivial sub-division of the diplomatic corps with their own *doyen*. [12] For example, against the background of the serious border clashes between the Soviet Union and the PRC in 1969, the senior Soviet service attaché in Tehran took the opportunity of a reception held by the Turkish military attaché to inform the US army attaché that his country would use tactical nuclear weapons against any major Chinese incursion into Soviet territory and that he expected that the United States would be their 'eventual ally' in the conflict.[13] In addition, service attachés might be asked to monitor the activities of any private military company based in their home state which is operating in the state of their accreditation; these companies are today extremely numerous and are also much involved in providing protection to diplomatic and consular premises.[14] And the defence sections of belligerent embassies in neutral states adjacent to the theatre of conflict, as we shall see in Chapter 4, are relied upon to cope with what at least in the past has been a particularly heavy duty: assisting escapers and evaders who have found their way into their parishes.

[10] McLachlan, *Room 39*, pp. 189–90.

[11] German Legation (Stockholm) to Air Attaché Group (Foreign Ministry, Berlin), 15 Sept. 1941, *DGFP*, pp. 508–9.

[12] Albeit in reference to the 'attaché corps' in a neutral state in peacetime (Sweden, 1970–3), a vivid account of the boozy intimacy that can be achieved by the service attachés of otherwise hostile states accredited to the same government, encouraged by the tendency of their hosts to treat them as a group on both professional and social occasions, is provided in the memoir of the British military attaché at Stockholm, Lt. Colonel Dan Raschen: *Diplomatic Dan*. On the attaché corps in pre-Second World War Japan, see Piggott, *Broken Thread*, pp. 70–5, 197–8, 278–80.

[13] Amembassy Tehran to State Dept., 4 Sept 1969, NSA, available at http://www.gwu.edu/~nsarchiv/NSAEBB/NSAEBB49/sino.sov.16.pdf

[14] HCPP (HC 922), 1 Aug. 2002: Ev 97, 2.3.2; HCPP (Cm 5642), Oct. 2002: Annex B.

With the great increase in the importance in armed conflict of its basic duties and the distinct prospect that its miscellaneous tasks might also multiply, it is hardly surprising that, in these circumstances, the defence section's overall numbers should usually swell dramatically, even coming to exceed those of the diplomats. A glance at the diplomatic service lists is sufficient to establish this point.

For example, the American embassy in Britain had only eight service attachés in 1937, two years prior to the outbreak of the Second World War, but this number had already risen to 12 by the beginning of 1940. By the end of 1943, by which time the United States had been fighting alongside Britain for two years, it had more than doubled and was only two short of the total of other regular diplomatic staff.[15] As for Britain itself, which at the end of 1943 had 107 service attachés worldwide (less than a fifth of which were by then burdened with side accreditations) compared to the 30 of 1931, the defence section of its embassy in Washington had more than tripled in size since 1939, despite the highly significant intelligence and related work being carried out in New York by British Security Co-ordination (see Chapter 4). As with the American embassy in London, it was by that time almost exactly the same size as the political section of the embassy.[16] Much later, against the background of the Vietnam War at the end of the 1960s, John Franklin Campbell noted that the Pentagon, lavishly funded and eager to increase its influence over foreign policy, employed '60 per cent *more* personnel within U.S. diplomatic missions abroad' than the State Department.[17]

As for the defence sections of belligerent embassies in strategically important neutral states, the US mission in Argentina in the

[15] There were 28 service attachés altogether: 22 military attachés, three naval attachés, and three air attachés (two War Dept. and one Navy Dept.). Side accreditations, which were not marked at this post in 1937, virtually disappeared altogether as German power spread across Europe, *Foreign Service List*, 31 Jan. 1944.

[16] Excluding the commercial section and the legal adviser, *FO Lists 1939* and *1944*.

[17] *The Foreign Affairs Fudge Factory*, p. 191.

Second World War may be taken as illustrative. At the beginning of 1940, there were only two service attachés in the American embassy in Buenos Aires; at the time of Pearl Harbor in December 1941, this number had already grown to five; and by the following July – with America itself now at war and anxious to pull Argentina in as well – Ambassador Norman Armour found himself with ten service attachés, again putting the defence section on a par with the political section.[18] The experience of the defence sections in the other US embassies in the important neutrals was very similar, except in landlocked Switzerland, where the Navy Department had no need of representation.[19] So, too, was the experience of the British embassies in the neutrals. At the British embassy in Turkey, for example, where Geoffrey Thompson arrived in May 1941 for a short spell as acting counsellor, what struck him most was the embassy's 'really formidable team' of service attachés; it was to become more formidable still, by the end of the war reaching twice the size of the diplomatic staff.[20]

A similar pattern can be seen, too, in the reverse situation: the case of embassies from neutrals to belligerents. This is a common occurrence when the neutrals have a close interest in the conflict concerned. For example, the number of military attachés at the British embassy in Turkey shot up during the Russo–Turkish War in 1877–8, and did likewise at the British legations in Tokyo and Peking during the Russo–Japanese War in 1904–5.[21] By the middle of the Second World War, the defence section of the Swedish legation in London – which had been strong for most of the jittery 1930s and was desperately anxious about British military plans for Scandinavia – had gone up from two officers in 1937 to five by 1943, and represented a third of the entire diplomatic staff; the number rose to six in the following year.[22] A further indication of

[18] *Foreign Service Lists*: 1940, 1942 and 1943.

[19] *Foreign Service List*, 1 Jan. 1943.

[20] *Front Line Diplomat*, p. 166. I have described the growth of the defence section at Ankara in *British Diplomacy in Turkey*, pp. 178–9.

[21] Berridge, *British Diplomacy in Turkey*, p. 44; Nish, 'British legations in Tokyo and Beijing during the Russo–Japanese War, 1904–1905'.

[22] *FO List*.

the Stockholm government's anxiety to strengthen this defence section was the presence among these new appointees of the 'very gifted and efficient' (and well-connected) Captain Count Oxenstierna as naval attaché.[23]

In the Western diplomatic tradition, the service attachés – like all other attachés – are required to accept the authority of the head of the mission in which they serve. However, their primary allegiance is to the military establishment on which they depend for their promotion, and it is to armed forces intelligence headquarters at home or to a defence ministry, or both, that they report. In the case of the United States, the CIA, which evolved in 1947 from the wartime Office of Strategic Services (OSS), also soon acquired the right to brief all newly appointed US service attachés on its 'collection requirements', so presumably they had to report to the agency as well.[24] The usual procedure has always been that these reports, which are sometimes of considerable political significance, should certainly be shown to the head of mission, who has a right to comment on them. However, in the past this rule was often ignored by service attachés and it would be surprising if this tendency were now extinct. Furthermore, armed forces personnel who are any good sometimes fit uneasily into the atmosphere and routines of an embassy (or too easily if they are not, or are close to retirement[25]), and can jeopardize a head of mission's own good relations with the local foreign ministry by engaging in illegal activities. When the defence section is large, it is not unusual to find it housed separately from the building containing the chancery, which was for example the case with the British mission in Berlin, the Japanese mission in

[23] Denham, *Inside the Nazi Ring*, pp. 68–9.

[24] http://www.foia.cia.gov/cgi/1950/Briefing_of_Service_Attaches_by_CIA_9_May_1950.PDF.

[25] The Church Committee found that many US service attachés were overly fond of representational and protocol duties, partly because the best officers were not attracted to the work (which presented poor promotion prospects) and partly because – as a consequence of this – a high proportion consisted of those on their last tours before retirement. In 1969, 38 of them had been dismissed outright for incompetence but even so little had changed, Church Committee Report, p. 353.

London in the 1930s and the Soviet mission in London during the Cold War.[26] It might even be based in a different city, as in the First World War, when the German military and naval attachés both had their own offices in New York while the embassy, of course, was located in Washington.[27] In short, for all of these reasons, service attachés are 'inclined to regard themselves as in, but not of, the Embassy.'[28] This can make for uneasy relations in the embassy under peacetime conditions, especially if the military establishment and the foreign ministry are tugging in different directions. This was notorious in the case of some German embassies – not least the one in London – in the years before and during the First World War.[29]

Against this background, it might be imagined that in war itself there is even greater potential for trouble between the defence section and the chancery because, as we have seen, the former is always greatly strengthened in these circumstances. But as it happens, this is not usually the case. One reason for this is that in these circumstances the diplomats tend to become more dependent on the defence section and thus less disposed to quarrel with it. To start with, the intelligence it provides will become more important as security worries – particularly in allied frontline states – inhibits the ability of the diplomatic staff to travel much beyond the embassy's walls. Sometimes, too, the embassy is dependent on the defence section for access to the local defence ministry and service chiefs, which is the more important because their political influence relative to that of the foreign ministry always tends to rise in war and near-war situations.[30] William Clark, the American ambassador in Delhi in 1989–92,

[26] Wark, 'Three military attachés at Berlin in the 1930s', p. 587; Berridge, *The Counter-Revolution in Diplomacy*, pp. 72–3; TNA, KV2/2471 (MI5 file on Matsumoto).

[27] Bernstorff, *My Three Years in America*, pp. 35–6.

[28] Hoare, *Ambassador on Special Mission*, p. 130.

[29] Cecil, *The German Diplomatic Service*, pp. 126–38; Bernstorff, *My Three Years in America*, pp. 36, 91–2.

[30] For example: Hoare, *Ambassador on Special Mission*, p. 50.

found this in regard to his own service staff and India's military establishment.[31]

Besides, the embassy's defence section is no more immune to the influence of local opinion – even to 'going native' – than its diplomats. A classic case in point is Major-General F. S. G. Piggott, who was twice military attaché at the British embassy in Japan (1921–6 and 1936–9) and was so devoted to the country that he could believe nothing bad of it. 'To the very last, indeed,' writes someone who knew him well, 'the "shadow" side of Japan continued to be invisible to him.'[32] Living in the same environment and mixing in at least some of the same local circles, service personnel and diplomats will inevitably tend to reinforce each other's views on the need to face local political and strategic realities. It was via this mechanism that the defence section of the British embassy in Ankara in the Second World War became an important ally of the ambassador in support of his view – against that of the prime minister, Winston Churchill – that Turkey's defences against German air attack were so inadequate that it would be disastrous to try to push it too quickly into the fight against Hitler.[33] In war conditions, too, and especially if the embassy is in constant danger of deliberate or accidental attack, there is always considerable pressure on all personnel to pull together – and much more willingness to cooperate in daily meetings of section heads with the chief of mission designed to ensure that each knows what they have to do to achieve the embassy's objectives.[34] If the chief of mission has great personal authority, like Ellsworth Bunker, who was US ambassador at Saigon in some of the worst years of the Vietnam War (see Chapter 5), so much the better. The need for a head of mission 'who could assert himself against an independent-minded military attaché' had been recognised by the German Foreign Office well before the

[31] Clark interview.
[32] Blacker, 'Two Piggotts', pp. 124–5.
[33] Berridge, *British Diplomacy in Turkey*, pp. 176–7, 200.
[34] Hoare, *Ambassador on Special Mission*, pp. 130–1; Berridge, *British Diplomacy in Turkey*, p. 179.

First World War.[35] In the end, then, in wartime there is usually a good working relationship between the chancery and the defence section, or at least better than might at first sight be expected.

It is important to add that close allies in a major conflict may be so anxious to coordinate military matters that an embassy defence section is totally inadequate to their purposes. As a result, the various branches of their armed services may agree to exchange their own permanent liaison missions or 'delegations' and poach the more able members of the staff of the embassy defence section. The result is that the remainder are relegated to largely representational duties and the task of keeping in touch with any smaller states to which they may be side accredited. Something like this was a marked feature particularly of Britain's military–military relations with the United States in the Second World War. Separate service liaison missions – known as the British Army Staff (BAS), British Admiralty Delegation, and Royal Air Force Delegation (RAFDEL) – were discreetly established in Washington while the United States was still neutral and blossomed after Pearl Harbor. They functioned collectively as the Joint Staff Mission – the embassy defence section writ large. Among other personnel changes, the former military attaché at the British embassy was made deputy to the new commander of the British Army Staff while the naval attaché stayed put and was accordingly 'lost to view'. [36] These permanent service missions quite dwarfed the embassy's rump defence section. At its high point in mid-1944 British Army Staff alone had 400 officers, 500 other ranks and over 1000 civilians (mainly locally engaged staff), spread over North America.[37]

[35] Cecil, *The German Diplomatic Service*, p. 128.

[36] McLachlan, *Room 39*, p. 52.

[37] TNA website, Admin Histories of BAS and RAFDEL; on RAFDEL, see also Guinn, *The Arnold Scheme*, p. 186.

Military advisers

Embassies in armed conflict, especially those of major powers in smaller friendly states, also have to cope with an influx of service personnel, usually only advisers, trainers or instructors, but sometimes major combat formations. Military advisers and even special forces officers may be formally attached (openly or under cover) to the embassy and, in the case of the United States, almost always have been, certainly since the Second World War.[38] If the influx of such personnel is a large one, the militarization of the embassy is by that degree further advanced.

The British embassy in Turkey in the Second World War is once more a case in point. Beginning in late 1937, there was a great increase in the number of British instructors attached to the Turkish armed forces. They attended embassy social occasions and, informally, were useful propagandists and information-gatherers. It is not surprising, therefore, that the British ambassador in Ankara, Sir Hughe Knatchbull-Hugessen, regarded them as members of his own staff – and therefore the main reason for the explosion in its size.[39] In fact, when the embassy did a head count in early 1944 of all those requiring foreign ministry identity cards, it was found that in November 1943 there had been 104 men and women nominally attached to the defence section, and in April 1944 160 – although the number of service attachés at the Ankara embassy during the war never exceeded 14.[40] But this was not all, for the headquarters for sabotage operations into the German-occupied Balkans of the Special Operations Executive (SOE), as also for its post-occupation contingency preparations in Turkey itself, was housed in the embassy's main consular post: the consulate-

[38] Under the typical mutual defense assistance agreement born of the Cold War era, the senior US officers in charge of a military assistance mission generally had full diplomatic status while its other members had the more or less limited privileges – depending on their rank – which corresponded to those of the different categories of non-diplomatic embassy staff, Prugh, *Law at War*, pp. 87–8.

[39] Berridge, *British Diplomacy in Turkey*, p. 179.

[40] Berridge, *British Diplomacy in Turkey*, p. 179.

general in Istanbul. SOE's Turkey section was disguised as the 'Shipping Department, Ministry of War Transport'.[41]

Like permanent service liaison missions to major allies, the arrival of military assistance missions and even more so large fighting formations, can swamp an embassy defence section, at best sidelining it and at worst making it seem an expensive bureaucratic irritant. In the latter event, it may be dissolved altogether, as happened at the US embassy in Saigon in the 1960s, where the US Military Assistance Advisory Group (MAAG) in South Vietnam – with which the embassy was obliged to work intimately in the 'US Mission' and which was soon to be absorbed by Military Assistance Command, Vietnam (MACV) – had grown to gargantuan proportions by 1963.[42] To take another example, in Afghanistan and Iraq, following the massive Western military interventions of 2001 and 2003 respectively, the British embassies also had no defence section.[43]

Sometimes it is agreed that the military visitors should install their headquarters in the embassy building or compound. For example, for some time after early August 1990 the British forces component of the anti-Iraq coalition being built up in Saudi Arabia was headquartered in the chancery of the British embassy in Riyadh; the Commander, British Forces Middle East (BFME), occupied the office next door to the ambassador.[44] The US ambassador to Saudi Arabia, Chas Freeman, and the Coalition

[41] Berridge, *British Diplomacy in Turkey*, pp. 182–93.

[42] Flott interview. However, following the Paris Peace Accords of January 1973 and the winding up of MACV, the defence attachés office (DAO) in the embassy took over the latter's headquarters, thus becoming 'The largest Defense Attaché Office in the world', Brown, Frederick Z., interview; see also Dunlop interview. This consisted largely of civilian employees of the Department of Defense but also 50 military personnel, Helble interview.

[43] Although by 2005–6 the head of each mission had acquired a solitary defence attaché, *Diplomatic Service List* 2003–6.

[44] Eventually, the British military HQ outgrew the chancery and moved to offices nearer to the main joint command centre in the Saudi Defence Ministry and the USAF headquarters, although Royal Air Force intelligence and elements of its communications remained in the embassy compound, Munro, *An Embassy at War*, pp. 79–80, 179.

commander-in-chief, General Schwarzkopf, were also 'co-located' in Riyadh during this war.[45]

Since the 9/11 attacks on the United States and the declaration of the 'War on Terror', many US embassies – not just those in Afghanistan and Iraq – have acquired an 'Office of Defense Cooperation' to coordinate new and lavishly funded security assistance programmes, not to mention teams of special forces officers and military propagandists ('public affairs' personnel). These US embassies have been christened 'command posts' in the War on Terror.[46] This is the militarization of the embassy taken to extremes, and sometimes this is underlined by the face its buildings present to the city in which it is located.

Intelligence officers under diplomatic cover

Civilian intelligence officers multiplied in the Second World War and some continued to use non-official cover as businessmen, journalists and so on.[47] Nevertheless, it is reasonably certain that the war years witnessed a relative increase in those given official cover in embassies and consulates, and not only in positions such as assistant commercial secretary, press attaché and vice-consul, where recruitment from outside the regular diplomatic service was quite common and would therefore be less likely to arouse suspicion. It is also reasonably certain that this trend continued afterwards. Intelligence officers operating under diplomatic cover usually work closely with the military component of the embassy. In the case of the British Secret Intelligence Service (SIS), which had long campaigned for diplomatic cover for its officers, this trend was given a strong push by the Bland report on the post-war organization of the service which was produced at the end of 1944.[48] Indeed, although he was an accomplished

[45] Freeman interview.

[46] 'Embassies as Command Posts in the Anti-Terror Campaign'.

[47] This sort of cover is also known as 'natural' or 'deep' cover.

[48] Previously, an SIS station chief regularly had cover as a Passport Control Officer (PCO), who in this capacity was attached to a consulate or consular

liar and notorious traitor to his country, there is no reason to doubt the assertion of the senior British intelligence officer, Kim Philby, that after the Second World War 'the great majority' of SIS officers serving abroad were posted in British embassies, where they were given the rank of first, second or third secretary, depending on their seniority, while a few were 'stashed away as simple attachés or as junior Information Officers.' At posts such as Paris and Washington, some were even appointed with the high rank of counsellor.[49] Philby himself had cover as a first secretary at the British embassy in Turkey while head of the SIS station in that country in the late 1940s.[50] Another colourful example is the master of the spy novel, David Cornwell, better known as John le Carré, who gathered the material for some of his writing (as well as material for other purposes) as an SIS agent with cover as a second secretary in the British embassy in Bonn in the early 1960s, and then briefly as a 'political consul' in the large consulate-general in Hamburg.[51] As for the operatives of the CIA, it is a matter of record that they, too, became heavily dependent on cover in US embassies and consulates, even though the resources available to the agency gave it more opportunities to provide

section but had neither diplomatic nor even consular status. PCOs had also become well known for what they really were, Jefferey, *MI6*, pp. 302, 314, 603–4; Andrew, *Secret Service*, p. 351.

[49] Philby, *My Silent War*, p. 124. The official history neither confirms nor denies Philby's claim that 'the great majority' of SIS officers were given diplomatic cover after the war but it provides examples of some who enjoyed this protection. Some others named simply as heads of station in a particular country can also be found in the *FO List*: for example, Tony Brooks, third secretary at Sofia; Nigel Clive, second secretary at Athens; and Rex Bosley, second secretary (information), at Helsinki, Jefferey, *MI6*, pp. 672, 674, 684.

[50] Berridge, *British Diplomacy in Turkey*, pp. 207–8.

[51] Author's official website. According to Cornwell's statement of services in the *FO List 1965*, he joined the Foreign Service on 27 June 1960, was appointed second secretary at Bonn not until a year later, and resigned on 29 February 1964. His time at Hamburg must have been very brief because there is no mention of his name on the list of consular staff there in either the *FO List 1963* or *1964*. If he had been he would not have been described as 'political consul' or 'consul (political)' but simply as 'consul', as opposed to 'consul (commercial)' or 'consul (information')'.

them with non-official cover.[52] There is no reason to suppose that the pattern was much different with other states. Why should this be so?

First, diplomatic cover gives maximum security to intelligence officers because of the privileges and immunities that come with it: maximum security to the secrets held in their heads and – since mission premises are inviolable – to those held in their files as well as to their equipment, especially their communications.[53] Even in states with large US military missions, where many CIA agents were also able to obtain cover, the CIA command post remained in the embassy.[54] Second, an official position in an embassy gives intelligence officers ready access – socially as well as officially – to at least some of the people on or from whom they may need to obtain information, and in many cases with whom they need to be able to collaborate. This is particularly true of those officers working for influential services like the CIA.[55] Third, the privileges of diplomatic status together with the vagueness of some embassy job descriptions (for example, 'first secretary') provide the intelligence officer with much greater mobility from day to day than that available to most working under non-official cover ('NOCs'), which is in any case much more difficult to set up and wearing on officers.[56] Fourth, the task of preserving diplomatic cover – even if they are worried about this – need not distract intelligence officers very much from their real work since a great deal of what, say, a political officer in an embassy would do is also what an intelligence officer would have to do anyway. The same is not true for most of those using deep cover, as in the case of the SIS officer appointed head of station in Tokyo in 1947 with cover as a

[52] Stockwell, *In Search of Enemies*, pp. 41, 49, 63.

[53] The protection afforded by *consular* status is still not as strong.

[54] Marks, 'How to spot a spook'.

[55] Stockwell, *In Search of Enemies*, p. 46.

[56] On the drawbacks of the CIA's huge 'proprietaries' (companies set up by the agency itself to provide cover for its officers as well as services in support of its special operations), see the Church Committee, Book I, Foreign and Military Intelligence, ch. XI. See also Stockwell, *In Search of Enemies*, pp. 112–13; and Dreyfuss, 'The CIA crosses over'.

university professor, who found he had insufficient time to serve in this capacity while carrying a full teaching load.[57]

Although the advantages of official compared to non-official cover for intelligence officers are, therefore, overwhelming, official cover is usually transparent to the local authorities. This is chiefly because embassies tend to be the subject of careful surveillance, intelligence officers with diplomatic immunity can be astonishingly careless, and diplomatic service lists sometimes make it child's play to form a shrewd idea of their identity.[58] However, this usually matters little since intelligence officers are handlers or case officers, rather than field agents, so it is unlikely that they will be caught 'red-handed'; if they employ 'cut-outs', although this is reputedly difficult, this will be less likely still.[59] In any case, intelligence officers based in embassies in friendly or neutral states usually have standing instructions not to work against their hosts, and actually introduce themselves to their local counterparts so that they can engage in joint action against common enemies – indigenous groups or states in the region.[60] In less friendly relationships, where good relations of this sort are impossible, there is nevertheless usually an understanding that each will be willing to extend diplomatic immunity to the officers of the other on the basis of reciprocity: unless they are caught red-handed or are appearing in threatening numbers, the local security service

[57] In the event another officer had to be '*more conventionally* installed in the British mission in Tokyo,' Jefferey, *MI6*, p. 704 (emphasis added).

[58] SIS officers at British embassies were often those among the few in the *FO List* who were given only 'local rank' (for example, as second secretary) and had either no 'statement of service' or a suspiciously truncated one. Similar clues in the Department of State's analogous lists made it possible also to be fairly sure of the identity of the CIA operatives given cover in US embassies, Marks, 'How to spot a spook'. Many of the US lists (*Register of the Department of State* and *Foreign Service List*) up to the mid-1960s can now be seen via a search on the 'Internet Archive' at http://www.archive.org/ On the traditional carelessness of CIA personnel, see Stockwell, *In Search of Enemies*, pp. 116–17.

[59] Jefferey, *MI6*, pp. 661–2, 672–3.

[60] Stockwell, *In Search of Enemies*, pp. 46, 49. Although today's friend may be tomorrow's enemy, and agent networks cannot be created overnight, Jefferey, *MI6*, p. 677.

will be unlikely to make a fuss about them for fear of provoking retaliation against its own.[61]

But matters are not always as cosy as this. In armed conflict, and especially where terrorist groups are active, the lives of intelligence officers are at risk if they are exposed. It is for these reasons that greater efforts are now made to conceal the identities of embassy-based officers even at a time when it has been accepted that there should in general be more transparency about secret intelligence organizations. Thus in the mid-1970s the US State Department ceased publication of the lists which made it possible to identify CIA officers without too much difficulty. The Church Committee on intelligence activities – at the request of the CIA – also deleted the section headed 'Support: Cover' from the chapter on the State Department in the published version of its final report which appeared in April 1976.[62]

Nor should it be forgotten that espionage is prohibited under diplomatic and consular law.[63] As a result, there has always been a fear on the part of heads of diplomatic missions that they will be embarrassed by the intelligence officers they are required to harbour. This is particularly true when they work for services which – like SIS and the CIA – have responsibility for special operations as well as intelligence-gathering.[64] After all, sometimes they do work against the country in which they are stationed, even when it is friendly. When the numbers of intelligence officers

[61] Berridge, *The Counter-Revolution in Diplomacy* ('Specific reciprocity and the 105 Soviet spies'); Marks, 'How to spot a spook'.

[62] Church Committee Report, p. 315 n 17a. The British *FO List* (later renamed the *Diplomatic Service List*) ceased publication after 2006, ostensibly only for reasons of economy.

[63] The VCDR (article 3) and the VCCR (article 5) both emphasize that missions are only entitled to obtain information on the receiving state by 'lawful means'. The charge of espionage – euphemistically described as 'activities incompatible with their status' – is a common reason for expelling diplomats, Denza, *Diplomatic Law*, pp. 77–8.

[64] During the Second World War British ambassadors had tended to see SIS officers as their allies against the far noisier SOE agents and accordingly treated them more indulgently. However, SOE was disbanded after 1945 and 'special operations' duties were given to SIS, Jefferey, *MI6*, pp. 628–9, 656, 660.

are excessive and their funds lavish, heads of mission also tend to fear that they will be by-passed or manipulated by them – even overshadowed by chiefs of station in their relations with the local head of state.[65] Long gone are the days when an ambassador could refuse on grounds such as these to give cover to any intelligence officers at all, as some British ambassadors did even after the Second World War. Nevertheless, some steps have had to be taken to provide them with reassurance. In the United States, this need became urgent following the exposure in the early 1970s of the extent and nature of the covert operations of the CIA, by which time more than a quarter of all US 'diplomats' posted abroad were members of the agency, which also controlled most diplomatic communications.[66]

In the United States, agreements have been negotiated between the intelligence community and the State Department about the percentage of intelligence officers able to enjoy cover at any given post.[67] A cap on numbers is important because the more intelligence officers are sheltered by an embassy or consular post, the more difficult it is to give them things to do to lend substance to their cover, the more they are likely to dominate embassy decision-making, and the more threatening the embassy will seem to the receiving state. Limits on numbers might also be part of tacit understandings between unfriendly states based on reciprocity. The requirement that no 'special operations' should be permitted without high-level political authorisation seems also to be a rule commanding some respect. Above all, there is the norm, strongly reinforced in regard to the CIA by the Church Committee's final report in 1976, that the chief of mission is indeed the chief and should, therefore, be given the kind of detailed guidance and political support needed for effective supervision of all intelligence officers – in their espionage activities as well as in special operations.[68]

[65] Stockwell, *In Search of Enemies*, p. 63; Church Committee Report, ch. XIV.

[66] Marks, 'How to spot a spook'; Church Committee Report, p. 315.

[67] Private information.

[68] Church Committee Report, pp. 308–15, 466–9.

Conclusion

In armed conflict, the basic duties of the embassy's defence section usually assume more importance and its miscellaneous tasks tend to multiply. As a result, it is common for its overall numbers to swell dramatically, sometimes exceeding those of the diplomats. Nevertheless, while service attachés are inclined to regard themselves as occupying a world of their own, which can produce tensions within the embassy in quiet times, their relations with the diplomats tend to improve in wartime, not least because in these circumstances their value becomes more obvious. As for the outer core of the military component, military advisers arriving in large numbers can strengthen the defence section, but in extremely large numbers can swamp it altogether and even lead to its dissolution. For their part, intelligence officers have tended to become an increasingly important auxiliary to the embassy defence section during armed conflict and in some circumstances probably dwarfed it in numbers. Diplomatic cover has overwhelming advantages for them, although its price is that they are usually well known to the local security services and – if they are not very careful – cause periodic tensions with the head of mission.

2 Embassies in Enemy States

Chapter Overview

When diplomatic relations between two states are severed as a prelude to armed conflict, as was traditionally the case, or are broken at some later point in the fighting, as has tended to be the case in recent times, any embassy involved is entirely at the mercy of a hostile government and its more or less aroused populace. In this situation, the receiving state usually isolates the embassy at once while its fate is determined. The decision might be that embassy staff are permitted to depart promptly or that they are to be interned until an exchange of diplomats with the sending state can be negotiated. Alternatively, in an encouraging development of recent times, diplomatic relations might not be broken at all, with the result that the embassies are left in place for the duration, although usually permitted to perform only the most limited diplomatic functions, if any at all. Which of these possibilities comes to pass is determined in large part by the nature of the relationship between the belligerents, but what happens to the diplomats, as well as to their property and the mission premises, is also shaped in some degree by international law.

The different circumstances in which a diplomatic mission might be terminated, and especially the extent and durability of privileges and immunities beyond this point, have always been important elements of diplomatic law and not especially controversial ones. Indeed, long before the Vienna Convention on Diplomatic Relations (1961) entered into force the rules were clearly and firmly established in customary law. As a result, they caused little debate either in the International Law Commission (ILC) when diplomatic law was being codified in the 1950s, or at the UN conference in Vienna in 1961 when the ILC's recommendations were considered. What do these rules say?

First, the diplomats must be permitted a speedy departure and given official assistance in this if they cannot do it under their own steam.[1] However, there is an important qualification to this rule. Locally engaged staff who are nationals of the receiving state – as most are – do not enjoy the right to depart with the foreign diplomats, let alone have assisted passage. This qualification was added at the Vienna conference at the instigation of the British delegation, which on this point was vocally supported among others by the Soviet Union and its allies.[2] Clearly, states do not relish the prospect of seeing their own citizens flee with the enemy, especially if they are of military age and carry with them valuable intelligence.

Second, the departing diplomats are still entitled to their full privileges and immunities until they leave the country even though their diplomatic functions have ceased. The only qualification to this rule is that they should not take too long about getting out: their immunities will be forfeit if they linger beyond

[1] VCDR, Art. 44. For brief discussion, see Denza, *Diplomatic Law*, pp. 481–3. Sometimes diplomats do not wish to return home on the outbreak of war, usually because they have disavowed the policies of their own government. Duly resigning their positions, they are treated as honoured guests by the receiving state. Such was the case with the heads of legation in London of Romania (Viorel Tilea, 1940) and Bulgaria (Nicholas Momtchiloff, 1941), Rendel, *The Sword and the Olive*, pp. 181–2.

[2] VCDR, Art. 44; *UN Conference on Diplomatic Intercourse and Immunities*, pp. 214–17.

'a reasonable period'.[3] This period varies greatly but states have tended to be relatively generous to those diplomats with the responsibility of winding up a mission.[4]

Third, the receiving state must 'respect and protect' the premises and any archives and other property the diplomats have had to leave behind. (However, this does not mean that the premises themselves remain inviolable indefinitely, that is, beyond the short period analogous to that in which the diplomatic staff are permitted to retain full immunities until they leave the country.)[5] Furthermore, the sending state may appoint a protecting power to look after them, as also to protect its other remaining interests.[6]

The initial siege

Even when the prompt departure of the personnel of an embassy is expected to be permitted in the event of hostilities, its numbers are usually run down. This is chiefly because dependants and non-essential staff are sent home or directed to other posts for safety reasons. However, it may also be because of pressure from a receiving state apprehensive about what a fully-staffed embassy – especially its service attachés and intelligence officers – might get up to in the meantime. Seven diplomats and a security guard were expelled from the Iraqi embassy in London on 3 January 1991– a month before relations between Britain and Iraq were finally broken in the Gulf War – as a result of 'near-panic' on the part of the British government that chemical or biological weapons might have been smuggled into the mission.[7] As for the Iraqi embassy

[3] VCDR, Art. 39.2.

[4] Denza, *Diplomatic Law*, p. 437.

[5] VCDR, Art. 45(a). The convention itself is silent on this point but this view is supported by state practice and by analogy from Art. 39.2, Denza, *Diplomatic Law*, p. 490.

[6] VCDR, Art. 45(b) and (c). This subject is discussed at length in Chapter 3.

[7] Urban, *UK Eyes Alpha*, p. 167; BBC Home, 'On this day, 1950–2005: 3 January' [www]. Subsequently, it was found to contain only conventional small arms and ammunition, probably for use against opponents of Saddam resident in Britain, *The Times*, 9 June 2005.

in Saudi Arabia at the same juncture, this was also reduced to a skeleton staff long before relations were formally broken between Riyadh and Baghdad.[8]

Immediately following the start of hostilities, restrictions are placed on the enemy embassy, although these tend to vary with the tone of the relationship, the political culture of the receiving state and the political weight of its foreign ministry – which, naturally more conscious of the implications of the principle of reciprocity, generally favours correct treatment of diplomats.

The first right to be restricted is freedom of movement. Even in the most liberal states the police presence around an enemy embassy is usually increased and elsewhere the military may be employed to guard it. Any gates on a perimeter boundary are locked and no-one is allowed in or out without special permission, and then often only with an escort. The American embassy in Rome and the Italian embassy in Washington enjoyed relatively liberal application of this general rule for some months following Mussolini's declaration of war on the United States in December 1941.[9] So, too, did the Japanese embassy in London during the same period, this on the testimony of what he thought was a secret letter to his father written during his later internment by the Western-educated Kaoru Matsumoto, an honorary attaché on the embassy staff:

> At first we were quite free to go out, and then after about a week [wrote Matsumoto], we were allowed to go out only with police escort, and then again changed as the police no doubt found escorting us rather troublesome. Allowed to go out for shopping etc. without escort once in 3 days. Every day walk in Hyde Park, but only in Hyde Park, without escort any time until the black-out time. We gave the word of honour not to go out of the Park. … I used this freedom fairly well and

[8] Munro, *An Embassy at War*, pp. 98, 283.

[9] SoS to Dip. Reps. in the American Republics, 18 Dec. 1941; Memo of Conversation, by Asst. SoS (Long), 12 Jan. 1942; Memo. by Keeley to Jones, 2 Feb. 1942; and Swiss Minister to SoS, 2 Mar. 1942, *FRUS, 1942*. Vol. I, pp. 288, 302–3, 307, and 323–4 resp.

> went to cinema, theatre, dined once and lunched once at a restaurant and even visited some friends![10]

The Allied embassies in Tokyo were not indulged to the same extent.[11]

Particular importance is also attached to cutting embassy communications. For example, within five hours of the expiry of the British ultimatum to Germany at 11am on 3 September 1939, all of the telephone lines of the British embassy in Berlin were cut;[12] in the four days following the Japanese attack on Pearl Harbor in December 1941 and the German declaration of war on the United States, first the telegraph office in Berlin refused to accept telegrams from the American embassy, and then its telephones 'mysteriously ceased to function';[13] and the embassies on each side of the line-up in the impending Gulf War in late 1990 and the first days of 1991 suffered a similar fate, although this conflict also demonstrated that, while their power source lasted, radios had made it more difficult for embassy communications to be cut altogether[14] – unless, that is, the embassy were to be entered and the equipment seized. In the Second World War, the Japanese authorities, without notice and only hours after the attack on Pearl Harbor, entered the still fully occupied American embassy in Tokyo and politely stole every short-wave radio set in the building.[15] Other enemy embassies suffered likewise at the hands of the Japanese. It is true that, in the first days of an embassy siege in the Second World War, it was not unusual to find that telegrams

[10] TNA, letter to his father, 15–19 Mar. 1942, Security Service: Personal file on Kaoru Matsumoto, KV2/2471.

[11] Craigie, *Behind the Japanese Mask*, ch. 22; Grew, *Ten Years in Japan*, pp. 493–5.

[12] Henderson, *Failure of a Mission*, p. 285.

[13] Kennan, *Memoirs*, p. 135.

[14] *New York Times*, 25 Jan. 1991; HCPP (143-I), 9 July 1991, pp. 16–25. On surviving radio-telephone links to embassies in Kuwait City: Munro, *An Embassy at War*, p. 121, and Bodine, 'Saddam's siege of Embassy Kuwait', pp. 123, 129. The US embassy in Kuwait City also discovered and reactivated a number of dormant local telephone lines which proved valuable.

[15] Grew, *Ten Years in Japan*, p. 494.

would still be accepted provided they were not in cypher but in the circumstances this was of very limited use.[16]

Occasionally an embassy might find that its other lifelines to the outside world are also severed. At the start of the Suez War in November 1956, all electricity to the British embassy in Cairo was cut off for two days.[17] Most draconian of all was the truly medieval siege laid to the embassies in Kuwait City which were rightly instructed to stay put, notwithstanding the demand issued by Saddam Hussein on 9 August 1990, following occupation of the capital by his forces a week earlier, that, since Kuwait was now a province of Iraq rather than a sovereign state, they had two weeks 'to either close, convert to consulates, or face being forced out, at gunpoint if necessary.'[18] Since any of their staff remaining after the deadline of 24 August would – in the Iraqi view – no longer be diplomatic officers, they would be liable to arrest and use as 'human shields' against the bombing of key installations, along with other Western hostages already being made to serve this purpose; meanwhile, they would be entitled to no special protection against popular hostility.

On expiry of the ultimatum, Saddam blinked at using force against the embassies in Kuwait and instead cut completely their telephone connections (hitherto only interrupted intermittently), electricity, water, food and medical supplies. The larger and better resourced embassies were able to hang on for some time and by various means – and varying degrees – to provide support to their nationals trapped (some in hiding) in the short-lived 'province', as well as symbolise resistance. However, most were forced to give up by early October and, after the French and Canadian embassies pulled out at the end of the month, only those of the United States and Britain remained. The Americans and the British managed to hold out until December, when – considering their jobs to have been done and it was likely that war was just a matter of time

[16] Grew, *Ten Years in Japan*, pp. 493–4; TNA, FO to Helsingfors, 1 Aug. 1941, FO371/29385.

[17] Trevelyan, *The Middle East in Revolution*, p. 117.

[18] Bodine, 'Saddam's siege of Embassy Kuwait', p. 114.

– they were permitted by the Iraqis to depart.[19] The Americans had survived with the assistance of a small generator and, above all, by successfully digging – against all the odds – a well which produced clean water at 200 gallons a minute;[20] the British, who had been growing their own vegetables, were inspired by the American example and successfully dug a well of their own.[21]

With war impending or actually begun, an embassy has certain immediate preoccupations which never vary, although other priorities depend to some extent on the discernable intentions of the receiving state towards it and its expatriate community. Always first in importance is destroying its codes, ciphers, classified papers and – in earlier times – such items as seals and consular service fee stamps. For this purpose, until the latter half of the twentieth century, open fires and iron wastebaskets usually sufficed very adequately.[22] In the embassy's last days, the smell of burning was always pervasive and the air thick with ash.[23] Since then, shredding machines and dedicated burn barrels have become popular, sometimes with sorry consequences. Apart from the fact that shredding machines usually depend on an externally supplied power source (unless the embassy has its own generator), the strips of paper produced by primitive versions can sometimes be re-assembled, as was notoriously the fate of the classified papers at the US embassy in Tehran in 1979.[24] By

[19] Bodine, 'Saddam's siege of Embassy Kuwait', p. 127; Munro, *An Embassy at War*, pp. 212–13. See also HCPP (143–I), 9 July 1991: Mins. of Ev., 24 Oct. 1990, p. 16. There was a rather sad sequel to the siege of the British embassy in Kuwait. At the end of the war the Special Boat Squadron was ordered to re-secure it but, suspecting it was booby-trapped, blew in the famous Lutyens front door. No one appears to have told them that the Indian janitor was on hand and would have opened it for them had he been asked, Billière, *Storm Command*, p. 308.

[20] Bodine, 'Saddam's siege of Embassy Kuwait', pp. 122–5.

[21] Billière, *Storm Command*, p. 184; Munro, *An Embassy at War*, p. 213.

[22] Non-confidential archives were traditionally sealed and either placed in a locked room or transferred to a more secure location, for example the mission of the protecting power.

[23] See the graphic description of the US embassy in Tokyo after Pearl Harbor, in Heinrichs, *American Ambassador*, p. 358.

[24] Tomseth, 'Crisis after crisis', p. 49.

contrast, sophistication can prove a problem with burn barrels since – unlike shredding machines – embassies are unlikely to gain familiarity with them by regular use. The few remaining staff of the US consulate-general in Can Tho in April 1975, at a point when it was feared the Viet Cong were closing in, had such difficulty in getting the contents of their unfamiliar model of burn barrels to ignite that, in desperation, they were about to hurl incendiary grenades into them when the barrels finally burst into flames. On this occasion, the air seems to have been thicker with expletives than with smoke and ash.[25]

The embassy also needs urgently to arrange and advise on the responsibilities of the protecting power appointed to look after its interests, often a neutral such as Switzerland or Sweden – or, in the first years of both world wars of the twentieth century, the United States (see Chapter 3). If it is told to expect a prompt departure, it must also agree with foreign ministry representatives the time and means of leaving – and, not least, who shall be on the list to travel, which is often a complicated and delicate matter:

> For days we and the Swiss laboured to get an agreed list. I refused to move [says Sir Humphrey Trevelyan, the British ambassador in Cairo at the time of the Suez War] without the staffs of the consulates in Alexandria, Ismailia and Suez, the Service Attachés who had been stationed with the contractors and the fifty-one Embassy employees held up in Alexandria.[26]

If harsh treatment of the members of the expatriate community is anticipated, the embassy is also under an obligation to give sanctuary to as many of them as possible. This was an especially urgent matter for the anti-Axis embassies in Tokyo after Pearl Harbor in December 1941, as for the Coalition embassies in Kuwait City – especially that of the United States – in August 1990.[27]

[25] McNamara, *Escape with Honor*, pp. 142–4.
[26] Trevelyan, *The Middle East in Revolution*, pp. 123–4.
[27] Bodine, 'Saddam's siege of Embassy Kuwait', pp. 116–21.

Embassy premises entrusted by a departing head of mission to a protecting power are not thereby guaranteed the 'respect and protection' required by the VCDR. Saudi security staff were well within their rights to give the Iraqi embassy in Riyadh 'a thorough going-over' after its staff had all left in early 1991;[28] as were British police officers in entering the Libyan mission in London in search of evidence following the departure in 1984 of its officers, one of whom was clearly responsible for shooting dead a policewoman from one of its windows during a demonstration outside the building.[29] However, the same can hardly be said for the Iraqi troops who occupied and looted the British embassy in Baghdad after its abandonment on the eve of the Gulf War in 1991 (see Chapter 5). It was no doubt in retaliation for this that, despite the fact that the Iraqi embassy in London was placed under the protection of Jordan, no particular care seems to have been taken by the British authorities to look after its premises. The police failed to prevent Kurdish protesters from briefly occupying the building in April 1991 and causing damage to internal fittings. Subsequently it was not only burgled but treated as a desirable residence by squatters and stripped of virtually everything bar some safes, which was just as well because one of them contained a stash of weapons. Whether the abuse and damage inflicted after April 1991 occurred during the long period of Jordanian protection up to early 2003 or in the period immediately afterwards, is not clear.[30]

Prompt, safe and dignified departures

The long-established custom that, on the outbreak of war, enemy diplomats have a right to expect a prompt, safe and dignified departure reflects the desire of states to secure, by reciprocity, the same treatment for their own diplomats. This anxiety to get

[28] Munro, *An Embassy at War*, pp. 283–4.
[29] Denza, *Diplomatic Law*, p. 490.
[30] guardian.co.uk 8 June 2005.

them home is prompted not only by concern for their safety, but also by a need to use them elsewhere. After all, diplomacy does not end with war: in relations with allies and neutrals it becomes more important, and the foreign ministry at home may also need strengthening. While foreign ministry personnel departments have good reasons for wanting their own diplomats back, security services might also have good ones for getting rid of the enemy embassy, especially if it still contains persons whose activities could be particularly dangerous in war, and whose confinement or closer watching would – should they remain – be an irksome burden. For example, when in 1941 Finland became a co-belligerent with Germany against Britain's new ally, the Soviet Union, and broke relations with Britain at the end of July (Britain and Finland did not formally go to war until December), one of the reasons that it was anxious to see the departure of the British legation in Helsinki was that it still harboured the rump of an important SIS station.[31] In the subsequent negotiations over the exchange of diplomats, this became obvious when the Finnish foreign ministry refused the legation's request to allow four of its members (some of whom, because of the previously close collaboration between SIS and Finnish military intelligence, it must have known or suspected to be SIS officers[32]) to be allowed to proceed directly to Sweden and there join the British legation in Stockholm. It was feared, confessed a senior official of the foreign ministry to a member of the US legation in Helsinki at the

[31] Jeffery says that all SIS staff in Finland were removed to Sweden during June and July 1941, *MI6*, p. 373. However, it is a more than reasonable inference that four likely SIS officers remained in the legation until it was finally closed and all of its members left for Lisbon in early September. This group included an archivist, two members of the passport control office (standard SIS cover; one of these men also had the rank of vice consul but is mentioned nowhere in the *FO List 1941*), and the superintending clerk of the military attaché's office – 'C. Cheshire', TNA, US Legation Helsinki to US Embassy London, 26 Aug. 1941, FO371/29386. In December 1942 'Cyril Cheshire' (is it not likely that they were one and the same?), described by Jeffery as a 'fluent Russian-speaking' former timber merchant, became PCO and head of the SIS station, *MI6*, pp. 378, 512–13.

[32] Jeffery, *MI6*, pp. 371–2.

beginning of September, that the British wanted them to go there 'for the purpose of continuing their activities vis-à-vis Finland.'[33] Similarly, during the Suez War in 1956, the British ambassador in Cairo soon realized that Nasser's government was anxious to see the back of his embassy, possibly prompted by a fear that it would organize a provocative incident in order to give the British and French forces an excuse to attack Cairo; or, alternatively, that it would make contact with the domestic opposition, which the ambassador believed would not have been difficult despite the siege of the mission.[34]

For reasons such as those outlined above, therefore, on the outbreak of the First World War states still generally played by the book. Special trains for departing ambassadors and their staffs were normally provided, and – although individual officials might prove truculent and urban mobs sometimes threatened to upset matters – they were usually shown the customary courtesies.[35] (The most notable exception was probably the treatment of the party of Jules Cambon, the French ambassador at Berlin, which was forced to depart Germany via the least convenient route, badly treated on the train, and then forced to pay for it in gold before being permitted to cross the frontier.)[36] A special train might not always have been needed by the diplomats but – with locked doors and blinds sometimes pulled down during the day – it provided an efficient means of shepherding them to the frontier. This not only made sure that they all left, but also avoided the risk of incidents should they have fallen foul of excited crowds if recognized while they were making their own way to the frontier. No obvious suspicion seems to have been attached to any delays, which were to be expected with the outbreak of war, and there appears to have been no attempt – certainly no routine attempt – to negotiate formal exchanges.

[33] TNA, Memorandum of the American Legation, Helsinki, 2 Sept. 1941, FO371/29388. This fear was well justified.

[34] Trevelyan, *The Middle East in Revolution*, pp. 117, 123.

[35] Frey and Frey, *The History of Diplomatic Immunity*, pp. 422–4.

[36] Gerard, *My Four Years in Germany*, p. 92; Rumbold, *The War Crisis in Berlin*, pp. 314–15; *The Times*, 8 Aug. 1914.

On the outbreak of the Second World War embassies in some of the key belligerent relationships still enjoyed the same system. Prompt departures were accorded without difficulty to Sir Nevile Henderson, British ambassador in Berlin, as also to Dr Theodor Kordt, the German chargé d'affaires in London. In Italy the retreating embassies benefited from the anxiety of Count Ciano, the *faux*-aristocratic Italian foreign minister, to demonstrate that he – if not Mussolini – knew how to behave like a gentleman, his Fascist contempt for professional diplomacy notwithstanding.[37] The departures in June 1940 of the parties of Sir Percy Loraine, the British ambassador in Rome, and Signor Giuseppe Bastianini, the Italian ambassador in London, were delayed by only about a week; and the special train taking home the party of the French ambassador at Rome, André François-Poncet, experienced only a similar short delay.[38] Even the departure of Count Werner von Schulenburg, the German ambassador in Moscow at the time of Hitler's 'surprise' attack on the Soviet Union on 22 June 1941, was delayed by little longer, despite the evil reputation for the treatment of diplomats that Stalin's regime has since acquired.[39] Perhaps the disposition to play by the rules shown by the Soviet foreign minister, V. M. Molotov, was encouraged by the fact that the German ambassador had warned him of Hitler's treacherous intentions.[40] The departure of Vladimir Dekanozov, the Soviet dictator's own ambassador in Berlin, was similarly quite prompt. It was over a month before the British legation was able to leave Helsinki and the Finns were able to leave London following the break in their relations at the end of July 1941, but the arrangements made by the Germans to take the British party by train from Lübeck to the Spanish frontier, en route to Lisbon, were carried

[37] *Ciano's Diary*, p. 262. See also Phillips, *Ventures in Diplomacy*, p. 168. On Ciano's attitude to professional diplomacy, see Gilbert, 'Ciano and his ambassadors'.

[38] Reid, *Winged Diplomat*, pp. 147–51. The French party arrived in Bordeaux on 17 June, just a week after the Italian declaration of war, Waterfield, *Professional Diplomat*, p. 276.

[39] Frey and Frey, *The History of Diplomatic Immunity*, p. 423.

[40] Gorodetsky, *Grand Delusion*, pp. 309–15.

out impeccably, as the Northern Department of the Foreign Office conceded with reluctant admiration.[41]

Other missions, such as the British embassies in Hungary and Romania, were permitted to withdraw safely before being firmly in the grip of an enemy and so avoided testing the respect of their hosts for international law. It must be added, however, that while the British legation in Bulgaria was similarly treated (as that country was being occupied by the Germans in March 1941), two time bombs in suitcases were smuggled on to the special train taking its staff to the Turkish frontier. One of these caused a number of deaths and many injuries when it exploded in the Pera Palace Hotel in Istanbul as the party led by the British minister, George Rendel, was unpacking. It seems likely, however, that this was either German-inspired or the result of Bulgarian private enterprise, because King Boris had arranged for the royal coach to be attached to the train for Rendel's convenience, while foreign ministry officials and the American minister in Sofia – who had assumed protection of British interests – had travelled on the train to the frontier.[42]

Despite the reasonable treatment of these particular embassies in the Second World War, the fact remains that many consular officials in the key belligerent relationships and embassies in others fared less well. This was because, by 1939, ideology and ethnic animosities had poisoned international relations, while the underpinning of cross-national aristocratic solidarity in diplomatic circles had been weakened. It was therefore more common than hitherto for enemy diplomatic and consular officials and their families to be interned until *formal* exchange agreements in which both sides could have confidence were negotiated, usually via third parties.

[41] TNA, mins. on docket N596 14 Oct. 1941 (folio 32), FO371/29388. The party, which numbered over 100, was escorted by an American diplomat as far as Frankfurt and by Baron von Bothmer of the Protocol Department of the German Foreign Office all the way to the Spanish frontier.

[42] Rendel, *The Sword and the Olive*, pp. 181, 185–92; *The Times*, 13 Mar. 1941.

Internment pending simultaneous exchange

It is one thing for enemy diplomats to be bottled up, more or less tightly, in their embassy for a few days while they have time to attend to their final duties and then pack up and finalize their travel arrangements. It is quite another for them to be left there for months, possibly even years. This is when temporary confinement becomes 'internment'.

Straws in the cold wind carrying the threat of internment were already obvious at the time of some of the prompt returns described in the previous section. For example, in June 1940 British consular staff from Albania were held for two days in an Ancona hotel 'as hostages for the departure from Malta of the Italian consular staff there, delayed by their own side's bombing' before being allowed to return to Britain with Loraine's party.[43] Furthermore, the ambassador's party from Rome, which sailed from Ancona in an Italian vessel, did not proceed home directly but via soon-to-be-popular Lisbon in neutral Portugal. Here, in the last week of June, it was exchanged for the party led by the Italian ambassador to Britain, which had arrived from the Clyde in a British ship two days earlier. Each party, which also included 'non-officials', transferred to its own flag vessel, which thereupon turned round and went home.[44] Applying the same principle to the departing French diplomats, the Italians held up their train for three days at Domodossola on the Swiss frontier pending arrival at its own point of entry into Switzerland of the train carrying the Italian diplomats from France, which had been delayed by the difficulty of gathering in Italian consular staff caused by the German invasion. The agreement was that the two trains were to move into Switzerland simultaneously, so only when news that the Italian party had also arrived at the frontier was the train carrying the French allowed to enter the Simplon Tunnel.[45] As for the return of the German diplomats from Moscow and their

[43] Grafftey-Smith, *Bright Levant*, p. 209.
[44] *The Times*, 25 and 27 June, 1 July 1940. See also papers in TNA, ADM199/1294.
[45] Reid, *Winged Diplomat*, pp. 149–51.

Soviet counterparts from Berlin, this depended on an agreement brokered by the neutral Swedes for a simultaneous exchange via neutral Turkey. This duly took place on 18 July 1941, when Schulenburg's party was handed over to the Turkish authorities at Leninakan (modern day Gyumri, in Armenia) and Dekanozov's was handed over to them at Svilengrad in Bulgaria, just across the border from Edirne.[46] This exchange – like the Franco–Italian one – was facilitated by the fact that scarce shipping, with all its attendant complications, was not required. In other circumstances, such exchanges did not prove so easy to arrange.

In fact, many diplomatic and consular officials had to wait for around half a year before being allowed to return home and some for considerably longer. Among the latter was the large British party gathered together by Germany from across occupied Europe and the smaller party of German consular officials and their families arrested by the British in neutral Iceland following its precautionary occupation in May 1940. It was the end of September 1941 before what proved to be only the first instalment of exchanges of members of these two groups – among which numbered the British ambassador in Brussels, Sir Lancelot Oliphant, and the German consul-general in Reykjavik, Werner Gerlach – was achieved.[47]

While waiting for their exchange to be agreed, some of the interned diplomats were effectively placed under house arrest in their own compounds. This was the fate of the Allied embassies in Tokyo.[48] However, with the exception of a few individuals (see p. 41 below), none of their staff seem to have been subjected 'to brutality, serious deprivation, or gross indignity'.[49] This at least was the experience of the American and British embassies in

[46] On this, see Koblyakov, 'On the way home from Berlin' (a valuable source for which I am indebted to Professor Geoffrey Roberts), and *The Times*, 24 July 1941.

[47] Oliphant, *An Ambassador in Bonds*; TNA, FO371/26375 and FO371/29307 [Annual Report for Iceland for 1940]; *The Times*, 25 Sept. 1941.

[48] Heinrichs, *American Ambassador*, pp. 358–9; Craigie, *Behind the Japanese Mask*, pp. 138–51.

[49] Heinrichs, *American Ambassador*, p. 359.

Japan and certainly of the American embassy in Italy. The staff of the Japanese embassy in London were also interned in their own building, although the acting consul in Liverpool and his secretary – second class citizens like all consuls at that time – were sent to an internment camp in Chelsea pending their despatch to the main British internment camp on the Isle of Man.[50]

A common alternative to being interned in their embassy buildings was for the diplomats, within a week or so, to be removed from the capital and confined, sometimes with other expatriates, in relatively commodious but secluded buildings in the provinces – here a spacious hotel, there a sanatorium. On his release, Oliphant – who experienced both sorts of accommodation – was on the whole very complimentary about his treatment by the Germans, and it was probably for this reason that the Central Department in the Foreign Office was anxious to severely restrict distribution of his report.[51] It did, after all, compare rather too favourably with the public account of the conditions of his own internment on the remote and over-crowded Isle of Man given by Gerlach on his own return home.[52] At the former Grand Hotel in Bad Nauheim near Frankfurt, where the US embassy staff were interned, many of the Americans complained endlessly about the food, although Leland Morris, the acting chief of mission, in voicing their feelings to the State Department in February 1942, acknowledged that their allotment amounted to 'one and a half times the normal German civilian ration'. Emotions at Bad Nauheim also ran high on another matter: 'No pressing or ironing or shoe polishing services are provided,' reported an anguished Morris, 'and persons are obliged to do their own work along these lines.'[53] It is little wonder that Morris's administrative officer, George Kennan, who had daily to bear the brunt of these complaints, became so sick of the majority of his compatriots

[50] TNA, letter to his father, 15–19 Mar. 1942, Security Service: Personal file on Kaoru Matsumoto, KV2/2471.

[51] TNA, min. of Makins, 2 Jan. 1942, FO371/26375.

[52] Oliphant, *An Ambassador in Bonds*, p. 215; see also p. 200.

[53] Huddle (Berne) to SoS (enclosing letter from Morris), 28 Feb. 1942, *FRUS, 1942*. Vol. I, pp. 319–21.

that when they finally got out he revenged himself upon them by leaving them locked on the train at the Spanish–Portuguese frontier while he ate a breakfast of eggs in the station buffet.[54] In the United States, Axis diplomats were corralled at comfortable and amply provisioned hotels in the mountains of West Virginia. On the basis of reciprocity negotiated via the Swiss – who were in charge both of German and Italian interests in the United States and US interests in Germany and Italy – freedom of movement was permitted in the grounds of these buildings, chiefs of mission were upon request permitted to visit the nearest town, and the internees were free to telephone or write to the Swiss and receive visits from them at all times.[55] The Japanese diplomats, whose protecting power was Spain and were placed at the Homestead Hotel in Hot Springs, seem to have lived under slightly tighter restrictions.[56] Following the severance of relations between America and Vichy France on 7 November 1942, Vichy diplomatic and consular staff in the United States whose allegiance to the Allied cause had yet to be determined were confined in the equally comfortable Hotel Hershey in Hershey, Pennsylvania.[57]

Sometimes, diplomats interned in the Second World War were if anything more angry with their own governments than with their captors. A cold contempt for the wartime State Department seeps from the pages of Kennan's memoirs. It ignored them until the end of April, he charges, although it could easily have communicated with them via the Swiss embassy. Furthermore, when the department did finally send a telegram, this was merely to inform the staff of the comptroller-general's decision (which it was clearly 'disinclined to challenge') that they would not be paid for the

[54] Kennan, *Memoirs*, pp. 137–8.

[55] Huddle (Berne) to SoS, 25 Dec. 1941 and SoS to Huddle, 26 Dec. 1941, *FRUS, 1942*. Vol. I, pp. 293–5 ; Kennan, *Memoirs*, pp. 136–9.

[56] Memo. by Asst. Chief of Protocol, 27 Dec. 1941, *FRUS, 1942*. Vol. I, pp. 385–6.

[57] The great majority were sympathetic and hence left at liberty, Memo. by Asst. SoS (Long) for Roosevelt, 'Exchange of French and American Official Personnel', 16 Dec. 1942, *FRUS, 1942*. Vol. I, pp. 374–7; 'World War II: The Vichy internment at the Hotel Hershey'.

period of their confinement because they had not been 'working'. Putting the need to appease Congress before the interests of its own employees, it also informed them that – contrary to the initial promise – half of the staff were to be left in German custody in order to free up space for Jewish refugees on the exchange vessel. Kennan and Morris managed to kill these proposals but the bitterness lingered.[58]

What is important to understand, however, is that the exceptional length – if not the conditions – of some of these internments is not necessarily an index of the retreat of diplomatic law in the face of the advance of mid-twentieth century barbarism.[59] It is evidence instead that there were sometimes exceptional difficulties not only in agreeing the terms of the exchanges of the interned diplomats, but also in implementing them. A closer look at the exchange of British and Allied diplomats under Japanese control and Japanese diplomats in the British Empire will illustrate these difficulties.

Exchanging British and Japanese diplomats in the Second World War[60]

At the time that Britain found itself at war with Japan following the attack on Pearl Harbor on 7 December 1941, it had a large

[58] Kennan, *Memoirs*, pp. 139–41; Harrison (Berne) to SoS (enclosing message from Morris, Bad Nauheim), 29 Apr. 1942, *FRUS, 1942*. Vol. I, pp. 361–2. On Bad Nauheim, see also Wolter, *POW Baseball in World War II*, ch. 8 [www].

[59] In *The History of Diplomatic Immunity*, Frey and Frey highlight some of the worst excesses against diplomats following the outbreak of the Second World War and see this as an index of the 'deterioration of the international order', pp. 422–4. It is, however, going too far in the opposite direction to maintain that no marked change of any kind occurred at this time, as is implied in the only statement on the subject, albeit a guarded one, in Roberts (ed.), *Satow's Diplomatic Practice*: 'These [customary] facilities for departure were uniformly granted in many States in Europe on the outbreak of the Second World War', 15.29.

[60] Except where otherwise stated, the following section is based on the extensive British files on this subject located in TNA: ADM199/1294, FO371/31739 and WO208/1478. Only exceptionally or in the case of quotations are citations from them made.

embassy in Tokyo. Excluding the ambassador, Sir Robert Craigie, the chancery and the defence section each had a staff of five, while six Japanese language specialists in the consular service staffed both the 'Japanese secretariat' and the commercial section. The registry itself had three officers. Altogether, including a large number of student interpreters, 29 diplomatic and consular officers were officially reported as in post at Tokyo.[61] With British ancillary staff and dependents added, there was a grand total of 74.[62] In addition, Britain had consular staff at eight provincial outposts, as well as numerous other officers in territories occupied by Japan. These included the sizeable staff of the British legation in Bangkok, which was headed by the old Siam hand, Sir Josiah Crosby, and the consulate-general in Saigon.

Following the outbreak of hostilities, staff and their families living outside the Tokyo embassy were hurriedly called into the compound and facilities that had previously provided accommodation for 30 persons thereafter needed to support 90. Vere Redman, the journalist who had been casually appointed press and information officer and was not on the diplomatic list, was suspected by the Japanese of spying and trying to stir up trouble between themselves and their German allies. As a result, he was forcibly removed from the embassy by the notorious *Kempeitai* and placed in solitary confinement in Sugamo prison in Tokyo.[63] As in the case of the American embassy in Tokyo, the premises were also invaded by the Japanese to search for radios and generally reconnoitre its interior. The British legation staff in Bangkok were also interned in their compound, although they obtained slightly

[61] *FO List 1941*. For some reason, Arthur de la Mare was not included, so the figure should really have been at least 30. See also Gore-Booth, *With Great Truth and Respect*, pp. 78–9.

[62] TNA, British Officials in Japanese Territory and Manchuria, 20 Dec. 1941, FO916/432.

[63] Cortazzi, 'Sir Vere Redman, 1901–1975', p. 293. Contrary to some more lurid stories, the ambassador – by his own account – had only been politely brushed aside when he had offered token physical obstruction to 'this high-handed arrest within the embassy' in order to signify that he had not acquiesced in it, Craigie, *Behind the Japanese Mask*, p. 144.

better treatment when the Japanese soldiers guarding them were replaced by Thai policemen.[64]

In London, the staff of the Japanese embassy was almost as large as the British embassy in Tokyo and had an even bigger defence section.[65] The Japanese mission as a whole was also more readily gathered up because only the consulate at Liverpool, already mentioned, was staffed by Japanese; the Thai legation was only small. Of the Japanese diplomats, only one was interned outside the embassy building. This was the honorary attaché, Matsumoto (see p. 26 above), who was in practice part cultural attaché and part press attaché. As the member of the Japanese embassy whose duties corresponded most closely to those of Vere Redman (and also because his suspected intelligence activities made him of great interest to MI5), on 24 December Matsumoto was arrested and sent to the internment camp at the Oratory Central School in Chelsea by way of reprisal for the British press officer's treatment.[66] Shigemitsu Mamoru, the ambassador, was more fortunate: he had departed for Tokyo some months before the outbreak of war.[67]

The issues on which agreement on a reciprocal exchange of diplomats with the Japanese was needed were – as we shall see – numerous and complex, and would have benefitted from being broached with the Japanese foreign ministry, the *Gaimushō*, well before the outbreak of war. Sir Robert Craigie was strongly of this view, although he also believed that a conciliatory approach to Japan was of 'vital importance'[68] and that raising the issue

[64] Crosby, *Siam*, p. 141.

[65] Three military attachés, three naval attachés and one air attaché.

[66] At the Oratory School Matsumoto, who spoke German and French as well as excellent English, and was reputed to have a 'fantastic memory', spent much time gleaning intelligence from the mixed bag of other internees and was soon regarded by MI5 as a 'menace'. Since it was impossible to segregate him from the others, on 25 June 1942 he was transferred to Brixton Prison, TNA, Security Service: Personal file on Kaoru Matsumoto, KV2/2471; see also Cortazzi, 'Sir Vere Redman, 1901–1975', p. 294.

[67] Best, 'Shigemitsu Mamoru and Anglo-Japanese relations', pp. 258; Craigie, *Behind the Japanese Mask*, p. 130.

[68] Best, 'Sir Robert Craigie as Ambassador to Japan, 1937–1941', p. 241.

of mutual evacuations too early ran the risk of suggesting that Britain regarded war as inevitable. As a result, while as early as May 1940 he had told the Foreign Office that it was on his mind and described the categories and rough numbers of evacuees for whom provision would have to be made, it was late December before he suggested that it was now time to open 'unofficial discussions'. However, the Far Eastern Department of the Foreign Office was unsympathetic. It admitted that an early agreement on reciprocal evacuation 'might obviate much last minute confusion and subsequent hardship' but thought this outweighed by the risk that seeking such an understanding would either savour of panic or be thought to suggest that Britain was bent on war.[69] To this position the Foreign Office remained super-glued to the end.

Following Pearl Harbor in December 1941, all arguments against opening negotiations for a formal agreement on reciprocal evacuations fell away. The Japanese embassy in London was now equally keen on the idea, as the British knew from an intercepted telegram which it had sent to Tokyo a week before the attack.[70] However, war conditions made communications between them difficult and to this was added the problem of having to deal via third parties. Moreover, the British and the Japanese had chosen different protecting powers: Argentina to protect British interests in Japan, and Switzerland to serve for Japan both in Britain and most of the rest of the empire.[71]

The first result of this situation was that opening messages crossed. On 23 December – slow off the mark compared to the Americans[72] – the Foreign Office despatched a brief, general

[69] See especially TNA, FO to Craigie, 2 Jan. 1941, ADM199/1294.

[70] Japanese chargé d'affaires in London to Tokyo, 1 Dec. 1941, TNA, HW1/296.

[71] The US government was in a similar position, with the Swiss legation in Tokyo representing its interests in Japan and the Spanish embassy in Washington representing Japanese interests in the United States. Both channels were used in the US–Japanese negotiations, which on at least one occasion caused difficulties, Grew, *Ten Years in Japan*, pp. 514–15. This problem, together with slow communications, was also picked out in a short post-mortem in the State Department on the delays affecting the first American exchange and projections for the second, *FRUS, 1942*. Vol. I, pp. 448–9.

[72] On 13 December, less than a week after Pearl Harbor, the State Department

proposal for a reciprocal exchange to Tokyo via Berne, while the Japanese submitted a plan of their own via Buenos Aires. The Japanese plan was superseded by a fuller version which arrived at the Foreign Office on 21 January, this time via the Swiss legation in London. That the Japanese had also decided to use the Swiss channel at this juncture was a relief to the Foreign Office, and at the end of April Camille Gorgé, the efficient if rather overbearing Swiss minister in Tokyo, was appointed in place of the Argentine ambassador to protect British interests.[73] But already protecting US interests in Japan, Gorgé had for some time been complaining to Berne that his small legation was seriously overstretched and that, while the *Gaimushō* was 'openly helpful', he was meeting 'incredible resistance among subordinates';[74] in any case, the foreign ministry appears not to have been well organized to deal with this sort of negotiation.[75] In short, communications with the Japanese were simplified by being concentrated in the hands of the Swiss but remained laborious.

In the middle of 1940, the Foreign Office had told Sir Robert Craigie that any negotiation for a reciprocal exchange between Britain and Japan following the outbreak of war would use as a model the agreement previously made with the Italians. Among other things, therefore, permission to leave Britain would be

sent off a message via the Swiss proposing an exchange at Lourenço Marques. It amplified this in a further message on 26 December, *FRUS, 1942*. Vol. I, pp. 378–9, 382–5 resp.

[73] Gorgé's personality led him to make enemies among his own staff as well as within the Tokyo diplomatic corps, and later in the war criticisms reached London that he had not been vigorous in protecting British interests, not least because before the war he had been legal adviser to the *Gaimushō*. These were dismissed by others, including Craigie, who spoke highly of him, TNA, FO (POW Department) to Washington, 1 Apr. 1944, FO916/1115. See also Craigie, *Behind the Japanese Mask*, p. 149; Gore-Booth, *With Great Truth and Respect*, p. 110; *The Times*, 30 Apr. 1942.

[74] Kirby, *Japan and East Asia*, pp. 165–6. The Swiss minister appears later to have received assistance from 'a number of keen, public-spirited Swiss residents in Japan who had volunteered for the work', Craigie, *Behind the Japanese Mask*, p. 149.

[75] Memo. by Asst. Chiefs of Special Division to Roosevelt, 16 Dec. 1942, *FRUS, 1942*. Vol. I, p. 448.

granted to all Japanese diplomatic and consular officials and their staff (including government employees on official missions but without diplomatic status), as also to any other Japanese national who so desired it, unless there were 'security reasons' for detaining them; the staffs of the embassy and consulates would be allowed to take out as much personal baggage as they desired; and there would be no interference with or sequestration of any property remaining in Japanese ownership, which would all be placed under the control of a protecting power.[76] The moment had now come to adopt these principles but Japan's expansion at Britain's expense soon weakened its hand and made this less easy in 1942 than had been anticipated in the middle of 1940.

Tokyo wanted one big exchange which involved nationals of all of the states with which they were at war or with which they had severed diplomatic relations, including the United States. This had the advantage of enabling the British to link their diminished bargaining power to that of the Americans, but inevitably meant delay while they concerted their negotiating positions.[77] Britain also had to consult Egypt, Iraq and the allied governments in exile in London, including the Free French National Committee, together with all of the dominions apart from Canada.[78] As a result, it was 7 February before the Foreign Office had produced a draft reply and the breadth of interests it touched then meant it was necessary to debate this in an ad hoc interdepartmental committee of the War Cabinet.

Attended by representatives not only of the Dominions Office, Colonial Office, India Office and Burma Office, but also of the War Office, Home Office, Ministry of War Transport, Admiralty and MI5, the committee met at the Foreign Office on 10 February.

[76] TNA, FO to Craigie, 16 July 1940, ADM199/1294.

[77] The American desire to incorporate the South American republics in their exchange with the Germans and the Italians also caused immense complications and delay. This exchange finally took place in Lisbon in the middle of May 1942, the American diplomats from Bad Nauheim still complaining about the food, *FRUS, 1942*. Vol. I, pp. 287, 310–41 *passim*, and *The Times*, 17 May.

[78] It was agreed that Canada should be part of the American wing of the exchange.

Here, further delay was caused because the Colonial Office successfully pressed for a radical extension of the agreement: its inclusion of colonial officials and other British nationals in the territories recently captured by the Japanese, including Hong Kong. This caused great unease in the Foreign Office, where it was believed that at best it would delay any reciprocal evacuation indefinitely and at worst wreck the emerging scheme altogether. This meant that the foreign secretary, Anthony Eden, had to raise the recommendation at the full War Cabinet on 16 February, where he managed to get it rejected.

As it turned out, the delay caused by the need to refer the draft British response to Japan's proposal to the full War Cabinet was of no consequence because, despite pressure from London, the State Department's general endorsement of the British attitude was not received until the end of February. It was, therefore, 6 March before the British response could finally be passed to the Swiss legation in London, although even by this time it had not been possible to secure the formal assent of all the dominion governments.

The first British message to the Japanese had referred to an exchange confined to diplomats and other officials because of the fear that the complications of dealing with non-officials (whose numbers were also much larger) would inevitably cause great delay if an attempt were made to exchange them at the same time. As a result, the British would have preferred a two-stage operation in which the officials were brought out first. However, they were well aware that this could lead to serious public criticism at home.[79] As a result, they now indicated a readiness to fall in with the Japanese idea that there should be a simultaneous exchange of officials and non-officials – on condition that the Japanese would provide two ships rather than the solitary vessel they had mentioned and that priority in the allocation

[79] In the United States, the threat of public hostility to any suggestion that diplomats were getting preferential treatment, whether in exchange arrangements or the draft, was feared even more by the Department of State, Kennan, *Memoirs*, pp. 139–41.

of available berths should be given to officials. The decision to seek an exchange of this sort was without doubt the single most important reason for the delay in agreeing and then implementing the exchange and was well understood – and accepted – by the diplomats themselves.[80]

The Foreign Office was also willing to concede the Japanese stipulation that the exchange of persons (official and non-official) should not be limited by numbers nor subject to enquiry 'into their value for war purposes'. All three of the main parties – the Americans, British and Japanese – also agreed easily enough that the place of exchange should be the port of Lourenço Marques in Mozambique, at that time a colony of neutral Portugal and roughly the same distance by sea from each of the countries concerned;[81] and also that Portugal should be asked to serve as guarantor of the exchange, to which it subsequently agreed. There was also no difficulty in agreeing that each should take responsibility for securing from their allies the necessary safe conducts for the exchange ships, as also in settling on such matters as the money and personal belongings that evacuees would be permitted to bring out.

This degree of common ground was encouraging, but on many details there were significant differences. The British worried particularly that the Japanese definition of 'officials' was too narrow and that it would prevent the repatriation of individuals such as Redman.[82] Nor were they inclined to fall in with the Japanese proposal that diplomatic and consular evacuees destined for new posts should be permitted to proceed to them directly, suspecting that Tokyo wanted this to help it reinforce missions

[80] Craigie, *Behind the Japanese Mask*, p. 149.

[81] A South American port would have been much more convenient for the Americans but this could have caused political problems so soon after the conclusion of the anti-Axis Rio Conference.

[82] The proposed British definition was 'officers from any part of the British Empire and all individuals employed in Diplomatic Missions and Consulates whether they possess diplomatic status or not, including Trade Commissioners and their staffs, judicial officers and their staffs and officials of His Majesty's Ministry of Works or other Ministries and their staffs'. Britain was willing to give 'an equally wide interpretation so far as Japanese officials are concerned'.

in enemy territory: all evacuees, they insisted, must first go to Lourenço Marques. The British also wanted all non-officials who wished to leave to be permitted to do so and not just – as the Japanese had proposed – 'non-permanent residents' and women and children among those who were permanent. They also wanted Indo–China, Thailand and the Philippines to be added to the territories from which British Empire nationals were to be evacuated (Tokyo had said that these should be confined to Japan, Manchukuo and occupied China) and in return offered to arrange that the exchange should cover Japanese nationals in the Netherlands, Belgian and Free French territories, Egypt and Iraq. The British also wanted representatives of the protecting powers – with unrestricted access to ships' radio facilities for communication with their governments in plain language – on all exchange vessels.

It was the second week of April before the full reply of the Japanese to the British counter-proposals found its way to the Foreign Office. Fortunately, this indicated their willingness to exchange about 1100 nationals and met almost all of Britain's objections to their original proposal.[83] By this time the British were also keen to settle. This was in part because of their growing fears for the treatment of their nationals held by the Japanese, concerning which worrying reports were arriving. But it was also because of the disturbing news received on 8 April that the State Department, whose own negotiations with Tokyo had been proceeding more quickly, was being tempted to fall in with a new Japanese plan to exchange first with the Americans and leave

[83] The main exception was that the Japanese failed to confirm the inclusion of certain named individuals (such as Redman) and categories of personnel, among the latter the wireless operators from Peking and Allied officials at Hong Kong. For their part, the Japanese appear to have accepted the position adopted by both the British and Americans that official evacuees could not be transferred under safe conducts directly to new posts (even in neutral countries) without having first to go to Lourenço Marques, although it was put to them that the reason for this was that the practical difficulties of arranging it 'would delay still further the completion of arrangements which under existing circumstances are already complicated', TNA, FO to Swiss legation, 4 Apr. 1942, ADM199/1294.

the British until later.[84] Accordingly, via the usual Swiss channel, the Foreign Office replied swiftly to the Japanese. Their latest proposals were generally acceptable, they were told; furthermore, Britain hoped to be able to provide more shipping than had been originally envisaged for the evacuation of Japanese nationals, especially from Australia, provided Japan reciprocated by putting on a second ship in order to permit the repatriation of more British nationals. In short, Britain proposed that the numbers to be exchanged in the emerging agreement should be doubled.[85] Tokyo was also urged to suggest an approximate date by which their vessels might reach Lourenço Marques. Reasonably confident that final agreement was now close, the Foreign Office increased its attention to the equally complicated practical arrangements needed to implement it. The question of towering importance here was shipping.

With huge demand on shipping for war purposes, the questions of where the exchange vessels were to come from and when they would be available were peculiarly difficult to resolve; and upon the answers to them – as well as whether or not the Japanese agreed to double the number of evacuees – turned not only the date when the exchange could be made, but how many non-official evacuees could be carried. The British problem was how to get the Japanese scattered across three widely separated locations to Lourenço Marques: the UK, India (where Japanese officials from the Straits Settlements were being concentrated) and Australia and New Zealand. It was made the more difficult because it was not known how many non-official Japanese would wish repatriation. The Japanese problem was equally severe, with British nationals (including the diplomatic and consular officials in Thailand and Indochina) needing to be picked up from many points across their recently much expanded 'co-prosperity sphere'.

[84] See also Memo. of Conversation by Asst. SoS (Long), 13 Apr. 1942; and Harrison (Berne) to SoS, 22 May 1942 and Hull to Harrison, 23 May 1942, *FRUS, 1942*. Vol. I, pp. 414–15, 422–3 resp.

[85] The Americans were also proposing to exchange double the numbers originally envisaged in their own negotiations with the Japanese, TNA, Dept. of State to US legation, Berne, 7 Apr. 1942, FO371/31739.

Following discussions between the Foreign Office and the Ministry of War Transport which started on 12 March and gathered pace in early April, a tentative British plan had emerged. This involved using two vessels: first, the large Swedish ship, S.S. *Gripsholm*, which would be chartered to carry 100 Japanese from the UK to Bombay, whence – having there picked up a further 1600 (later revised downwards) – it would re-cross the Indian Ocean to drop them all at Lourenço Marques (a journey estimated to take about ten weeks), finally returning to London with 1100 British evacuees from Tokyo dropped there by a Japanese vessel; and second, a British troop-ship, to bring between 400 and 2000 Japanese nationals from Australia to Lourenço Marques before proceeding to Canada. (Since the trooper could not divert to the UK, this still left the problem of getting the extra British nationals out of Portuguese East Africa, and required still more temporary South African hospitality.)

Unfortunately, on 20 April it was learned that the Americans had already snapped up the *Gripsholm*, as well as the only other large Swedish vessel available, the *Drottningholm*, which it planned to use for the repatriation of Axis officials on the Atlantic crossing. This development threw the British into temporary confusion. In early May, at which point the Foreign Office was hopeful that the exchange would take place at the beginning of July, the first alternative in prospect – with some assistance from the Americans – was the Argentine vessel, the *Rio de la Plata*. This was well equipped; however, it was not very large and could not be obtained immediately. Then the Egyptian S.S. *El Nil* (220 passengers) also became available. But both together would not provide the capacity of the *Gripsholm*. In the end, the *El Nil* was chartered for the UK–Lourenço Marques run in preference to the Argentine vessel, while troopships were used for the rest.

Meanwhile, despite a prod from the Foreign Office on 4 May, it was a month before the Japanese – who were no doubt having their own problems – broadly accepted Britain's proposal to double the size of the exchange. They would repatriate the larger total of 1700 British and Allied nationals on two ships, the *Kamakura Maru* and the *Tatuta Maru*, which would arrive at Lourenço Marques on 10 July. The British and American exchanges should still take place concurrently. All of the officials to be repatriated would be carried on this occasion, while those non-officials left behind would be taken on a subsequent voyage. Just over a week later they also agreed to include Redman and several other named officials in the exchange.

Unfortunately, some groups and named individuals were still missing from the Japanese list, notably Commander Woolley, the naval staff officer at the consulate-general in Shanghai, and two Australian officials – the official representative in Singapore, Vivian Bowden, and the consul in Timor, David Ross. They had also failed to confirm that they would give priority – as had been requested – to those British nationals who were suffering imprisonment. The Foreign Office anticipated that it would take two to three weeks to clear this up, not least because Canberra was particularly angry about Bowden and Ross and was refusing to release the 25 Japanese officials it held against only some eight Australian nationals if these two were not returned as well. The Foreign Office also complained to the Japanese that their laggardly reply had made it impossible for Britain to make 'detailed' shipping arrangements. For all of these reasons, the date on which it was hoped the exchange might take place receded: the earliest that the British could contemplate was now 15 August. As expected, the Americans did not feel able to wait this long and agreed to the Japanese suggestion to make their own rendezvous at Lourenço Marques on 10 July.

In light of the British suggestion of 15 August as the exchange date, in the second week of June the Japanese replied that their own vessels would arrive at Lourenço Marques five days later, adding that they would now be providing accommodation for 1800 evacuees, not 1700 as originally stated. This was close enough, but the Foreign Office waited until 2 July before sending off confirmation that Britain would reciprocate on the number and aim for the same date – adding, however, that Britain's commitment to 20 August was conditional on the return of Woolley, Bowden and Ross, together with priority for those suffering imprisonment. In practice, this meant a deadline for the Japanese of 13 July, since if the *El Nil* did not sail from the UK on that date it could not arrive at Lourenço Marques by 20 August.

Just two days after belatedly serving this notice on Tokyo (but probably before it had arrived), the Foreign Office learned from the Berne legation that the Japanese had now announced that the British party would not leave Tokyo before 7 September. 'FO are making urgent enquiries of Berne – it looks as if this ditches whole scheme', someone in the Admiralty scribbled on a copy of the telegram in which this alarming news was conveyed.[86] Clearly, the Japanese had decided to give the British some of their own medicine. Tired of waiting for the British response to their suggested date of 20 August for the exchange, they used exactly the same language that the British had used to them when – on an earlier occasion – London had shown impatience with Tokyo. Due to British tardiness, they said, they had been unable to make the 'detailed' shipping arrangements needed for the exchange to proceed smoothly. There was, nevertheless, some consolation for the Foreign Office in the message in which this language was used: it now appeared that 7 September was the date being proposed for the exchange at Lourenço Marques, not the departure date of the exchange ships from Japan. The relief felt at this notwithstanding, the Foreign Office countered with a proposal for the exchange to take place on 27 August, warning that further delay would so upset the 'complicated shipping arrangements' necessary that even more delay might well be the result.[87] A week later a neat compromise was achieved: the exchange would take place in two stages, the first on 27 August and the second on 7 September, 900 persons being exchanged on each occasion.

Meanwhile, agreement had been reached between Britain and its allies on their individual quotas of non-nationals to be evacuated and the Dominions Office had managed to persuade the Australians to drop their threat to scupper the whole arrangement if the Japanese would not return Bowden and Ross.[88] As a result,

[86] TNA, Berne to FO, 3 (received 4) July 1942, ADM199/1294.

[87] TNA, FO to Berne, 7 July 1942, ADM199/1294.

[88] By this time they would have known that Ross had escaped and no doubt feared that Bowden was dead, as unhappily proved to be the case.

all now looked set for the exchange to go ahead. There were, however, to be further difficulties to overcome.

As the evacuees were being marshalled for boarding, there were arguments over Swiss reports that certain individuals were being excluded, and over the implementation of the agreement on priorities for non-officials. There was also anxiety that atrocity stories appearing in the American press would threaten the second stage of the exchange. And then there was the extremely important need to do whatever was possible to ensure the safety of the exchange ships on their voyages. This meant sharing knowledge of the markings on their hulls and superstructures, which included on both sides amidships the word 'DIPLOMAT' painted in large letters; at night they were also to be floodlit. Knowledge of their routes and speeds also needed to be shared, not least because safe conducts had to be secured from the belligerent powers with warships and submarines operating in the waters through which the exchange ships would have to pass. Obtaining safe conducts was obviously vital and delays in obtaining these – sometimes because applications were not accompanied by sufficient information – held up some sailings. Ideally, too, it was desirable that warships and submarines should signal their understanding that an exchange vessel had been granted a safe conduct. 'Safe conduct ships have been sunk before now', the Foreign Office told its consul in Lourenço Marques, when urging him to impress on nervous Indian evacuees the advantages of returning to the sub-continent on a ship in convoy rather than wait forever for one with a safe conduct.[89]

The American–Japanese exchange had already taken place successfully at Lourenço Marques in the space of under four hours on 24 July.[90] This was later than envisaged because of last minute hitches, mainly to do with passenger lists, and the American diplomats did not finally reach New York until 25 August – a total journey time of over two months since they had boarded their

[89] TNA, FO to Lourenço Marques, 7 Sept. 1942, ADM199/1294.

[90] Preston (Lourenço Marques) to SoS, 28 July 1942, *FRUS, 1942*. Vol. I, p. 440.

exchange ship in Yokohama harbour.[91] The two-stage timetable agreed with the Japanese by the British also slipped somewhat but not seriously. The British consulate-general at Lourenço Marques – which had recently been strengthened – had also learned some good lessons from the American experience about how to handle the exchange.

Meanwhile, as they waited for the interminable exchange negotiations to conclude, life for the senior British diplomats at least had been tolerable. According to Craigie, relations with the police had improved as a result of pressure from the foreign ministry, occasional visits to town had been allowed, and in early July – in the interests of his health – he had even been permitted a fortnight's break at a mountain resort two hours' drive from Tokyo, where he met some other Allied heads of mission.[92] But the general experience had been one of tedium and frustration and they were greatly relieved to be heading for home. Redman had been returned to the embassy just before the departure and was carried on board on a stretcher.[93] On 30 July the *Tatuta Maru*, transporting the British diplomats and other nationals, departed Yokohama and on 27 August arrived on schedule at Lourenço Marques.[94] The *El Nil*, which was carrying the Japanese contingent from Britain (including Matsumoto), arrived four days later. Presumably because of this failure of the vessels to coincide, and notwithstanding the recent agreement between the British and the Japanese that only those not proceeding on a repatriation ship should be allowed ashore, at least the senior diplomats were permitted shore leave on the basis of reciprocity.[95] On 28

[91] Heinrichs, *American Ambassador*, pp. 361–2; Bohlen, *Witness to History, 1929–1969*, p. 115.

[92] Craigie, *Behind the Japanese Mask*, p. 150.

[93] Craigie, *Behind the Japanese Mask*, p. 151; de la Mare, *Perverse and Foolish*, p. 80.

[94] *The Times*, 29 Aug. 1942.

[95] Craigie is altogether vague on the procedural details of the exchange at Lourenço Marques, which would seem to confirm that the senior officials were given preferential treatment, *Behind the Japanese Mask*, p. 155. It would in any case have been impossible to provide accommodation on shore for all of the evacuees.

August, the day after their arrival at Lourenço Marques, the British heads of mission evacuated from Tokyo and Bangkok gave a press conference at the British consulate-general. According to the report in *The Times*, Craigie thanked the Portuguese, Swiss and Argentine governments for their assistance in arranging the exchange, declined to comment on the Japanese treatment of prisoners and internees, and emphasized the determination of all the returning Allied nationals to throw their weight once more into the war effort. It was, said the engagingly cynical Malcolm Muggeridge, the local SIS officer, 'a kind of diplomatic incantation; like a monsignor splashing holy water over a missile site'.[96] After their later arrival, the Japanese diplomats were observed by Muggeridge being entertained by the Italian consul-general, Umberto Campini, at the Polana Hotel – their faces 'frozen in their wonderment' at his 'Mussolini-like gestures'.[97]

The theatricality continued when the formal exchange took place under the eyes of the Portuguese delegate. In what was later described by Paul Gore-Booth as a 'solemn ceremony', the British diplomats and their fellow nationals walked off 'Gangway A' of the *Tatuta Maru* (it is not clear whether Craigie and Crosby had been smuggled back on board in order to be able formally to disembark) while simultaneously their Japanese counterparts boarded it via 'Gangway B'.[98] This vessel then returned to Japan. In due course the British party boarded the *El Nil*, which duly retraced its route to Liverpool, arriving there in early October.

In sum, the periods of internment for the diplomats had been long but not because of any wish on the part of either the British or the Japanese that this should be so. Rather, it was a result of many quite different factors. First among these was without doubt the agreement that 'non-officials' should, as far as this was

[96] Muggeridge, *Chronicles of Wasted Time, vol. 2*, p. 170.
[97] Muggeridge, *Chronicles of Wasted Time, vol. 2*, p. 172.
[98] A similar, if not identical procedure, which took four hours to execute on 24 July, had been employed for the exchange of the American and Japanese internees between the *Asama Maru* and the *Conte Verde* on the one hand, and the *Gripsholm* on the other, Melbourne, *Conflict and Crises*; and Hemingstam, 'Drottningholm and Gripsholm'.

possible, be evacuated at the same time as the diplomats and other officials. Since the non-officials on both sides – but especially on the British – were scattered far and wide, gathering them in was a time-consuming business. Then there were the almost equally demanding tasks of concerting positions with allies and negotiating such sensitive points as passenger lists, markings on the exchange vessels, routes and ports of call, and date and place of exchange. To make matters worse, this all had to be done via third parties because of the political problems of seeking agreement before war had commenced, with the added difficulty presented to communications over long distances by war-time conditions. In addition to this there was the acute problem of finding ships at a time when military demands for them had priority and sinkings were mounting all the time. Securing safe conducts confirmed by receipt of acknowledgements from warships and submarines active on the chosen routes was not exactly a business that could be achieved overnight either; and in any case could not be sought until sailing dates were definitely fixed. In the circumstances, it was something of a miracle that it was only ten months before all of the diplomatic and consular staff and their families were safely home.

Preserving diplomatic relations

Following the Second World War, as explained in the Introduction, states resolved to settle their disputes by force of arms normally fought shy of formally 'declaring war'. This made it easier to remain in diplomatic relations even after armed conflict had broken out. The consequence of this was that rather than being swiftly repatriated or allowed to return only after a lengthy period of internment, the staff of embassies and subordinate posts could sometimes find themselves in the hitherto unknown situation of being required to carry on with their diplomatic and consular duties as best they could while their states were effectively at war. The period during which they would be permitted to do this might last for only a limited period following the start of a conflict but sometimes extend over its full duration – always provided there were reasonable assurances of the safety of the staff.[99] This has not happened very often but the fact that it happens at all is testimony to the courage of the men and women who serve in these missions and to the value of their work. The experience of the belligerent embassies in the limited but savage Sino–Indian border war from 20 October to 21 November 1962 is the first instance worthy of note.[100]

During the period of tension prior to the outbreak of this conflict there had been angry opposition demands in the Indian parliament for the closure of the influential Chinese embassy in Delhi,[101] and ambassadors had been recalled by both sides. Dependants and non-essential staff had also been sent home.[102] Neither embassy had a direct telecommunication link with its home ministry and at the start of the war the Peking post office refused any longer to send the Indian embassy's coded telegrams to New Delhi;[103] it

[99] Gore-Booth (ed.), *Satow's Guide to Diplomatic Practice*, p. 155; Dembinksi, *The Modern Law of Diplomacy*, p. 96; Denza, *Diplomatic Law*, pp. 477, 485.

[100] Another candidate for this title is Britain's undeclared war with Vichy France from July 1940 until its German nemesis late in 1942. However, it was France's consulates in Britain which remained in business rather than its London embassy, which was closed following Marshall Petain's severance of diplomatic relations with the UK after the attack on the French fleet at Mers-el-Kébir on 3 July 1940. On what is nevertheless an instructive case, see Atkin's outstanding account of the Vichy consulates in Britain in ch. 4 of his *The Forgotten French* (the provincial consulates were closed in 1941 but the consul in London was allowed to remain until well into 1942, and was Vichy's de facto diplomatic representative in Britain). Anyone who has any illusions about the extent of the fighting between Britain and Vichy should read Smith, *England's Last War against France.*

[101] Xiaohong Liu, *Chinese Ambassadors*, p. 133.

[102] There is some haziness about when this occurred. Banerjee, whose record is not always accurate, says the staff of both embassies was reduced to 15 on a reciprocal basis shortly after the start of the war in October, *My Peking Memoirs*, pp. 68–9; however, this probably occurred earlier. On the wartime embassies generally, see Banerjee, *My Peking Memoirs*; Damodaran, 'Diary of an old China hand' and Rana, 'A young Indian diplomat in China in the 1960s and 1970s'; *The Times*, 22 and 23 May, 7 Dec. 1962; Gore-Booth (ed.), *Satow's Guide to Diplomatic Practice*, p. 190; Bhutani, *Clash of Political Cultures*, pp. 128–32.

[103] Banerjee, *My Peking Memoirs*, p. 68; see also Bhutani, *Clash of Political Cultures*, pp. 183, 191–2.

would be surprising if the Indian government had not retaliated in kind. The Indian embassy was also handicapped by the absence of any fluent Chinese-speakers on its staff. Nevertheless, both missions were permitted to remain open throughout the conflict and the Indians were able to send telegrams via the British and Yugoslav embassies.[104] The Indian embassy also benefited from the unusually good personal relations between the chargé d'affaires, P. K. Banerjee, and a number of prominent Chinese, notably the premier, Zhou En-lai. Indeed, the embassies were the conduit for the exchange of several messages between Zhou En-lai and the Indian prime minister Jawaharlal Nehru during the fighting – and for the exchange of more immediately afterwards.[105] These were usually initiated by late-night summonses from Zhou to Banerjee, the timing of which was construed by the Indians as 'harassment' and prompted reciprocal nocturnal treatment of the Chinese chargé d'affaires in Delhi[106] – but they were effective. With the assistance of the Chinese foreign ministry and the temporary shift of attention to the threat of global nuclear war posed by the eruption of the Cuban missiles crisis, the Indian embassy also gave a semblance of business as usual – even if, like the Chinese embassy in Delhi, in reality it was in something of a deep freeze.[107] For example, on 5 November, in a routine diplomatic ritual, Banerjee was called to the foreign ministry to hear a protest over India's closure and 'forcible take-over' of the Bank of China's Calcutta branch and Bombay agency.[108] What purposes did the continuing operational presence of these missions serve? Aside from facilitating high-level communication between the two governments, it signalled the determination of both parties to keep their military conflict limited; in other words, it gave substance to the claim of each to have been forced reluctantly into the fighting and to be anxious for a quick settlement.[109] In practical

[104] Banerjee, *My Peking Memoirs*, p. 69.
[105] Banerjee, *My Peking Memoirs*, *passim*.
[106] Information kindly supplied by Kishan Rana.
[107] *The Times*, 7 Dec. 1962.
[108] *The Times*, 6 Nov. 1962.
[109] *The Times*, 31 Oct. 1962.

terms it also enabled the conduct of normal business to resume more quickly than would otherwise have been the case. It is interesting that some time prior to the outbreak of war, Banerjee, who had been a university teacher of international law before entering the foreign service, had discussed – and agreed – with Nehru the point that in modern conditions there were no legal obstacles to preserving diplomatic relations during a war.[110]

In the very next year the same thing happened in the 'Confrontation' between Indonesia and Malaysia, supported by Britain.[111] This was caused by the openly declared determination of the charismatic but erratic Indonesian president, Dr Sukarno, to 'crush' the new federation of Malaysia announced on 16 September 1963. Malaysia had a defence agreement with Britain – which had been the midwife of the new state – and to Sukarno was therefore nothing but a vehicle for the neo-colonial encirclement of Indonesia, the most obvious threat from which was on the shared island of Borneo.[112] Immediately the new state was proclaimed, therefore, the chancery of the British embassy in the Indonesian capital, Djakarta, newly built only a year earlier, was attacked and severely damaged by a large mob; two days later rioters returned to finish the job, terrorizing the staff (a small number of whom were injured before they were rescued by the police), ransacking the offices, torching the building and placing the Indonesian flag on its charred shell.[113] A similar fate was met by many embassy staff houses, as well as by private property owned by British citizens and the British consulate at Medan in north Sumatra; many British company properties were at the same time occupied

[110] Banerjee, *My Peking Memoirs*, pp. 91, 144.

[111] I am grateful to John W. Young for drawing this case to my attention.

[112] On the background to and course of this conflict, see Easter, *Britain and the Confrontation with Indonesia, 1960–1966*; Phillips, *Envoy Extraordinary*, ch. 9; and Healey, *The Time of My Life*, pp. 229–31, 285–9.

[113] This account of the events of September 1963 is based largely on the British ambassador's diary, 16–27 Sept. 1963 and Gilchrist to Butler, 3 Mar. 1964 (repr. in Confidential Print], both held in CAC Cam., GILC/13; see also *The Times*, 17, 19 and 20 Sept., 1 Oct. 1963. The British Council's office in Djakarta was unaccountably overlooked in this orgy of destruction but all of its offices in Indonesia were ordered to be closed a year later, *The Times*, 13 Aug. 1964.

by their employees. The residence of the ambassador, Sir Andrew Gilchrist, was spared because it was of historical importance to Sukarno but also suffered the ignominy of having its Union Jack replaced by the Indonesian flag. Only a 24-hour watch on the burnt-out chancery (entry to which was prohibited to embassy staff on the pretext that it was unsafe), together with a show of strength by friendly members of the diplomatic corps and prompt action by the military attaché, Colonel Becke, enabled the British to foil a subsequent attempt by the Indonesians to break into the chancery's three strong-rooms. These had survived the fire and contained its most sensitive documents.[114]

The ambassador, who had himself been hit by stones in the final attack on his embassy and concluded that the Indonesian government was unwilling to conduct business with him, recommended his own recall.[115] But, aside from the personal question, it was not a British reflex to cringe in the face of physical threats or renounce the use of an embassy in an important state. There was an evacuation of British nationals to orchestrate, consular protection to provide for the many choosing to remain, and extensive British commercial interests to look out for, in particular a new agreement due to be concluded in only a few days between British and American oil companies and the Indonesian government 'on comparatively favourable terms'. Despite the 'outrage' of the attack on the embassy, therefore, the foreign secretary, Lord Home, secured the agreement of the cabinet to his view that 'we should avoid, if possible, any rupture of diplomatic relations.'[116] The Indonesians also eventually apologized for the affair and offered guarantees for the future safety of British lives and property. In any case, the Foreign Office was not optimistic about the availability of any effective protecting power other than the Americans should a rupture be forced on them, and Washington wanted the British to remain in Djakarta.[117] As a result, the embassy was left in

[114] These documents were retrieved and incinerated at the US embassy.
[115] TNA, CAB128/37 CC(63), 54th Conclusions, 5pm, 19 Sept., 1963, min. 2.
[116] TNA, CAB128/37 CC(63), 53rd Conclusions, 10.30am, 19 Sept., 1963, min. 1; see also FO to Djakarta, 17 Sept. 1963, PREM11/4310.
[117] TNA, Ormsby-Gore (Washington) to FO, 20 Sept. 1963, FO371/169948. See

place with Gilchrist still as its head.[118] After a few days in the Hotel Indonesia followed by a short period packed into his residence, the chancery and other departments gradually moved into a set of miscellaneous buildings along one edge of the residence garden. Here they remained, with makeshift defences and without a strong-room, throughout the whole period of 'Confrontation' – and well beyond.[119]

In its personnel, too, the British embassy in Djakarta had become a shadow of its former self.[120] By noon on 21 September, by which time the evacuation to Singapore was complete, well over half of the staff as well as all dependants had departed. Among those evacuated was Anthony Bottrall, the political warfare specialist from the Foreign Office's secretive Information Research Department (IRD) sent out earlier in the year to encourage anti-Communist propaganda in Indonesia and whose role it was later feared might have been exposed by the seizure of IRD papers during the looting of the embassy.[121] Left behind were the ambassador, the four service attachés, key members of the chancery and various others, including the archivist, a communications officer, the chaplain and two chancery guards – 19 in all. By the following April it had partially recovered its support staff (tripling the number of chancery guards) but by 1965 it was still down by over 50 per cent on the 1963 numbers of what Gilchrist called his 'front-line troops' – that is, those with 'political/repre-

the other papers in this file on the difficulties anticipated in finding an alternative protecting power.

118 The Malaysian embassy closed but the Australian embassy also remained open, despite the fact that Australian troops came to fight alongside the British in Borneo, Phillips, *Envoy Extraordinary*, p. 72.

119 At the end of the Sukarno era full compensation was agreed and the embassy building – the shell of which had survived – was fully rehabilitated, HCPP (666), 26 Oct. 1967, pp. 23–4; Phillips, *Envoy Extraordinary*, p. 73.

120 Except where otherwise indicated, this account of changes in the embassy and of its functions during the period of 'Confrontation' is based on CAC Cam., 'List of Embassy Staff Evacuated to Singapore', nd; 'Staff Remaining – Djakarta, 21 Sept. 1963'; 'British Embassy, Djakarta. List of UK Based Staff … as at April 27th 1964'; and 'British Embassy, Djakarta – Modus Operandi', ca. 1965, GILC/13.

121 See papers in TNA, FO1110/1663.

sentational functions'. How many of the staff – if any – were SIS officers is impossible to tell but it is well known that the service played an important role in this conflict.[122] Staff turnover was also exceptionally high, which, together with the loss of the mission's archives (which made 'reading in' by new staff impossible), meant that continuity was hard to preserve. Meanwhile, the ambassador, who was the target of both great personal animosity reaching to Sukarno himself and repeated manoeuvres to secure his recall, could communicate with the president only via another (unnamed) ambassador who happened to have his ear.[123] Gilchrist did not actually get an opportunity to talk to Sukarno directly until May 1965 – the first time since presenting his credentials over two years earlier – when by chance he was able to corner him alone at a reception at the Austrian embassy.[124] The embassy functioned in these difficult circumstances by cutting out 'frills' and abandoning some tasks altogether, in particular commercial reporting and political warfare (Bottrall having departed for Singapore).

In the days immediately following the sacking of the British embassy, the belief was briefly held in London that the Indonesians were about to initiate a breach in relations themselves and staff of their London mission were seen removing 'secret papers'.[125] In the event, however, all that happened was that in the following May their ambassador departed for another post and the London

[122] Easter, *Britain and the Confrontation with Indonesia, 1960–1966, passim.*
[123] CAC Cam., 'The Corps Diplomatique', GILC/13. In 1964, one of Gilchrist's own senior colleagues (almost certainly the new counsellor, Gerald Rodgers) thought he should be replaced, informing the head of Personnel Department in the FO that the ambassador was too dull and unimaginative to promote the political solution to confrontation that was so badly needed, CAC Cam., anon to Muirhead (FO), 31 Mar. 1964, GILC/13. It is also clear from Gilchrist's papers at this time that periodically he also thought he should be replaced – but because of the animosity towards him, not because he was dull and unimaginative!
[124] CAC Cam., Gilchrist to Peck (FO), 19 May 1965, GILC/13.
[125] TNA, FO to UK Mission (New York) for SoS, 25 Sept. 1963, FO371/169948.

embassy was left in the hands of a chargé d'affaires;[126] oddly, the size of the embassy's defence section was also reduced.[127]

In short, then, labouring under marked handicaps although they were, the embassies remained in place in both Djakarta and London and thereby helped both to mask and keep the lid on what is now known to have been an ugly, secret guerrilla war in the jungles of Borneo which at one time threatened to escalate into open, all-out war.[128] But this was by no means all they did. The British embassy in Djakarta kept the Foreign Office in London and the British Commander-in-Chief in Singapore as fully informed as possible on developments in Indonesia's foreign policy, internal politics (including the physical health of Sukarno, in which there was great interest) and military activities; exerted such pressure as it could on Indonesian ministries on matters affecting British interests (including commerce, which continued much as before); provided consular services; and far from least – indeed a 'weighty commitment', according to the ambassador – provided the propaganda agencies of Malaysia as well as Britain (the Political Warfare Co-ordinator of which, Norman Reddaway, was based in Singapore) with the materials which formed 'the basis of their output'.[129] Since it was widely appreciated that no military solution to 'Confrontation' was possible, this was vital to the form and timing of Britain's attempts to undermine Sukarno's regime. Finally, the British embassy provided what seems to have been the key channel for promoting understandings between

[126] This was a minister plenipotentiary, Suyoto Suryo-di-Puro. An ambassador was not restored to the embassy until October 1966. This was General Ibrahim Adjie, who – interestingly enough to mention – had been military attaché at the Indonesian embassy in Belgrade from 1956 to 1959: *FO List 1965*; *The Times*, 13 Feb. and 15 May 1964; 28 Dec. 1965; 12 Aug. and 27 Oct. 1966.

[127] Four service attachés are recorded in the *FO List 1964* but only two in the *FO List 1965*.

[128] Easter, *Britain and the Confrontation with Indonesia, 1960–1966*, ch. 5.

[129] CAC Cam., 'British Embassy, Djakarta – Modus Operandi', ca. 1965, GILC/13. On the propaganda value of Gilchrist's 'Sitreps' (situation reports) see also Reddaway (Office of the Political Adviser to the C-in-C, Far East, Singapore) to Gilchrist, 18 July 1966, GILC/13; and Easter, *Britain and the Confrontation with Indonesia, 1960–1966*, p. 168.

London and the Indonesian army generals who gradually eased Sukarno out and in the course of 1966 brought 'Confrontation' to an end.[130] It would be surprising if the full complement of service attachés which had remained at the British embassy throughout the conflict had not had a hand in this. It is reasonable to infer that at least some of these functions were fulfilled for its own government by the Indonesian embassy in London, assisted by the fact that it worked under fewer handicaps.

During the short Indo-Pakistan wars in August–September 1965 and December 1971, the same pattern of missions remaining in place was once more observable. Perhaps it was not entirely coincidental, either, that in 1965 Gopalaswami Parthasarathi, the Indian high commissioner in Karachi,[131] had been in charge of the Indian embassy in Peking prior to his recall in 1961; and that Arshad Husain, in charge of the Pakistan high commission in Delhi, was a first cousin of an Indian ambassador.[132] Nevertheless, below the surface the picture was somewhat different from that evident in the Sino–Indian conflict in 1962; there were also significant variations between the 1965 and 1971 Indo–Pakistan wars.[133]

On the outbreak of neither war were diplomatic relations simultaneously severed, although as soon as hostilities commenced the missions on both sides (including consular posts) had their telephone links cut, all staff and their families were in effect placed under 'house arrest' and no unauthorized visitors were permitted. However, on 6 December 1971, only a few days after the second war broke out,[134] Pakistan *did* formally sever diplomatic

[130] Easter, *Britain and the Confrontation with Indonesia, 1960–1966*, pp. 170, 181, 190; Phillips, *Envoy Extraordinary*, pp. 72–4.

[131] J. K. Galbraith, at the time US ambassador in Delhi, had a long talk with Parthasarathi before he left for Karachi and recorded in his diary that he was 'a reasonable man who will work for Indian–Pakistani reconciliation', *Ambassador's Journal*, p. 383. He was still in Karachi in 1965 because the Pakistan foreign ministry – with the diplomatic missions in its wake – did not move to the new capital of Islamabad until after the war, in November, *The Times*, 26 Feb. 1966.

[132] This was Azim Husain, ambassador to Switzerland, *The Times*, 26 Apr. 1968.

[133] cf. Denza, *Diplomatic Law*, p. 485.

[134] It was publicly declared on 7 December.

relations with India, ostensibly because of the latter's recognition of the breakaway state of Bangladesh earlier in the day.[135] In these circumstances the wartime mission of neither state was able to do any political or consular business. In fact, in 1971 the only reason they remained was that trust between the Indian and Pakistan governments was at such a discount that neither party would permit the departure of mission staff from its own territory until – as in the Second World War – it had cast-iron guarantees that its own diplomats would be returned safely at the same time; and, following Swiss intervention, they were exchanged very shortly after the fighting stopped.[136] On the other hand, in 1965 – when India and Pakistan remained in diplomatic relations throughout the fighting and the wartime diplomats were not afterwards repatriated – it seems clear that in late October–early November at least the Indian embassy in Karachi played a role in negotiation of the Indo–Pakistani agreement on the exchange of internees that bore fruit as early as mid-December 1965.[137] However, in 1965, if not in 1971, it also seems clear that keeping missions in place was more important as a means of signalling the anxiety of both sides to keep the fighting limited. There must at any rate have been some good reason for it because Pakistan, with far less provocation, had no hesitation at the same juncture in severing diplomatic relations with Malaysia for failing to lend it moral support.

Finally, lest it be thought that preserving diplomatic relations and operational embassies in armed conflict was a transient fashion of the 1960s which fizzled out in the early 1970s, let the Gulf War of 1990–1 be recalled. In this conflict the US-led coalition began its bid to drive the forces of Saddam Hussein out of Kuwait with a massive aerial bombardment of Iraq in the early hours of 17 January 1991. However, although Coalition embassies in Baghdad were closed shortly before the attack, Iraq was determined to keep

[135] *The Times*, 7 Dec. 1971; Dembinski, *The Modern Law of Diplomacy*, p. 96; and information kindly supplied by Kamal N. Bakshi, India's assistant high commissioner in Karachi during the 1971 conflict.

[136] Information kindly supplied by Kamal N. Bakshi.

[137] *The Times*, 28 Oct., 5 Nov. and 20 Dec. 1965.

its own embassies in their capitals open as long as possible.[138] As late as 24 January it even sought the permission of the British government to appoint a *new* ambassador. This was declined by John Major's government, but the Iraqi embassy in London remained open until the first week of February, when Saddam finally broke relations with Britain.[139] Other Iraqi embassies in coalition states also remained open until early February and diplomatic relations between the United States and Iraq were not severed – also on the initiative of Baghdad – until 9 February. Dr Abdul Razzak Al-Hashimi, Iraq's most senior diplomat at a foreign posting, did not leave his embassy in Paris until 18 February, barely a week before the start of the ground war.[140] There is no doubt that the propaganda activities of its embassies was believed to be of enormous value by Saddam Hussein's government in January–February 1991 (his ambassadors were constantly to be seen making his case on television sets), and was the main reason why they were kept open for so long.[141]

Conclusion

Following the outbreak of armed conflict and the initial isolation of an embassy finding itself on enemy territory, mission staff may be permitted to depart promptly, be interned for a long period until a formal exchange of diplomats is negotiated, or be left to get on with their business as best they can. The first of these three possibilities was the norm in the First World War. In the Second World War it was still not unusual, but was being replaced by internment pending formal exchange. During the 1939–45 conflict the treatment of interned diplomats was rarely bad, and when

138 'For tactical reasons the FCO did not go for a formal breach in relations [at the time the British embassy in Baghdad was closed], and left the onus to do this on the Iraqis', Munro, *An Embassy at War*, p. 228.

139 Munro, *An Embassy at War*, p. 283.

140 *The New York Times*, 25 and 30 Jan. 1991; *The Seattle Times*, 19 Feb. 1991; U.S. Dept. of State (Office of the Historian), *A Guide …: Iraq* [www].

141 Taylor, *War and the Media*, pp. 97–8, 106–7.

internment was protracted it was not a symptom of any descent into barbarism. Instead, it was usually because of the political need to include non-officials as well as officials in the exchanges and the exceptional difficulties presented by wartime conditions of agreeing their terms via third parties and then carrying them out, often over very great distances. When diplomatic relations are not broken on the outbreak of armed conflict – an encouraging development of more recent times – and working embassies are left in place, this is usually because of a desire on the part of both parties to minimize the significance of the fighting and certainly to signal an intention to avoid all-out war. This can also have other practical advantages, notably in the fields of intelligence-gathering and propaganda.

3 Neutral Embassies to Belligerents

Chapter Overview

Adjustments in the shape, size and priorities of the embassy of a neutral state to a belligerent depend chiefly on its vulnerability – and the vulnerability of its operations – to the fighting, the nature and extent of the general disruption caused by wartime conditions, the likely outcome of the conflict and the response to this prospect of the government at home. A neutral embassy in a belligerent remote from the front line and not vulnerable to accidental attack from the air is unlikely to be dramatically affected by the war. By contrast, a neutral mission finding itself more exposed will usually have to send home dependants and non-essential staff and, with a skeleton operation, concentrate solely on the core functions of preserving communications, consular and commercial work and war reporting. Whether exposed to the fighting or not, how effectively it is able to pursue these task also depends on how the neutrality of its government is seen by the belligerent. Few are ever regarded as strictly impartial; so is it seen as a friendly or an unfriendly neutral? When a neutral embassy accepts the role of protecting power for the interests of one or more enemy states, the impact of the war is particularly great. The embassies of neutral protecting powers do work of great value and as a result will be given disproportionate attention in this chapter. However, it is important to remember that historically they have represented only a small minority of neutral embassies to belligerent states – and since the Second World War have been absent altogether from most international armed conflicts and all major ones.

Helping expatriates

The first priority of the neutral embassy on the outbreak of war is ministering to the needs and anxieties of the expatriate community. While its members will be unlikely to suffer the official maltreatment which belligerent nationals might expect, they might well risk being caught up in any fighting or – in some circumstances – be mistaken on the streets for belligerent nationals or suspected of sympathising with them. When the expatriate community of a neutral state is large the task of responding to its demands can seem daunting to its embassy, especially if the outbreak of war is relatively sudden. This was the case with the embassy of the neutral United States to Germany at the start of the First World War in August 1914. The American ambassador, James W. Gerard, a New York lawyer and active member of the Democratic Party with no diplomatic experience prior to his appointment to Berlin in July 1913, found his embassy 'overrun with Americans' as soon as war seemed imminent. Thousands of them besieged the building, most needing passports and money (German banks had stopped cashing cheques and letters of credit) and all wanting seats on special trains to Holland and sea passages home. The first room inside the embassy entrance became a ticket office, while a relief committee and banking office were established in the ballroom. To cope with this dramatic upsurge in consular work, Gerard not only had to draft the entire staff of the embassy but also enlist volunteers, among them an

11-year old child who happened to be staying in his residence at the time.[1]

Similar scenes were no doubt witnessed at some of the other embassies similarly placed in this conflict, as in others afterwards; fortunately, they do not normally last for very long. In other embassies, especially those with well-laid evacuation plans, matters usually proceed in more orderly fashion. This was certainly true of the evacuation of Americans from Egypt from the port of Alexandria during the Suez War in the late autumn of 1956, in which the United States was to all intents and purposes neutral. It was also carried off despite the fact that the evacuation convoy had to depart from Cairo while the British were bombing targets in and around the city. It helped that the US embassy had a consulate-general at Alexandria and that the Egyptian authorities were cooperative.[2]

Reporting the war

In wartime, when changes affecting the fate of nations can occur suddenly, intelligence on the intentions and military capabilities of belligerents is particularly important to all neutrals whose territory, commerce or other vital interests overseas are exposed to the conflict. Usually they require this intelligence chiefly in order to know which side is most likely to win, because only if they know this will they be in a position to adopt a posture appropriate to the protection of those interests. But they might also find it extremely useful in modifying their own defence forces, especially if there is a possibility that at some point in the future they will have to confront one of the current belligerents themselves.

Powerful neutrals tend to assume a policy of benevolent neutrality to the party which seems most likely to lose, especially if a victory by either party would jeopardize a power balance in which they have an interest or if for some other reason the

[1] Gerard, *My Four Years in Germany*, pp. 96–8.
[2] Hart interviews, Hare interview.

prospective loser attracts its sympathy. Considerations of both sorts were in evidence in the attitudes of the United States in the early years of both world wars in the twentieth century and in the terrible Iran–Iraq war when, in 1982, it began to seem that Iran might win.[3] In the Kosovo War in 1999, the PRC tilted markedly to the Milosevic regime because, like Serbia, it too had restive minorities and wished to see no precedents established for successful Western-led interventions to protect them. By contrast, neutrals which are weaker relative to the parties to a conflict are more inclined – in order to forestall an attack – to tilt to the side of the prospective winner, as was the case with a number of neutrals in the Second World War. In the end, weak and powerful neutrals alike may need to abandon neutrality altogether in order to get the result they want.

In obtaining the information they need to adjust their policies to suit their interests, the diplomatic missions of neutrals in the capitals of the major belligerents have usually played a key role. Indeed, it is one of the main reasons why some choose to stay on – not all do – despite the considerable difficulties of obtaining intelligence in some circumstances and the dangers faced by embassy staff, especially if an air war develops. For example, even after the United States had tilted towards Iraq in the latter's war with Iran, the US embassy in Baghdad – which had re-opened in 1984 – could not get access to the war zone and its service attachés were closely watched. As for the chief of its political section, apart from official contacts, he had to rely for his information mainly on visiting journalists, other members of the diplomatic corps and authorized travels in the countryside with his family. Meanwhile, Iranian Scud missiles were falling randomly on Baghdad.[4] As for the Chinese embassy in Belgrade during the Kosovo War, this was widely suspected of exploiting its position to gain intelligence on NATO military technology, and paid the price in the form noted

[3] The United States was 'officially neutral' in this conflict but the US ambassador in Baghdad from 1984–8 says that 'my longer term requirement was [to] do everything that we could to help within legal limits to make sure the Iraqis didn't lose the war', Newton interview. See also Rankin interview.

[4] Rankin interview; see also Newton interview.

at the start of this book (p. 1).[5] Nevertheless, neutral embassies do not always find intelligence as difficult to obtain as the Americans did in Baghdad, and even in such instances they usually have one advantage: the anxiety of the belligerent host government to court a weighty or strategically significant neutral in the hope that it might be won over, or won over more completely. For the embassies of such states, the doors of highly placed persons will usually be open, while the movements of their staff in these states or in territories they have occupied will in most cases be relatively unimpeded. This is readily seen in two other instructive examples: the US embassy at Rome and the Swedish legation at Berlin in the Second World War.

In January 1940, still six months before Benito Mussolini's Fascist Italy entered the war on Hitler's side, the US embassy at Rome was presided over by William Phillips. A Harvard-educated New Englander who had been chief of mission in Rome since 1936 (it was a post he had sought), Phillips was a senior and well connected career diplomat – 'one of our most competent', noted Roosevelt's secretary of state, Cordell Hull.[6] According to a contemporary *Time* magazine article, he was suave and gracious and second only to Sumner Welles in the State Department for 'tall, aristocratic elegance'; in disposition, it added, he was a 'patient, conservative diplomat who has never ruffled feathers nor interfered with history.'[7] Phillips had a diplomatic staff of 15, eight of whose members were service attachés, among whom the largest number represented the Navy Department. The embassy also had a four-man consular section, and nine consular posts scattered across the country. The latter included a consulate-general at Milan and another – by far the largest – at the port of Naples, which was soon to become a vital node in Axis communications in the eastern Mediterranean and the most heavily bombed Italian

[5] *The Observer*, 17 Oct. 1999.

[6] Hull, *The Memoirs*, pp. 509, 1491. On leaving Rome, Phillips was briefly with the OSS in London, then the president's personal representative in India, and after that political adviser to General Eisenhower.

[7] *Time*, 21 Dec. 1942; see also Bohlen, *Witness to History*, p. 38, for a similar description.

city in the Second World War.[8] At the end of May 1940, Phillips believed that the United States should immediately make up its mind to enter the war.[9] Furthermore, when Italy entered the fray in June and the Allied missions departed, the ambassador found himself increasingly isolated, with Mussolini himself refusing to see him any more because of the hostility of the American press and the increasingly anti-Axis posture of the Roosevelt administration. Since the ambassador believed that Italy's policies were being directed by Hitler, he also thought it pointless and demeaning to be an ambassador in what was in effect nothing more than a German province, especially since there was not even an American ambassador in Berlin any more.[10] Accordingly, he repeatedly urged his recall. The US embassy in Rome, like the one in Berlin, he thought, should be left to a chargé d'affaires – 'all that was really necessary to preserve the contacts'.[11] But it was not to be. Despite long periods of home leave which he obviously hoped would become permanent, at Roosevelt's insistence he remained head of the mission until the United States entered the war at the end of 1941.

Despite the handicaps under which Phillips came to labour, he continued to have easy access to the Italian foreign minister and son-in-law of Mussolini, Count Ciano, and got on with him well enough. On 22 April 1940, Ciano recorded in his diary that Phillips 'more and more reveals himself to be a friend and a gentleman', and noted on the outbreak of war between their countries on 11 December 1941, following Pearl Harbor, that 'Phillips is an honest man, and he loves Italy. I know that for him this is a day of

[8] *Foreign Service List*, January 1 1940 (Washington: GPO, 1940). A year later, there had not been much change, *Foreign Service List*, 1 January 1941.

[9] Phillips to Hull, 28 May 1940, *FRUS, 1940*. Vol. I, p. 235.

[10] Phillips, *Ventures in Diplomacy*, p. 175.

[11] He had an able and experienced number two in Alexander Kirk who could readily take over. Kirk had served as a junior under Gerard in Berlin in the First World War, had been in Rome before, and had actually been chargé d'affaires in Berlin on the outbreak of war in September 1939, Phillips, *Ventures in Diplomacy*, pp. 131, 174–205 *passim; Register of the Department of State*, 1 Nov. 1941, p. 154.

mourning.'[12] As for his own view of the foreign minister, Phillips wrote in his memoirs that 'in spite of his dissipation and conceit, he had remained helpful, even friendly to me during the difficult months of 1941, when most Italians had avoided me.'[13] This relationship and the numerous private interviews through which it developed, was no doubt an important reason why Roosevelt insisted on Phillips remaining at his post. For this not only gave the president – who was anxious to keep Italy out of the war for as long as possible – an effective channel to the foreign minister's ear but also enabled him, via the ambassador's reports, to gain insight into Ciano's mind.[14] The ambassador's reports, which were also eloquent on the state of Italian public opinion, continued to be of 'great use.'[15] Clearly, too, their value must have increased as it became more and more likely as 1941 progressed that the United States would be drawn into war with Italy on the side of Britain, for the British themselves no longer had diplomatic resources there and SIS found it virtually impossible to penetrate.[16] It is unlikely that this point was lost on Phillips but it was certainly one with which he had some difficulty in coming to terms.[17]

In any event, there were numerous other sources of information on Italy on which the American ambassador could draw. Other ambassadors were one of them – for example, the Greek minister on the Balkan situation and the Chinese chargé d'affaires on Axis moves in the Far East.[18] American correspondents were

[12] *Ciano's Diary*, pp. 237, 408.

[13] Phillips, *Ventures in Diplomacy*, pp. 203–4.

[14] Although Phillips himself doubted – at least at the beginning of 1940 – that this access had the further and critical advantage of giving him indirect access to Mussolini's own thinking, Phillips to Hull, 28 Feb. 1940, *FRUS, 1940*. Vol. I, p. 12.

[15] Roosevelt to Phillips, 24 May 1941, quoted in Phillips, *Ventures in Diplomacy*, p. 191.

[16] Jeffery, *MI6*, pp. 423–7.

[17] Recording his feelings after Roosevelt's strong anti-Axis Labour Day address in 1941, Phillips wrote: 'What a strange [not a valuable] position I was in! An Ambassador accredited to the military partner of the Axis, while my country was determined to "crush" the Axis and all of their forces!', Phillips, *Ventures in Diplomacy*, p. 199.

[18] Phillips, *Ventures in Diplomacy*, p. 174 and Phillips to Hull (various), *FRUS*,

regularly tapped by Phillips for information.[19] There are also oblique references in his memoirs (and guarded but slightly more revealing ones in despatches from the embassy published later) to important intelligence obtained from a number of other contacts, one of whom was a friend also in the confidence of someone in the German embassy;[20] although even before the outbreak of war Phillips had noted 'the extreme reticence observed by Italians generally when speaking with foreign diplomatic representatives in regard to international politics.'[21] His embassy staff, particularly his numerous service attachés, would have had their own sources of information, perhaps most especially the military attaché, Colonel Norman Fiske, who had spent several years at the Rome embassy in the mid-1930s (including two months with the Italian army on its Ethiopian campaign) and re-joined it in October 1940.[22] But his most important sources were probably the officers in the extensive American consular network spread over Italy, especially those based in the ports, as most of them were.

The consuls kept Phillips informed of the popular mood in their districts, for example that the heavy British naval bombardment of military targets in and around the port of Genoa on 9 February 1941 had provoked more anger at the government for bringing on this state of affairs than at the shelling itself, and supplied such specific information as that in Milan the Germans were acquiring control of the iron and steel mills.[23] It was, however, undoubtedly their ability to report on ship movements and military activity at

1940. Vol. IV, pp. 273–85.

[19] Phillips, *Ventures in Diplomacy*, pp. 174–87 *passim*.

[20] See especially Reed (chargé d'affaires at Rome for a period during 1940) to Hull, 14 Aug., 21 and 26 Oct. 1940 (forecasting Italian moves against Greece), *FRUS, 1940*. Vol. III, pp. 532, 542 and 545 resp.; Phillips to Hull, 27 and 29 Jan. and 10 Mar. 1941, *FRUS, 1941*. Vol. II, pp. 640–1, 661 resp. This routine caution was just as well because, according to Ciano, Italian military intelligence had got hold of the embassy code and was reading all of Phillips's telegrams, *Ciano's Diary*, 30 Sept. 1941, p. 378.

[21] Phillips to Hull, 5 July 1939, *FRUS, 1939*. Vol. I, p. 663.

[22] Kirk to Hull, 22 June 1936, *FRUS, 1936*. Vol. III, p. 77; *Register of the Department of State*, 1 Nov. 1941, p. 119.

[23] Phillips, *Ventures in Diplomacy*, pp. 177, 179.

the ports which was their greatest value and this is why it was not long before the Italian authorities – who had no illusions about the sort of things that consuls got up to[24] – moved against the American consuls. Just three days after the attack on Genoa, when new restrictions were also imposed on the movements of diplomats, it was announced that all consulates other than those of Germany were to be moved from the ports of Palermo in Sicily and Naples 'to a place as far north as Rome or farther north, and to a place which was not on the sea coast;'[25] and also that consular officers were no longer free to leave their cities of residence without prior notification.[26] The Italians protested that these steps were not anti-American because they were aimed at the consulates of all foreign governments, but this was obviously disingenuous. Aware that Italian officials at American ports and on the Canadian border might obtain information which the United States in its turn might wish to conceal, for example on the supplies being shipped to Britain, the State Department retaliated by imposing similar restrictions on them and requiring the closure of the Italian consulates at Detroit and Newark.[27] At the beginning of May, an Italian foreign ministry official alleged openly that advance information provided to the British by a US consular officer in Naples had been responsible for the sinking some time earlier of two Italian ships and that all 'American consular officers in Italy were spies'.[28] On 19 June 1941, the American embassy in Rome was told that, due to the 'wholly illicit' information-gathering in which the remaining American consular posts on Italian territory were

[24] Although his remark was provoked by a trivial incident concerning the American consul at Naples and a beggar, on 5 March 1940 Ciano confided to his diary that 'as Minister for Foreign Affairs I shudder at the sources of information used by consuls, naturally including our own consuls', *Ciano's Diary*, p. 216.

[25] Memo. of Conversation [with Prince Colonna, the Italian ambassador], by Asst. SoS (Long), 12 Feb. 1941, *FRUS, 1941*. Vol. II, p. 793.

[26] Phillips, *Ventures in Diplomacy*, p. 178.

[27] 'Closure of Italian Consular and Other Offices in the United States and of Similar American Offices in Italy', *FRUS, 1941*. Vol. II, pp. 793–801; Hull, *The Memoirs*, p. 926; *The Times*, 7 Mar. 1941.

[28] Phillips, *Ventures in Diplomacy*, p. 189.

engaged, they were all to be closed and their staffs withdrawn by 15 July.[29] In his memoirs, Phillips claims that this was a 'German-inspired' move prompted by anger at the announced closure just days earlier of all German consulates in the United States, which might be true but it does not follow that the Italians did not have their own reasons for quickly agreeing.[30]

What of the intelligence-gathering activities of the Swedish legation in Berlin? Until well into 1942, Sweden lived in constant fear of German occupation, a fate already suffered by its Scandinavian neighbours. As a result, discerning the Nazi leader's plans was obviously a major priority for the legation. Fortunately, since Sweden was important to the Nazis as a vital source of strategic materials, particularly iron ore and ball bearings, and contained a large reservoir of pro-German sentiment, this did not present it with any major difficulties.[31] The legation was further assisted by the fact that Arvid Richert, who had been Swedish minister in Berlin since 1937 and was to remain there throughout the war, did not – like most Swedish officials – conceal his enthusiasm for a German/Finnish victory over Russia in June 1941;[32] nor was he – any more than his political counsellor, Eric von Post – the sort of diplomat to embarrass his hosts by making a fuss about such a matter as the extermination of the Jews, a Nazi policy of which the legation certainly had knowledge at least as early as August 1942.[33] Richert had 'friendly and confidential contacts' with men such as Ernst von Weizsäcker, number two at the German foreign ministry until 1943, and Werner

[29] Phillips to Hull, 19 June 1941, *FRUS, 1941*. Vol. II, p. 800.

[30] The State Department promptly retaliated by requiring the closure of all Italian consulates (and all other official Italian agencies) in the United States by the same date as that stipulated by the Italians for the departure of the Americans. All of the consuls (including those in and from Germany) were duly exchanged in Lisbon, Phillips, *Ventures in Diplomacy*, pp. 193–4; Welles to the Italian ambassador, 20 June 1941, *FRUS, 1941*. Vol. II, p. 801; *The Times*, 26 July 1941.

[31] This according to the Swedish foreign minister, as reported in Hägglöf, *Diplomat*, pp. 80–1, 141.

[32] Hägglöf, *Diplomat*, p. 164.

[33] Lewandowski, 'Early Swedish information'.

von Grundherr, chief of its Scandinavian desk;[34] he routinely reminded Weizsäcker of the 'German orientation' of the policy of his foreign minister.[35] Swedish businessmen and senior officials such as Gunnar Hägglöf, head of the foreign trade section of the Swedish foreign ministry, who were regular visitors to Berlin, also had talkative high-level contacts.[36] And then there were the Swedish consuls, particularly important among them Karl Yngve Vendel, who in January 1940 was transferred from Holland to the consulate at Stettin, Germany's most important port on the Baltic and not a great distance from Berlin.[37] Gathering intelligence on German military preparations – from his many friends and acquaintances in official circles as well as by direct observation – was Vendel's principal assignment, and he was good at it.[38]

Well placed as it was to gather intelligence, it is not surprising that, in the first days of April 1940, the Swedish legation in Berlin generated a 'flood of telegrams and letters' arriving in Stockholm warning of German attacks on Denmark and Norway, which duly took place only a short while later.[39] A little over a month

[34] Hägglöf, *Diplomat*, p. 156. In 1952 Grundherr, then West Germany's ambassador to Greece, was named by a cross-party Bundestag committee as one of four members of the foreign ministry whose war record was sufficiently unsavoury to warrant his discharge, *Time*, 28 July 1952.

[35] Weizsäcker memorandum, Berlin, 2 Aug. 1940, *DGFP*, no. 279, p. 403.

[36] Hägglöf, *Diplomat*, *passim*.

[37] As a rule, the relatively unknown and unobtrusive consul is readily shifted by neutrals to sensitive spots in wartime. Gerald Fitzmaurice, chief dragoman of the British embassy in Constantinople, was diverted from home leave to serve as acting consul-general in Tripoli during much of the Italo–Turkish War in 1911–12. This was a conflict in which Britain was neutral but greatly interested. Fitzmaurice moved around and met people with no difficulty and sent numerous detailed reports to the Foreign Office on the progress of the fighting, Berridge, *Gerald Fitzmaurice*, pp. 169–71.

[38] It was also Vendel who revealed to Richert and von Post what was really happening to the Jews. This information was contained in a report which he wrote up in the legation following an approved visit in August 1942 to the estate in east Prussia of one of his key contacts, Count Heinrich von Lehndorff, where he appears to have been introduced to General Henning von Tresckow – both key figures in the secret opposition to Hitler in high military circles in Germany, Lewandowski, 'Early Swedish information'.

[39] Hägglöf, *Diplomat*, p. 139. See also Lewandowski, 'Early Swedish

after this, against the background of the perilous position of the German foothold at Narvik in northern Norway, the legation confirmed the rumour that German forces were concentrating for an attack on Sweden itself.[40] Then, in early 1941, it also contributed substance to a rumour which this time materialized and, in so doing, carried the hope of diverting the storm: that, anticipating a long conflict in view of the likely entry of the United States into the war, Hitler was thinking seriously of seizing the main productive areas of the Soviet Union before Stalin's urgent programme of rearmament made the risk too great.[41] For its pains, the Swedish legation in Berlin – like the Chinese embassy in Belgrade many years later – subsequently suffered serious damage by aerial bombardment, as will be seen shortly.

Commercial work

By the beginning of the twentieth century, it had long been established that, as a general rule, a private individual or corporation of a neutral state had a right to trade with or make loans to any belligerent, except in two main circumstances. The first was that the goods shipped should not be 'contraband of war'; that is, should not help to sustain its war effort. But how was contraband to be defined? About armaments there could be little argument, but about many other goods – foodstuffs for example, because soldiers need to eat – there could be, and was, a great deal. The second proviso was that any attempt to 'trade with the enemy' – however innocent – might be prevented if a blockade was in place. But why should a neutral not be able to get goods that it needs from a belligerent? What is the legitimate geographical range of a blockade, and for how long might it be rightfully enforced?

information'.

[40] Hägglöf, *Diplomat*, p. 146. Anxiety on this point was relieved when the Allies decided to abandon the Narvik campaign.

[41] Steinhardt (Moscow) to SoS, 24 Mar. 1941, *FRUS, 1941*. Vol. I, p. 133. Operation 'Barbarossa' was launched against the Soviet Union by Hitler on 22 June 1941. See also Lewandowski, 'Early Swedish information'.

These and a host of other questions concerning neutral rights have always caused political controversy in war. In addition, belligerents locked into protracted conflicts have tended to extend state control over their foreign trade and the exchange of foreign currency needed to finance it. Among other things, this has helped them, either via barter or pre-emptive purchase, to secure vital raw materials from neutrals and, in the process, deny these items to the enemy; neutrals have usually been obliged to reply in kind, harnessing the influence and machinery of the state to their own side in negotiations. War also causes inevitable dislocation to trade by the destruction of transport facilities, communications and so on, and often requires political intervention if priority treatment in commercial dealings is to be secured. For all of these reasons, therefore, it is not surprising that the embassies to belligerents of neutral trading states have always been required to give a markedly higher priority to commercial questions than was customary for them in peacetime.

In the First World War, the American ambassador in Berlin, Gerard, soon found himself heavily engaged in commercial negotiations with the German government. Involving him in discussion with the head of the department of the interior, the foreign minister, the chancellor and the emperor himself, these negotiations were always difficult and frequently unsuccessful. On the supply side, they featured chiefly the anxiety of the United States to secure from Germany such important items as dyestuffs, potash (used for the manufacture of explosives as well as fertilizer), beet-seed and cyanide (employed in the treatment of gold and silver ores) – in all of which Germany held a strong market position.[42] The US embassy also had such commercial tasks as securing export permits or compensation for American-owned property seized by the Germans following their occupation of Belgium.[43] But, above all, it had responsibility for handling all of the numerous and complicated issues which arose from the deadly risks run by American flag vessels and American passengers and

[42] Gerard, *My Four Years in Germany*, pp. 186–91.

[43] Gerard, *My Four Years in Germany*, p. 195.

cargoes on British flag vessels entering the 'war zone' around the British Isles announced by Germany in February 1915. For this meant a blockade enforced by ruthless submarine warfare. 'From then on', wrote Gerard afterwards, 'we had constant cases and crises', a development heralded most dramatically by the sinking of the luxury Cunard liner, RMS *Lusitania*, in the following May, in which well over 100 Americans lost their lives. Securing redress for losses and demanding restrictions on the freedom of German submarines to torpedo merchantmen and passenger vessels without warning was made the more difficult because of the resentment in Germany at the American 'contraband of war' being supplied to Britain in this transatlantic trade. On these grounds, the Kaiser himself refused to see Gerard for long periods.[44] It is true that the embassy had some successes. Among these was its role in the delivery of what was in effect an ultimatum from the US president, Woodrow Wilson, following the sinking of the *Lusitania*, which led to the temporary abandonment of the campaign of unrestricted submarine warfare. Nevertheless, it was helpless to prevent its resumption at the beginning of February 1917, which was the occasion for the severance of diplomatic relations with Germany by the United States.[45] Its declaration of war followed on 6 April.

As for the Swedish legation in Berlin during the Second World War, already mentioned, this was constantly engaged in commercial discussions with the German authorities. These were always likely to be frequent and sensitive because Germany was Sweden's most important trading partner, while Germany came to regard Sweden as its most vital supplier: 'hinterland and supply base of our fighting forces', as Karl Schnurre, number two to Germany's blockade minister, Karl Ritter, put it in September 1941.[46] But what made them even more so was that, following its occupation of Denmark and Norway in April 1940, Germany

[44] Gerard, *My Four Years in Germany*, pp. 154–5.

[45] Gerard, *My Four Years in Germany*, chs. 12 and 17; Liddell Hart, *History of the First World War*, pp. 213, 216.

[46] Schnurre and Wied (Stockholm) to Berlin, 20 Sept. 1941, *DGFP*, no. 343, p. 539; see also Schnurre and Wied to Berlin, 19 Sept. 1941, *DGFP*, no. 336,

secured control of the sea lanes between the Baltic and the North Sea, and was thus in a position to cut off altogether Sweden's maritime trade, which was based on Gothenburg.[47] Meanwhile, the British had imposed their own blockade in the North Sea of ports serving Germany. The upshot was that the Swedes faced a double blockade. After securing the agreement of the British in November 1940 to permit a limited number of sailings, in February 1941 the Swedes finally made a similar breakthrough in Berlin, without which the British agreement would have been useless.[48] This freed up the Gothenburg traffic after a fashion, although it remained prone to interruption. Later in the war, the Swedes were compelled by the British – then joined by the Americans – to adopt a stiffer attitude in their economic relations with the Germans. In return for Allied promises of vital commodities such as petroleum for their armed forces (much of which ended up fuelling Swedish convoys of German supply ships in the Baltic), in a highly complex tripartite agreement signed in London on 23 September 1943, the Swedes made significant concessions. Having already at the end of July cancelled their agreement to German transit traffic to and from Norway, they undertook to extend to the Germans no further credits, while generally reducing exports to them – especially of iron ore – and prohibiting the export of other strategic items altogether.[49]

It is true that the Swedish legation in Berlin was not the most prominent instrument of Swedish–German trade negotiations. In view of the degree to which their economic fates were entwined, it had actually been agreed early on that Sweden and Germany should each establish a permanent trade delegation dedicated to periodic negotiations, and after the agreement for 1941 this machinery was central to the annual revisions of their

p. 533. Schnurre, who held the rank of minister, was head of division W IV in the Economic Policy Department of the German Foreign Ministry.

[47] Hägglöf, *Diplomat*, pp. 107, 117–18,

[48] Hägglöf, *Diplomat*, pp. 157, 159–60.

[49] 'Sweden – War Trade Agreement between the United States, the United Kingdom and Sweden', *FRUS, 1943*. Vol. II, esp. pp. 806–15; Hägglöf, *Diplomat*, pp. 170–4.

trading and payments arrangements until 1943, when the last bilateral agreement, for 1944, was concluded.[50] Sometimes the German delegation, headed by Dr Alex Walter of the German ministry of food and agriculture, would fly to Stockholm,[51] while sometimes the Swedish team, headed by Gunnar Hägglöf, would fly to Berlin; their stays in the respective capitals were lengthy. It is also true that, as Germany was increasingly the *demandeur*, the German legation in Stockholm was also extremely active in commercial matters, as well as in others such as the transit across Sweden of troops and war material. Nevertheless, it is equally clear that the Swedish legation in Berlin supported Hägglöf during his stays in the German capital and held the fort for him in the intervening periods. In both roles, it appears that the key part was played, as might have been expected, by Torsten Vinell, the legation's commercial counsellor, who was formally a member of the Swedish delegation.[52] Furthermore, the agreement freeing the Gothenburg traffic in February 1941 took the form of an exchange of notes between Arvid Richert and Rudolf Leitner in the German foreign ministry,[53] and it would be extremely surprising if the Swedish naval attaché – formally detailed as the point of contact in the legation for the German naval high command in connection with the Gothenburg traffic[54] – was not

[50] *Sweden and Jewish Assets*, pp. 2.29, 2.30.

[51] Sometimes Schnurre would fly in and take over the leadership of the German delegation ('government committee') from Walter when it was already ensconced in Stockholm, a practice to which the minister, Prinz Viktor zu Wied, objected. This was not only because he had complete confidence in Walter, but also because, as he told Weizsäcker in urging him to put a stop to this practice, every time a special representative applied for a visa at the Swedish legation in Berlin the Swedes pressed the alarm button. 'I have just learned', he added in a mournful postscript to the message containing this plea, 'that Herr Schnurre will arrive here in the next few days', Wied to Weizsäcker, 7 Dec. 1941, *DGFP*, no. 558, p. 977.

[52] Walter and Wied to Berlin, 22 Sept. 1941, *DGFP*, no. 347, p. 548. See also *Sweden and Jewish Assets*, *passim*.

[53] *DGFP*, p. 115 n 3.

[54] Official Minute on the Results of the Discussions conducted in Berlin from July 4 to July 8, 1941, regarding the Continuation of the Göteborg Traffic, *DGFP*, encl. with no. 91, p. 117.

a regular member of the Swedish delegation which held the brief for this.[55]

It is testimony to the importance attached by Sweden to maintaining a diplomatic presence in the German capital for commercial as well as other reasons that the legation, which stood on the Tiergartenstrasse, was not abandoned despite the increasing dangers it faced from Allied bombing raids on Berlin. (The consulate-general in Hamburg was also highly vulnerable.) On the night of 22 November 1943, in the course of a massive British raid on the centre of the capital, the legation – along with a number of other diplomatic missions and official buildings – was completely destroyed. Fortunately, a strong shelter under the building recently completed withstood the blast and no member of the staff was injured.[56] Nevertheless, it was a ragged-looking legation party which was at the airport to greet Hägglöf when his delegation – held up in Malmö while the raid lasted – arrived in Berlin afterwards in order to tackle the tricky question of the implications for Swedish–German trade of the tripartite agreement signed in London two months earlier. The rest of the legation, about a hundred people in all, had already been evacuated to Altdöbern, 80 miles from Berlin near the Saxony border.[57] However, the nucleus of the legation remained in the centre of the capital, where it was installed in temporary accommodation on Rauchstrasse. During another raid on Berlin on the night of 16 December, all of the widows of this building were blown out, and in the course of a further bombing attack on the night of 15 February 1944 it was severely damaged by fire.[58] It must have been after these events that more of the legation staff were dispersed to locations outside Berlin, but a small nucleus still remained in the capital until it was finally occupied by the Russians in the spring of 1945. It is as well that the minister had

[55] The Swedish delegation which renegotiated the Gothenburg traffic agreement in Berlin in July 1941 was headed by a rear-admiral.

[56] *The Times*, 24 Nov. 1943.

[57] Hägglöf, *Diplomat*, p. 190.

[58] *The Times*, 18 Dec. 1943 and 17 Feb. 1944.

an unflappable disposition, although he was not among the final hold-outs in Berlin.[59]

Protecting foreign interests

In addition to having to devote extra energy to consular work, commercial work and intelligence gathering – all in circumstances far more difficult than in peacetime – a neutral embassy is sometimes also instructed by its foreign ministry to take over the protection of the interests of one or more states at war with the state to which it is accredited, the embassy or embassies of the former having been closed; it may also have to take charge of the interests of other neutrals, whose embassies have been evacuated because of the difficulty of maintaining them in wartime conditions.[60] This work brings with it obvious burdens and risks for what is traditionally known as the 'protecting power'. What are they and why, nevertheless, are they sometimes taken on?

Even the resources of the embassy of a large neutral will be stretched if it has to become a protecting power, especially in a general war in which it has agreed to act in this manner for more than one state. In the First World War, the American embassy in Berlin, for example, was required to assume protection of the interests of Britain (including the dominion of Canada), Japan, Romania, Serbia and San Marino;[61] and when the United States itself entered the war in February 1917, the Spanish embassy, which

[59] Hägglöf, *Diplomat*, pp. 146, 190; *The Times*, 4 June 1945; TNA, Swedish Legation (London) to FO, 12 Mar. and 15 Apr. 1945, and Mallet (Stockholm) to FO, 23 Apr. 1945, FO371/48039.

[60] The institution of the protecting power has its origins in the sixteenth century and had survived the birth of nationalism to become firmly established by the second half of the nineteenth century. By far the best account of this is to be found in Franklin, *Protection of Foreign Interests*, chs. 1 and 2. Franklin was an academic, but during the Second World War had worked in the State Department and then seen military service. He completed this book after returning to the State Department at the beginning of 1945.

[61] And France, too, where Spain was not in charge, Franklin, *Protection of Foreign Interests*, p. 246; see also Gerard, *My Four Years in Germany*, ch. 10.

was already protecting French, Belgian and Russian interests, had to take over Japanese, Serbian, Romanian and American interests as well, which indirectly also massively increased the workload of the Spanish legation in Berne.[62] Until December 1941 in the Second World War, the US embassy in Berlin had to protect the interests of even more foreign states;[63] the burden of this was made even heavier when, at the insistence of the German authorities, in the summer of 1940 all ten of the US consular posts in Germany were closed down, leaving the Berlin post to pick up all of their work which could not be liquidated altogether.[64]

On top of the additional burden, taking on the protection of 'enemy' interests means that the neutral embassy runs the risk of having its impartiality called into question, with the consequence that its ability to advance the interests of its own state may be markedly reduced. It was fear of this which led the American minister at Brussels, in the event to no avail, to advise the State Department against accepting the request that he should take over protection of German interests in Belgium on the outbreak of the First World War: 'intense hostility in Belgium to Germans', he said, 'would largely nullify my efforts on behalf of our own and other interests'.[65] In February 1916, it was the strong feeling of the US ambassador at Vienna that this sort of fate had actually befallen his own mission.[66] Courting the risks of being a protecting power is the less easy for the neutral

[62] Protection of British interests was transferred to the Dutch legation, SoS to Gerard, 3 Feb. 1917, *FRUS, 1917*, pp. 585–6. On the Berne legation, see Reynoso, *The Reminiscences of a Spanish Diplomat*, ch. 15.

[63] Britain (including India and all British overseas possessions and mandated territories), Australia, New Zealand, Canada, France, Belgium, Luxembourg and South Africa, Franklin, *Protection of Foreign Interests*, p. 261.

[64] Kennan, *Memoirs*, pp. 105–6.

[65] Quoted in Franklin, *Protection of Foreign Interests*, p. 94.

[66] The American embassy to Germany's ally, Austria–Hungary, had taken over protection of the interests of France, Britain, Italy, Japan, and San Marino; see Franklin, *Protection of Foreign Interests*, pp. 101–3, 243. In much more recent times, Sweden – for long a popular choice as a protecting power – has shown itself particularly sensitive to the risk of compromising its reputation for impartiality by taking on this kind of responsibility, Roberts (ed.), *Satow's Diplomatic Practice*, pp. 226–8.

embassy to swallow when it also receives complaints about its activity – as it occasionally does – from protected powers (sometimes known as 'powers of origin') – usually that it is being dilatory or over-cautious in caring for their interests. Such charges against Camille Gorgé, the Swiss minister in Tokyo in the Second World War whom we have come across before (see p. 44 above), reached Washington and London in early 1944, although they were dismissed as unfair by the Foreign Office.[67] So why do neutral states sometimes agree – albeit often with some reluctance – to become protecting powers?

The long and the short of the answer to this question is that it is seen as enlightened self-interest – and is not so expensive as might at first be imagined; nor need it be so risky as in the past it has sometimes proved. It is enlightened because, as we shall see, it helps to preserve the fabric of diplomacy itself and meet urgent humanitarian needs; it also positions the neutral as a possible mediator in the search for peace. As the US State Department replied to its minister in Brussels in early August 1914, instructing him to accept the German request for US protection:

> In this critical hour it becomes necessary for our Government to render every assistance that a neutral can render, not only as an international duty, but that we may be in a better position to exert our influence for peace.[68]

As for the self-interest of a neutral state served by adoption of the role of protecting power, this has two aspects. First, to be asked to assume the responsibility is a mark of respect for its diplomacy and enhances its prestige. This has always been a powerful motive behind international mediation, to which the work of a protecting power is akin and sometimes leads, as when Switzerland was the protecting power for both sides in the India–Pakistan War in the

[67] TNA, POW Dept. (FO) to British Embassy Washington, 1 Apr. 1944, FO916/1115. Similar accusations surface in peacetime as well as in war; see Young, *Twentieth-Century Diplomacy*, p. 222.

[68] Quoted in Franklin, *Protection of Foreign Interests*, p. 94; see also p. 7.

early 1970s.[69] Second, it multiplies those in debt to the neutral, among whose number may be a state from which it might need the same favour itself at some point in the future; and, even if not from one of them, it might need it from another state applying principles which it has helped to reinforce through its own work as a protecting power. For example, after lengthy periods of initial neutrality in both world wars of the twentieth century, during which it was the most important protecting power, the United States then became the most protected state after entering those conflicts as a belligerent. In the First World War it became reliant on Spanish missions to protect its interests in Germany, Austria and Belgium, and on the Swedish mission to protect them in Turkey. In the Second World War, it was Switzerland on which the United States came to depend for the protection of its interests in enemy states after it entered the conflict in the days following Pearl Harbor.

Customary practice, shaped so much by that of the United States since the Franco-Prussian War of 1870–1 and soon displaying 'a remarkable degree of international uniformity',[70] has also evolved in such a way as to minimize the risks to neutral states in taking on the role of protecting power – in peace, as well as in war. This is clearly seen in the provisions on the subject contained in the US State Department's current *Foreign Affairs Manual*, which show few changes to the basic principles codified by Franklin in 1947.[71] One rule is that the protected power should reimburse the protecting power for all expenditure on its behalf, other than that incurred in the use of its staff's time. Another, and even more important, is that those in charge of foreign interests within the mission of a protecting power do not, ipso facto, become *official representatives* of the protected power. This fundamental rule is expressed in a number of secondary ones, among them that protecting power embassy staff are never accredited as diplomatic or consular

[69] Probst, 'The "good offices" of Switzerland and her role as protecting power', p. 26.
[70] Franklin, *Protection of Foreign Interests*, pp. 5, 39–44.
[71] US Dept. of State, 7 FAM 1000.

officers of the protected power; that in general the embassy never communicates directly with the protected power but indirectly via its own foreign ministry, and certainly never takes instructions from it; that, except in extremis, it should never agree to store on its own premises the property (including the archives) of a protected power's mission; that it should never present a formal claim or make a démarche on behalf of the protected power unless it is clear beyond doubt that it is acting in this regard merely as a messenger; and generally that the embassy is never expected to do anything on behalf of the protected power which is contrary to the interests of its own state.[72] Not surprisingly, unless the prospective protecting power is only to provide informal good offices, and providing that the local power is not expected to resist the arrangement, a bilateral agreement making clear all of this and more – notably the services needing to be performed – is usually necessary.[73] When Turkey accepted, probably with some trepidation, to be the protecting power in Tripoli for the United States (and various other states) when the Libya crisis worsened in early 2011, final agreement on the terms of its role were not announced until 20 March – over three weeks after the US embassy was closed.[74] (In an 'extreme emergency' such as a natural disaster, however, a US post can itself extend protection to another state without going through the usual procedure and the same reflex is probably a feature of most other diplomatic services.)[75]

In some circumstances, there is also open a special possibility that greatly eases the risk that a neutral protecting power might come to be seen by the local power as an enemy by another name, and also makes a mediating role more likely.[76] This is the

[72] US Dept. of State, 7 FAM 1013, 1036–8, 1042. See also Franklin, *Protection of Foreign Interests*, pp. 136–48.

[73] US Dept. of State, 7 FAM 1013. If the need is urgent a US post may extend protection without going through this traditional routine.

[74] See US Dept. of State, Special Briefing on the Suspension of United States Embassy Operations in Libya, 25 Feb. 2011; Daily Press Briefings, 3, 21 and 22 March 2011; and *Daily News & Economic Review* [*Hürriyet*], 20 Mar. 2011.

[75] US Dept. of State, 7 FAM 1032.

[76] ICRC, Commentary on Article 8.

arrangement by which a neutral might be the protecting power for both sides. The case of Switzerland in the India–Pakistan War of 1971 has already been mentioned and is far from a rarity. For example, in the Sino–Japanese War from 1894–5, the US mission at Peking became the protecting power for Japan in China while the US mission in Tokyo looked after Chinese interests in Japan.[77] And in the First World War, 'both sides-protection' of this sort was actually very common, largely because the United States was neutral for so long and popular with most parties, as we have already seen. For example, its missions protected British interests in Germany and German interests in Britain, British interests in Turkey and Turkish interests in Britain, British interests in Austria–Hungary and Austro–Hungarian interests in Britain, and so on.[78] The same pattern was equally apparent in the Second World War, particularly as the conflict spread and fewer neutrals were available to share the load. At one point in the war, Switzerland alone had charge of the interests of no fewer than 35 belligerents.[79]

Finally, it is important to note that it has long been common to permit the foreign interests section of the embassy of the protecting power to be assisted by a small number of locally engaged staff of the protected state and sometimes even by a few of its home-based consuls. For example, in the early stages of the First World War, the British section of the US embassy in Constantinople was staffed by four British consuls (plus a clerk) and the former British embassy's native dragoman;[80] in 1941, the Finns and the British reciprocally agreed (albeit with difficulty and on a smaller scale) a similar Finnish element in the Swedish legation in London, and

[77] Franklin, *Protection of Foreign Interests*, pp. 62–5. In the event, the United States offered to mediate in this war, Pooley (ed.), *The Secret Memoirs of Count Tadasu Hayashi*, p. 49.

[78] Franklin, *Protection of Foreign Interests*, pp. 95–7, App. I.

[79] ICRC, Commentary on Article 8, footnote 3.

[80] However, by one means or another, the Turks had managed to get rid of all of these bar the dragoman by the middle of 1915, Berridge, *British Diplomacy in Turkey*, pp. 124–7.

the same sort of British element in the US legation in Helsinki;[81] and, when the British embassy in Tripoli was 'temporarily closed' on 26 February 2011, its locally engaged pro-consul was transferred to the Turkish embassy, which immediately assumed protection of British interests in Libya.[82] Since the 1960s, even a few diplomats of a departing embassy have sometimes been allowed to remain and assist the neutral embassy which has taken charge of its interests (although this has been far less common than in the case of peacetime interests sections[83]). A striking instance of this was provided by the arrangement for diplomatic and consular protection agreed between Britain and Argentina following the outbreak of war between them over the Falkland Islands/Islas Malvinas in April 1982. The British interests section of the Swiss embassy in Buenos Aires, which took charge of British interests in Argentina, was staffed first by two and then (after the war) by more British diplomats.[84] As for the Argentine interests section in London, which enjoyed the protection of the Brazilian embassy, this appears from the start of the war to have had four Argentine diplomats.[85] Arrangements of this sort do not eliminate

[81] This was agreed only with difficulty; see the papers in TNA, FO371/ 29385 and 29386.

[82] A pro-consul is the senior administrator of a British consular post; this one was elsewhere described as one of the embassy's 'vice-consuls'. See 'Foreign Office update on situation in Libya', 26 Feb. 2011, FCO website http://www.fco.gov.uk/en/news/latest-news/?view=News&id=557562982;'Libya: the consular response', 3 Mar. 2011, FCO website http://www.fco.gov.uk/en/news/latest-news/?view=PressS&id=560403482.

[83] On this new kind of interests section generally, see Denza, *Diplomatic Law*, pp. 492–6; Wylie, 'Protecting powers in a changing world'; Berridge, *Diplomacy*, pp. 209–15.

[84] The two British diplomats who remained in Buenos Aires during the fighting were the recently appointed political counsellor (and number two) at the former British embassy, and the deputy administration officer and vice-consul. By 1985 a first secretary, an accountant and an archivist had been added to the British staff of the British interests section, which remained in the chancery, *DS List*, editions 1982–5; *The Times*, 6 and 30 Apr. 1982, 4 Nov. and 29 Dec. 1983.

[85] The Argentine interests section consisted of a counsellor, a first secretary, a first secretary (consular), and a first secretary (commercial affairs), *The London Diplomatic List*, Aug. 1982–Dec. 1986. It was based in the former ambassador's

the chances of friction between the staff of the protecting power and officials of the local power because the former still have to act as the channel of communication of the interests section to the local foreign ministry,[86] but they might reduce it. More importantly, they reduce the burden on the protecting power (making it possible even for a small and weakly staffed embassy to take on the role) while at the same time reassuring the protected power that its own interests remain in the care of its own staff.[87]

Unfortunately, the burdens and political risks of accepting a protecting power mandate are not the only obstacles to employing the system in international armed conflict, so reducing them only attacks part of the problem. After the Second World War, largely because of the ideological temper of the times and the more casual approach to the start of fighting, it became quite common for warring parties to decline to request a protecting power in the first place. Sometimes this was because they had not actually severed diplomatic relations. At others, it was because appointment of a protecting power would imply recognition of one party as a state when this was precisely the issue over which the conflict had commenced. Alternatively or in addition, it was because it would admit the existence of an armed conflict and thereby invite the charge that the state or states in question were in contravention of Article 2 (4) of the UN Charter which prohibits the use of armed

residence. According to Raymond Probst, a senior Swiss foreign ministry official at the time, there was 'a mutual agreement [between Britain and Argentina] permitting four diplomatic and four consular officers of each of the conflicting parties to remain on the spot at the disposal of the protecting diplomatic mission', 'The "good offices" of Switzerland and her role as protecting power', p. 26. However, these agreed staffing rights were clearly not immediately exerted to the full.

[86] Although this was also the case with the British interests section in the Swiss embassy in Buenos Aires during the Falklands War and for a long time afterwards (diplomatic relations were not re-established until 1990), it did become possible for its staff to have direct contacts with non-official Argentines, including members of parliament, HCPP (31–ii), 15 Nov. 1982: Q90; and HCPP (408), 13 May 1987: pp. 52–3.

[87] This point and the preceding one featured prominently in FO discussions of the most suitable protecting power for Britain when it seemed that Libya might sever relations with it in 1971; see papers in TNA, FCO39/883.

force. Occasionally, too, it was because of the impossibility of finding a third party regarded as neutral by both parties to the conflict.[88]

It is for reasons such as these that neutral states were not pressed to become protecting powers in many of the international armed conflicts of the second half of the twentieth century, and not at all in its most brutal and dangerous wars: the Korean War, the Vietnam War, the Iran–Iraq War and the numerous Arab–Israeli wars. The result was that a serious bid was made to deal with the difficulties which had led to this situation at the diplomatic conference held in Geneva in the mid-1970s, which – at the instigation of the ICRC – once more revisited the question of international humanitarian law.[89] Among other things, the first treaty to issue from the conference reaffirmed the importance of the system of protecting powers; clarified its compulsory character and insisted on the urgency of appointments to the role from the very start of a conflict; required states unable to agree on protecting powers to collaborate with the ICRC in finding suitable candidates and, failing this, to accept the ICRC itself as a substitute; ruled that acceptance of protecting powers did not affect the legal status of the parties to the conflict ('or of any territory, including occupied territory'); and stated that the appointment of protecting powers was entirely consistent with the continuation of diplomatic relations.[90]

Protecting powers had not been entirely moribund during international armed conflicts before they were strengthened by this treaty in 1977. They had been used in the Suez War in 1956, the India–Portugal conflict over Goa in 1961, and – as already

[88] ICRC, Commentary on Article 5.

[89] Formally, this was the Diplomatic Conference on the Reaffirmation and Development of International Humanitarian Law applicable in Armed Conflicts, Geneva, 1974–7.

[90] Protocol additional to the Geneva Conventions of 12 August 1949, and relating to the Protection of Victims of International Armed Conflicts (Protocol I) and Annexes I and II (1977). The key article is Article 5, which is reproduced in Appendix 2.

mentioned – the India–Pakistan War in 1971.[91] Since 1977, they have been employed in the Falklands/Malvinas War in 1982 and the Libya conflict in 2011, as already mentioned. They were also in play in Belgrade during the conflict between NATO and the Federal Republic of Yugoslavia (FRY) over Kosovo from 1998 until 2000.[92] Switzerland was also engaged by both sides in the Russia–Georgia conflict over South Ossetia, although not for some months after the very short battle between them in August 2008 was over. There is, therefore, perhaps no need to be quite so pessimistic about the future of the wartime protecting power as some are inclined to be.[93]

What are the most important duties of the neutral protecting power in wartime? These are numerous, and vary in their complexity and potential to cause tension between the protecting power and the local power. The most straightforward and least likely to cause trouble is the duty to serve as a channel of communications between the protected state and the local power, for

[91] In the Suez War, Switzerland was appointed the protecting power for both Egypt and France, and Egypt and Britain; but Egypt refused any arrangement with Israel. Over Goa, Brazil was the protecting power for Portugal in India, while Egypt performed the task for India in Portugal. In the India–Pakistan War, Switzerland was the protecting power for both sides, Forsythe, 'Who guards the guardians', pp. 46–7; ICRC, Commentary on Article 5.

[92] For example, the Brazilian embassy became the protecting power for Britain, while the Swiss embassy took over French interests, Fischer, 'Switzerland's good offices', p. 9. In anticipation of NATO strikes against military targets in Serbia, the British embassy was closed in October 1998 but diplomatic relations were not broken until March 1999. As soon as the British diplomatic and consular staff left Belgrade, the Brazilian embassy provided whatever help it could to the relatively small number of British nationals who chose to remain, but did not formally become the protecting power for Britain until either March or October 1999 (both dates can be found in FO statements). In either event, the British interests section of the Brazilian embassy contained no British staff – or at least not, it seems, until a few weeks before diplomatic relations were resumed on 17 November 2000. The Cyprus high commission in London became the protecting power for FRY interests in Britain. See BBC News, 12 Oct. 1998 http://news.bbc.co.uk/1/hi/uk/191763.stm; HCPP (HC 246), 20 Mar. 2001, para. 25; HCPP (Cm 5220), July 2001, p. 3; House of Commons Hansard Written Answers for 18 Jul 2000, col. 141W.

[93] For example, Wylie, 'Protecting powers in a changing world', p. 13.

example in the exchange of proposals and counter-proposals between them in the negotiation of an exchange agreement, as we have seen in Chapter 2. Other messages may deal with complaints of violations of international humanitarian law (previously the laws of war), the sailings of hospital ships, safe conducts and the preliminary terms of surrender.[94]

The custodianship which the protecting power must assume of the protected state's diplomatic premises, together with their contents (including any archives left behind), is another task which is relatively uncomplicated.[95] It can also have advantages, especially if they are spacious, well-equipped and conveniently located; this is because it is customary that, should this be desired, these premises – or at least a part of them – will be occupied by the section of the protecting power's mission dealing with the interests of the protected state. For example, in the Second World War, the State Department gave a blanket authorisation to the Swiss officials in charge of US interests 'to utilize wherever and whenever necessary any American diplomatic or consular premises in their custody.'[96] Similarly, when the Polish government took over the protection of American interests in Iraq shortly after the 1991 Gulf War, the Polish chief of the small US interests section, which included locally engaged as well as Polish staff but no Americans, was permitted to employ the large, former US embassy in Baghdad. (He was still rattling around in it until just weeks before the final showdown between Saddam Hussein and the Western-led coalition of his enemies in March 2003.)[97] Likewise the Algerian embassy, which was given charge

[94] Franklin, *Protection of Foreign Interests*, p. 234.

[95] The custodianship of property may be more so if, with the encouragement of the protected state and the agreement of the local authorities, the protecting power also assumes the protection of other official or semi-public property of the protected state; if the departing diplomats have left behind a considerable amount of personal property; and if private citizens of the protected state also have a great deal of property at the mercy of the local authorities, Franklin, *Protection of Foreign Interests*, pp. 190–206.

[96] Franklin, *Protection of Foreign Interests*, p. 183.

[97] It was 'temporarily' closed at the beginning of February 2003, *Los Angeles Times*, 8 Feb. 2003 (actually, 7 February). The Russian embassy took charge of

of Iraqi interests in the United States, was allowed to take over the former Iraqi embassy in Washington to employ as an Iraqi interests section.[98]

Nevertheless, having charge of the protected state's diplomatic premises can bring problems. These are most likely to occur when passions are high and in states where mob violence is readily aroused, and especially if – save perhaps for the presence of a resident custodian[99] – embassies are left empty. For example, only two days after the US mission in St Petersburg had taken charge of German interests following the outbreak of the First World War, a large mob was allowed to invade and wreck the interior of the German embassy. This prompted the US chargé d'affaires to charge the Russians with 'criminal negligence' and hint that satisfaction would be demanded.[100] Almost a century later, a similar insult was offered to Turkey when, following the closure of numerous embassies in Tripoli in late February 2011, about three weeks prior to the launch of UN-sanctioned air strikes against Colonel Gaddafi's forces led initially by France and Britain, it agreed to protect the interests in Libya of the United States, Britain, Italy and Qatar.[101] Immediately after the air strike on 1 May, which reportedly killed several members of Gaddafi's family, mobs attacked all of their embassies, the police melted away, and most were ransacked and then burned out. While the protected states

British interests in Iraq but did not take over the British embassy building. This remarkable footnote to the end of the Cold War was not publicized at the time and has been barely noticed since. It was mentioned by the British minister for trade in the House of Lords in 2002, Lords Hansard text for 8 Jan. 2002, col. 435 (www).

[98] CBS News, 'An embassy in limbo', 14 Jan. 2001 (Greg Myre, Associated Press); US Department of State Dispatch, 13 May 1991, p. 347. The important difference between these arrangements was that the Iraqi interests section in Washington was staffed by Iraqis.

[99] A member of the locally engaged staff of the departed mission appointed as caretaker of its buildings and grounds.

[100] Franklin, *Protection of Foreign Interests*, pp. 91–2.

[101] The willingness of the Turks to offer protection to Italian interests in Libya has a certain irony because this was an Ottoman Turkish province until it was wrested from the Turks by the Italians in a particularly brazen land-grab in the years immediately prior to the First World War.

seem to have been agreed that there was little that the Turks could have done about it, this unchecked rampage can have done little for relations between Ankara and Colonel Gaddafi's government. On the following day, the Turkish embassy was itself closed (although its consulate in rebel-held Benghazi remained open) and its staff withdrawn to Tunisia. The official reason given was the deteriorating security situation in the Libyan capital, which was plausible enough, but – aside from the insult – it may also have had something to do with Turkey's bid to mediate a solution to the crisis, which was not being helped by identification with the interests of such prominent NATO member states.[102]

The inviolability of diplomatic premises together with the hostile environments in which they are sometimes located, has meant that they have often housed stores of weapons, whether for use by military guard units permitted by the receiving state or by the diplomats themselves, including intelligence officers and members of special forces working under diplomatic cover. Frequently, too, they have held illegal telecommunications equipment and even explosives.[103] And what one state practices with its own missions abroad is very readily assumed to be practised by others. Since, furthermore – until this was ruled out by the Vienna Convention on Diplomatic Relations (1961) – it was customary to permit a receiving state to enter diplomatic premises if they were believed to represent a threat to public health and safety,[104] there has always been a strong temptation on the part of the authorities of that state to enter and search the diplomatic premises of a recently departed enemy, even though the protecting power might have gone to the lengths of erecting its own flag

[102] *Sunday's Zaman*, 2 May 2011; *Hürriyet Daily News*, 4 May 2011.

[103] Berridge, *British Diplomacy in Turkey*, pp. 177–93.

[104] Even under the VCDR, vacated diplomatic premises in the care of a protecting power can be legally entered by the authorities of the receiving state after a 'reasonable period' since they are no longer being used for diplomatic purposes and thus fail to meet the definition of 'diplomatic premises' contained in the convention. However, the receiving state still has an obligation to 'respect and protect' them, Roberts (ed.), *Satow's Diplomatic Practice*, p. 223.

over them in order that there should be no misunderstanding about whose protection they enjoyed. This is the sort of thing that can cause political temperatures to rise. For example, in the early days of the First World War, the Turks entered the British embassy in Istanbul in search of a clandestine radio without even giving any warning of their intention to the American ambassador, Henry Morgenthau, under whose protection the mission had been placed. No wireless was discovered, but what they did find in a locked room was a small arsenal: 80 rifles, 90 pistols and 9,000 rounds of ammunition. This could have caused tension between the Turks and Morgenthau, since he had previously sought to discourage them from entering the building. Fortunately, he had good personal relations with them and resolved the matter by turning over the whole arsenal to the Turkish Ministry of War before re-sealing the building.[105] Other American ambassadors fell victim to similar 'embarrassing incidents' in the first days of the Second World War. As a result, the State Department issued a general instruction that any US diplomat assuming protection of a foreign mission 'should first cause to be removed therefrom all weapons and dangerous material'; if this should prove impossible, the local authorities would have to be allowed to search the premises themselves and remove any such stocks as they might find.[106]

More routinely complicated and likely to cause protracted difficulties between the protecting power and the local power than either of the foregoing duties is that of helping with the repatriation of official and non-official nationals, the former category including diplomatic and consular officers. As it happens, it was under this heading that, shortly after taking charge of US interests in Libya in March 2011, the Turkish embassy scored a quick success in helping to secure the release and repatriation of four *New York Times* journalists who had been seized and physically abused by pro-Gaddafi forces only days earlier.[107] But protecting

[105] Berridge, *British Diplomacy in Turkey*, p. 126.

[106] Franklin, *Protection of Foreign Interests*, pp. 184–5.

[107] *The New York Times*, 21 Mar. 2011; *CNN World*, 21 Mar. 2011; US Dept. of

powers usually have it much harder than this. Their work of this sort began on a significant scale in the Franco-Prussian War of 1870–1, when two innovations coincided: the expulsion of enemy consuls on the outbreak of war and 'the imposition of stringent measures on enemy aliens'.[108] It climaxed in the Second World War when exchange agreements for official and non-official nationals – themselves negotiated with the assistance of protecting powers, as already recalled – provided for the repatriation of many thousands of people. If the immediate withdrawal of the diplomatic staff of an enemy embassy was allowed, there was usually little more for the protecting embassy to do than to serve as observers in order to ensure that this was safe and dignified. If, on the other hand, the diplomats were interned (a common occurrence in the Second World War, as we have seen in Chapter 2), it fell to the protecting embassy to visit them as often as possible in order to ensure that they were well treated, assist with their letters home, keep them informed of any negotiations for an exchange and generally try to keep up their morale. But, in the Second World War, it was the much more numerous and geographically scattered non-official enemy nationals who caused the biggest headaches for the embassies of the protecting powers. Those wishing to be repatriated had to be identified and passenger lists compiled suitable to the terms of the exchange agreements, which always had a ceiling on berths because of limited transport, and usually had priority categories as well. As can be imagined, in wartime conditions this was demanding work. It was also customary that an officer of the protecting power's mission would travel on the ship or train carrying the evacuees to ensure that the terms of the agreement were faithfully carried out.[109] Today, the information generated on expatriate communities with the assistance of warden networks, the ease of transferring it electronically to the protecting power

State, Daily Press Briefing, 22 Mar. 2011.

108 Franklin, *Protection of Foreign Interests*, pp. 27–9.

109 Franklin, *Protection of Foreign Interests*, pp. 207–8.

and far better communications should make all of these burdens – except the last one – easier to bear.[110]

There are always enemy aliens (especially those holding dual nationality) who wish to remain, and for these the embassy of the protecting power must – if so requested – exercise consular functions.[111] Notable among the consular functions is the distribution of relief funds (and perhaps pensions) to distressed nationals, which Franklin describes as 'among the most important and technically difficult duties performed by the neutral diplomat or consul in charge of the interests of a major belligerent.'[112] Another consular function which can be a matter of life and death on a massive scale is the issuing of passports and visas. A special kind of passport was the letter of protection, or *schutzbrief* (also known as the *schutzpass*), pioneered by Carl Lutz, chief of the Department of Foreign Interests of the Swiss legation in Budapest in the latter half of the Second World War. This letter provided a guarantee that the bearer was under the protection of Switzerland until the person whose name it bore was able to leave Hungary. This enabled many thousands of Jews to escape the country, and was later adopted by the consulates of other neutrals in Budapest to protect Jews from deportation. As the representative of the protecting power for Britain (among many other states), Lutz also issued Palestine certificates which helped many Jewish children to depart for Palestine.[113]

Last, but far from least, the protecting power's embassy has the duty of ensuring that the treatment of prisoners of war (POWs)

[110] A cardinal point in the standard Emergency Action Plan for US embassies is that they should: 'Give a list of the names and addresses of all U.S. nationals remaining in the area to the representative of the protecting power', US Dept. of State, 7 FAM 1071.4.

[111] According to the FO, a 'significant number' of British nationals who did not wish to be evacuated from Libya during the crisis in that country in early 2011 were actually dual nationals, 'Libya: the consular response', 3 Mar. 2011, FCO website, http://www.fco.gov.uk/en/news/latest-news/?view=PressS&id=560403482

[112] Franklin, *Protection of Foreign Interests*, pp. 218–19.

[113] United States Holocaust Memorial Museum, http://resources.ushmm.org/inquery/uia_doc.php/photos/10897?hr=null

and civilian internees meets the minimum standards required by the Geneva Conventions (1949). POWs first came on to the radar of protecting powers on a significant scale in the Russo–Japanese War in 1904–5, and then on a major scale (as did civilian internees) in the First World War, the consequence of which was that the role of protecting powers in the inspection of POW camps was legally recognized in the Geneva Convention of 1929 and, indeed, expanded – although some important states, among them Japan, had objected.[114] This convention was applied in the Second World War and, by analogy to it, civilian internees as well as POWs were taken under the wings of protecting powers in most belligerent states. It was therefore no surprise when the revision of the Geneva Conventions in 1949 also provided a legal basis for the role of protecting powers in regard to civilian internees, as well as further stiffening their position relative to scrutiny of the treatment of prisoners of war.[115]

In regard to POWs and civilian internees, the embassy of the protecting power has two main functions: first, providing a channel of communication between the protected power and the local power on this matter, as on others; and second, the inspection of POW and internment camps. It is the latter which is the most challenging because camp commandants can be hostile and, in particular, unwilling to allow private interviews between prisoners and embassy staff, as prescribed by the Geneva Convention. Furthermore if the embassy inspectors confine themselves simply to reporting back to the protected state, and if they report maltreatment, the only result is likely to be retaliation against prisoners or internees of the local power. Instead, the wisest approach – at least in the first instance – is to attempt to persuade the local officials to mend their ways. As Franklin says:

[114] This was the Convention relative to the Treatment of Prisoners of War. Signed at Geneva on 27 July 1929, it is now usually referred to as the second Geneva Convention. See Franklin, *Protection of Foreign Interests*, pp. 77–9, 94–100, 115, 219–20; and Wylie, 'Protecting powers in a changing world', pp. 9–10.

[115] ICRC, Commentary on Article 8; Convention (IV) relative to the Protection of Civilian Persons in Time of War. Geneva, 12 August 1949, article 9.

> In this manner he actually serves as an informal arbiter, helping to standardize the interpretations of the pertinent conventions or agreements and to bring the treatment of prisoners and internees to the level of the highest, rather than the lowest, common denominator between the belligerents. The effectiveness of such activity is greatest in those instances in which one neutral state serves as the protecting power for both belligerents … .[116]

The task of seeking to ensure that POWs and civilian internees are treated in accordance with the terms of the Geneva Conventions has sometimes been shared by the embassies of protecting powers with the International Committee of the Red Cross – and sometimes surrendered to it, with the embassy concentrating on the protection of political and economic interests, as when Switzerland was the protecting power for both sides in the India–Pakistan War in 1971.[117]

Conclusion

The highest priority of the neutral embassy on the outbreak of war is ministering to the needs and anxieties of its own expatriate community, although this soon passes. More enduring in importance is the need for it to provide intelligence on the military fortunes and political resolve of its belligerent host and, depending on circumstances and in case of future need, intelligence on the military capabilities of those attacking it. For the embassies of weighty or strategically placed neutrals, the doors of highly placed persons will usually be open, while the movements of their staff in these states or in territories they have occupied will, in most cases,

116 Franklin, *Protection of Foreign Interests*, pp. 226–7. See also ICRC, Commentary on Article 5; and Gerard, *My Four Years in Germany*, ch. 10 ('Prisoners of War').
117 Forsythe, 'Who guards the guardians?', pp. 46–7. Moreover, in the many conflicts – including non-international armed conflicts – in which protecting powers are notable by their absence, the ICRC acts as a legally recognized 'substitute' for a protecting power,

be relatively unimpeded – unless and until courting them has clearly failed. Commercial questions also tend to be a significantly higher priority for neutral embassies in armed conflicts because of the common attempts of belligerents to encroach on neutral rights to trade with 'enemy' states, and the general tendency of the state in wartime to seek greater control of commerce. If the embassies of neutral states also have to become protecting powers, they not only have a heavier burden to shoulder, but risk their reputation for impartiality with the host state. When they agree to it nevertheless, it is chiefly because it is seen as service to an institution which one day they might need themselves, because it is a way of earning gratitude, and because when – as gradually became more common during the twentieth century – an interests section staffed by officers of the protected power is permitted the burden is much reduced. Changing circumstances following the Second World War meant that neutral states were called on far less frequently to become protecting powers in international armed conflicts, and not at all in its most brutal and dangerous wars. However, they did not escape the duty altogether, and as recently as 2011 a (relatively) neutral embassy – that of Turkey – was seen taking it on in Tripoli. Among the numerous responsibilities of the neutral protecting power's embassy, the most important is usually the protection of detained enemy civilians and prisoners of war. That neutrals often attach high importance to the work of their embassies in belligerent states – whether their attitudes towards the latter are cool, strictly impartial or benign – is proved no more eloquently than by the high risks of devastating accidental attacks on their premises which they all have to run. This is well demonstrated by the fate of the Swedish legation in Berlin during the later stages of the Second World War and the Chinese embassy in Belgrade during the Kosovo War in 1999.

4 Belligerent Embassies to Neutrals

Chapter Overview

Belligerent embassies in neutral states do not usually find their work radically skewed from the normal unless their hosts are close to the front line or are, for some other reason, of strategic importance to the warring parties. But, in a general war, such neutrals might well be numerous; a few are usually present even in regional conflicts, where it is more difficult to avoid taking sides. Neutral states of strategic significance during the Second World War included Switzerland, Sweden, Ireland, Turkey, Spain, Argentina, Portugal, Italy until June 1940, and – until December 1941 – Thailand, Japan and the United States. In the Vietnam War, Cambodia – until the overthrow of Prince Sihanouk in March 1970 – was a case in point; while further examples were provided by Iran and Jordan in the first Gulf War in early 1991. How might powerful belligerents react to such states? In light of this reaction, how do their embassies usually adjust to their new role, and which tasks require priority?

Powerful belligerents confronting the problem of a strategically placed neutral state within their reach always have the option of trying to bring them into the war on their own side by means of heavy diplomatic and economic pressure, subversion and inspired coup d'état, or invasion and outright occupation, in all of which – even the last – their embassies may play an important role. However, the belligerent states may decide that the first two tactics are unlikely to work, and that the last – as Hitler concluded in regard to Switzerland at the beginning of the 1939–45 war – is too costly. In any case, belligerents may also decide that, even if a neutral could be manoeuvred or forced into the war, this would not be a good idea, especially if it is militarily unprepared. In such circumstances, the former neutral might either require the support of resources (including military equipment) better used elsewhere, or be exposed to devastating and possibly terminal attack by the enemy.

Whether because bringing the strategically placed neutral immediately into the war is too costly to achieve or in principle inadvisable, the belligerent embassy will normally be instructed in the meantime to secure its 'benevolent' neutrality. This should enable the embassy to obtain a disproportionate share of any commodities of military significance its state may need from the neutral, and also mean that the latter will turn a blind eye to, or even lend it discreet assistance in, the discharge of certain special, war-related responsibilities. But fostering a benevolent attitude on the part of a neutral is no straightforward task, especially since the embassies of rival belligerents will be engaged in the same exercise.

The problem with a gentle approach to a neutral by a belligerent embassy is that it might expose its head of mission to the charge of localitis by politicians at home and even colleagues at other posts angered by the 'fence-sitting' posture of the government to which it is accredited. The personal hostility of the British prime minister, Winston Churchill, to the neutrality of Turkey in the Second World War was no secret, and it is evident that he thought the British embassy in Ankara too sympathetic to its attitude. A similar reputation was acquired by the US embassy in Amman during the Gulf War. Indeed, Chas Freeman, the US ambassador in Riyadh during the latter conflict remarked afterwards – tongue rather obviously in cheek – that:

> Our embassy in Amman appeared to endorse Jordan's special pleading [about the embargo against Iraq] to such an extent that I considered persuading the United States Navy to refrain from air strikes on our embassy there to be one of my greater achievements.[1]

On the other hand, perhaps fearful of the charge of localitis, a belligerent embassy may be tempted to go too far in the opposite direction in order to make the neutral discreetly salute the right flag: apply heavy diplomatic and economic pressure and even intervene in local politics. The resentment caused by such tactics may easily drive the neutral into the arms of the enemy. This is a real risk for the heavy-handed belligerent in at least three circumstances: first, if the enemy seems likely to win, which was the risk for Britain in regard to neutral Turkey in the first years of the Second World War, Hitler's prospects then looking so good; second, if there is traditional nationalist antipathy to the belligerent applying the pressure, as was the case for the United States in regard to neutral Argentina in the same conflict;[2] and third, if there is strong sentiment on the streets of the neutral state in favour of the enemy – irrespective of its military prospects – as was the case for the Coalition states in regard to Jordan in the Gulf War in 1990–1, where there was popular sympathy for Saddam Hussein.

To avoid the twin risks of failing to secure benevolent neutrality either by being too gentle or too heavy-handed, the belligerent embassy needs to use exceptional tact in its relations with the neutral government, extend to it what assistance it can, and keep

1 Freeman interview.

2 In this case, the performance in 1945 of America's non-career ambassador at Buenos Aires, Spruille Braden, the US 'bull in the Latin American china shop', is instructive, *Time*, 5 Nov. 1945.

the more gung-ho members of its own staff in check. At the same time, the embassy needs periodically to remind the neutral that if it does not join the right side in time its interests will be ignored in the framing of the peace settlement. It also needs to take seriously its propaganda in the neutral state.

Propaganda

With the Second World War looming, Captain Sidney Rogerson, director of publicity at the British chemicals giant, ICI, predicted that the 'neutral zone will be the great battle-ground of propaganda, where both sets of combatants will fight each other with all their energies and every known method.'[3] And so it proved. Furthermore, while radio broadcasters, foreign ministry press departments (briefing foreign correspondents), film-makers and others at home acquired a major role in foreign propaganda – or, as this got a bad name, 'information work' and later 'public diplomacy' – the embassy was by no means displaced altogether. Indeed, its press attachés became the mission's 'principal propaganda field agents'. In British embassies in the Second World War, this meant advising London on how to adjust general propaganda themes to local circumstances – for example, the need to avoid any emphasis on the defence of 'democracy' as a war aim in the Portugal of the dictator Dr Salazar, and the importance of soft-pedalling Anglo–Soviet collaboration in Russo-phobic Sweden. Press attachés were also responsible for organizing the channels through which propaganda materials should flow (some embassies set up their own cinemas in order to show suitable films to selected audiences), and then for reporting on its effects.[4] It would be surprising if this were not illustrative of a general pattern, then and since.

[3] *Propaganda in the Next War*, p. 138.

[4] Cole, *Britain and the War of Words in Neutral Europe*, pp. 3, 11, 54, 87. The British embassy in Djakarta played exactly the same role during the 'Confrontation' with Indonesia in the early 1960s (see p. 63 above).

Other things being equal, it is inevitable that neutrals are disposed to act most benevolently to the belligerents in whose favour the tide of a war is running most strongly. As a result, apart from parading the virtues of its own state and the vices of its enemies, the belligerent embassy in the capital of a neutral state – or, indeed, that of a wavering ally – has always been required to boast about its country's military victories and make excuses for its defeats, while advertising the acquisition of new allies and minimising the value of any who might have departed. This also helps to keep up the morale of the expatriate community and any internees (on which see below).

The extent to which a belligerent embassy can conduct propaganda in a neutral state depends – aside from the resources available to it – on the strength of the receiving state's attachment to neutrality and other local circumstances. For example, in the Second World War, most if not all of the missions of the major belligerents in Argentina and Turkey – where, in both states, politics was volatile and censorship uncertain – were allowed to conduct relatively vigorous propaganda campaigns. In Buenos Aires, Axis propaganda was so extensive as to be a source of real and mounting concern to the Americans, while at the same time the British ambassador himself – who had the advantage of a party-loving Anglo–Argentine press attaché, popular with journalists[5] – had no difficulty in getting anything he wanted published in its leading newspaper, *La Prensa*.[6] In Turkey, the British embassy, although slow off the mark compared to the Germans – relying initially mainly on a few films and the supply of materials to the Turkish press – eventually ran a reasonable operation. As well as preparing and distributing better materials, this involved bribing local journalists and achieving a limited degree of coordination over the propaganda activities of the numerous British secret agencies operating in the country – including the ostensibly

[5] This was S. R. Robertson; see his rather bombastic *Making Friends for Britain*.

[6] Kelly, *The Ruling Few*, p. 313, also pp. 290–1.

independent but in fact British intelligence-run news agency, Britanova.[7]

In the United States, the legal constraints on propaganda conducted directly or overseen at arm's length by foreign missions were even fewer. However, stimulated by the isolationist tradition in the United States, here there was an entrenched idea that it was only cunning British propaganda that had inveigled America into the First World War against the nation's interests; and, as war in Europe once more loomed in 1938, pressure began to mount in Congress – with support in the State Department – for heavy legislative restriction on all foreign propaganda activity within the country's borders. This persisted through the neutrality period and beyond Pearl Harbor.[8]

The result of this hostility was that British propagandists in the United States, no less than those of other belligerents, had to be very careful. British propaganda, the overriding aim of which was to get America into the war as soon as possible, was initially low-key and passive; only after Franklin Roosevelt had been re-elected as president in November 1940 and public opinion in the United States – owing largely to propaganda emanating directly from London – had begun to shift to stronger support for Britain, was it gradually able to become more open and aggressive.[9] Britain's *acknowledged* propaganda machine in the United States was directed by the embassy in Washington (which had acquired its own press office) but had its operational centre in New York, the media capital of the country.[10] This began to

[7] This was launched in December 1939, Barker, *British Policy in South-East Europe in the Second World War*, p. 44.

[8] Cull, *Selling War*, pp. 19–20, 95–6, 144–5, 189–91.

[9] However, the speeches during 1940 of the British ambassador, Lord Lothian, also had some effect.

[10] This seems to have been an instance of a more general tradition. In the First World War, the unofficial German 'Press Bureau' was also established in New York, with the added advantage for the German ambassador, Count Bernstorff, that it distanced him from German propaganda as well as relieving him of the personal conduct of it which he had begun to find a serious hindrance to performance of his diplomatic role, Bernstorff, *My Three Years in America*, pp. 33–6.

crank up in October 1940, and by April 1941 had evolved into a unified structure called British Information Services (BIS), only the director of which held diplomatic rank.[11] Britain's *unacknowledged* propaganda machine, which was a wing of British Security Co-ordination (see below), evolved in parallel with BIS and was also based in New York. In the event, the neutrality of Roosevelt's administration became progressively more benevolent towards Britain, especially during the course of 1941, and British propaganda inside the United States had helped.[12] However, it took Pearl Harbor to propel it into war.

By contrast to belligerent embassies in Argentina, Turkey and even in the United States, those in the strategically vital European neutrals in the Second World War – Sweden, Portugal, Spain and Switzerland – had to be more circumspect. Censorship was generally tight in all of them, although in General Franco's Spain – where 'non-belligerency' was the watchword rather than 'neutrality', and the generalissimo's Blue Division was fighting alongside German troops on the Russian front – the propaganda directed by the German embassy had a virtually free run, whereas that of Britain and the United States was regularly harassed.[13] However, in Switzerland, neutrality was a religion and propaganda by any of the belligerent legations sacrilege. Here, the opportunities for the conduct of propaganda were restricted further in the case of the Allied missions because

[11] On the complex evolution of the British propaganda machine in the US, which began with the establishment in New York in 1920 of the British Library of Information as a branch of the FO's News Department, see Cull, *Selling War*, pp. 10–11, 118–22, 127–31.

[12] On charges of espionage as well as 'un-American' propaganda, in June 1941 the German Library of Information, which had been established alongside the German consulate-general in New York in 1936 and appears to have been modelled on its British counterpart, was ordered to close and along with it all German consular posts in the United States: *The Times*, 17 June 1941; Special Committee on Un-American Activities (1938–1944).

[13] Hoare, *Ambassador on Special Mission*, pp. 134–6, 201–4. In 1941, the British embassy – particularly its press annex – was the target of violent demonstrations, Cole, *Britain and the War of Words in Neutral Europe*, pp. 92–3, 97–8. See also Hayes (Madrid) to Jordana (Spanish foreign minister), 19 Mar. 1943, *FRUS, 1943*. Vol. II, p. 598.

Axis encirclement of the country created great problems for the supply of propaganda materials, especially films and newsreels, from home.[14] It was in these circumstances that the press attaché at the British legation in Berne had to place great reliance for anti-Axis propaganda on the sale two or three times a week of a bulletin summarising English news obtained by wireless from the Ministry of Information in London. 'To keep on the right side of the Federal authorities', wrote the British minister afterwards, '...we would neither sell nor advertise, nor send a single copy to anyone who did not apply for it in writing'.[15]

Espionage and special operations

It is the stuff of legend that, in wartime, neutral states are major scenes of intelligence activity, special operations and strategic deception. All belligerents have a diplomatic and consular presence in them which they can employ to provide cover for their intelligence officers (see Chapter 1), as well as a secure base for an enlarged embassy defence section. Particularly attractive to belligerent espionage are powerful neutrals, a decision on the part of any one of which to shift to belligerency – or just tilt more to one side rather than the other – might be expected to determine the outcome of the war. But also attractive are those smaller neutral states near to a major target of military, commercial and political intelligence gathering, be it the front line, a major belligerent (together with any of its occupied territories), a vital supply route or an air corridor. This is because the geographical proximity of a secret intelligence war station to its targets makes most

[14] Kelly, *The Ruling Few*, p. 274; Cole, *Britain and the War of Words in Neutral Europe*, p. 144.

[15] He claimed, nevertheless, that it was in great demand by the Swiss and soon had a circulation of more than 80,000 – 'superior, I believe, to that of any Swiss newspaper', Kelly, *The Ruling Few*, pp. 274–5; see also Cole, *Britain and the War of Words in Neutral Europe*, pp. 49, 80, 100–1, 120. Resort was had to a similar device by the British embassy in Madrid, Hoare, *Ambassador on Special Mission*, pp. 134–5.

forms of human intelligence-gathering easier, whether it is eaves-dropping, planting agents, communicating with agents in place and resistance groups in enemy-occupied territory, or simply gathering material from open sources.[16] Even more attractive to intelligence agencies are those neutrals close to two or more major targets.

In the Second World War, the port of Lourenço Marques in neutral Portugal's colony of Mozambique was a scene of *modest* intelligence activity because Allied convoys on the Cape route had to pass through the Mozambique Channel, where they were easy targets for German U-boats if knowledge of them could be obtained beforehand.[17] But the Swiss capital of Berne was a scene of *fevered* intelligence activity because Switzerland had a common frontier with Nazi Germany, was close to the front line in Europe and lay astride the vital supply route between Germany and its Axis ally, Italy; it was also a supplier itself of important war materials to Berlin, and an ideal point from which to supply weather reports of great value to Allied air crews on bombing runs to the Axis countries. In northern Europe, the position of Stockholm, the capital of Sweden, made it probably even more important from an intelligence point of view: 'by far the best observation post into Hitler's Europe'.[18] In the view of the British naval attaché in Stockholm, Captain Henry Denham, it was in consequence 'the cockpit for both British and German intelligence.'[19]

In the Second World War, the diplomatic and consular posts of belligerents in neutral states were stiff with intelligence officers. For example, the SIS station in New York, which in 1939 was

[16] Hagglöf, *Diplomat*, p. 169; Wylie, 'SOE and the neutrals', p. 167; Berridge, *British Diplomacy in Turkey*, pp. 180–93; Hyde, *The Quiet Canadian*; Harrison, 'On secret service for the Duce'; O'Halpin, *Spying on Ireland*, pp. 169–71, 198–200, 245–6, 276.

[17] On the rivalry there between Axis and British intelligence officers operating under consular cover, see Harrison, 'On secret service for the Duce', and Muggeridge, *Chronicles of Wasted Time*, pp. 142–86.

[18] McLachlan, *Room 39*, p. 194.

[19] Denham, *Inside the Nazi Ring*, p. 18.

still small and relatively insignificant, was soon to become 'the most important single overseas SIS station of the Second World War'.[20] 'British Security Co-ordination' (BSC), as this station was eventually styled, was directed by the Canadian businessman, William Stephenson, who took over as British passport control officer in New York in June 1940; his deputy had cover as a consul;[21] it was funded directly by the British embassy in Washington. Nominally charged with providing security against Axis sabotage to essential war supplies in the United States destined for Britain, under the talented, energetic and amazingly well-connected Stephenson, BSC grew into a small and highly successful, all-purpose empire. Well before the United States abandoned neutrality, it was already working in close collaboration with the FBI and Colonel 'Wild Bill' Donovan, the founding spirit of the OSS, which was the forerunner of the CIA. BSC not only specialized in obtaining intelligence on enemy-controlled businesses and neutral, as well as hostile embassies in the United States, but also ran covert propaganda and special operations, and engaged in high-level lobbying to get America into the war.[22]

Meanwhile, in the Swiss capital, Berne, the relatively large British legation included three service attachés and enjoyed the assistance of an interned RAF squadron leader as well.[23] It also supervised a network of provincial consular posts with a collective staff much larger still.[24] SIS, for which Switzerland was the main base for operations against Nazi Germany (the Netherlands had been another before it was overrun), had its agents concentrated in the consulates, particularly those in Zurich and Geneva.[25] In the US legation in Berne, Allen Dulles, later the director of the CIA,

[20] Jefferey, *MI6*, p. 438.

[21] This was C. H. ('Dick') Ellis, *FO List 1941*.

[22] Jefferey, *MI6*, pp. 439–55.

[23] Reid, *Winged Diplomat*, p. 185.

[24] Excluding those at Berne, in 1941–2 there were 31 British consular officers scattered across Switzerland at nine different posts, which represented a 70 per cent increase on the pre-war number, *FO Lists 1938* and *1942*.

[25] Jefferey, *MI6*, pp. 378–9, 507; Andrew, *Secret Service*, pp. 358, 381; Reid, *Winged Diplomat*, pp. 153–4, 171.

was nominally 'special assistant to the minister for legal affairs' but in reality station chief of the OSS.[26] In the German legation, one of the two counsellors, Sigismund Freiherr von Bibra, ran all of the German agents in Switzerland.[27] At the German legation in Stockholm, the most effective Abwehr officer was the mission's press secretary.[28]

What of the obstacles to the work of intelligence officers such as these? As might be imagined, they were not as great as those faced by embassy propagandists, and it seems clear that most were able to supply much valuable information to their governments.[29] Nevertheless, this was rarely obtained without some difficulty because all of the major neutrals had their own security services and these disliked the idea of foreign intelligence officers operating freely on their territory; the neutrals' security services were also under constant pressure from each of the belligerents to clamp down on the activities of the other. As a result, intelligence operations were under constant close surveillance (the Swiss intelligence service actually penetrated the important SIS station in Zurich [30]) and sometimes foreign intelligence officers were expelled, as happened to the German naval attaché in Stockholm.[31] Inevitably, however, the local security services tended to come down harder on some belligerent intelligence operations than on others. For example, well aware that the only belligerent by which they were threatened with invasion was Germany, the Swiss recognized an 'identity of interest' in the gathering of military intelligence on Germany with the Allied intelligence services and, at least in the case of the British,

[26] Srodes, *Allen Dulles*, p. 227; Dulles, *The Craft of Intelligence*, pp. 80–2.
[27] Reid, *Winged Diplomat*, p. 172.
[28] Denham, *Inside the Nazi Ring*, p. 45.
[29] For example, the invaluable intelligence on German naval movements in northern waters provided by the British naval attaché in Stockholm, Captain Henry Denham, which, among other things, led to the sinking of the *Bismarck*. Ludovic Kennedy provides a useful summary of this in his foreword to Denham's *Inside the Nazi Ring*.
[30] Jefferey, *MI6*, p. 379; see also McLachlan, *Room 39*, p. 185.
[31] Denham, *Inside the Nazi Ring*, p. 44.

this made for generally 'smooth relations' between them.[32] By contrast, in Sweden, while there was little love for the Nazis and nervousness about Hitler's intentions, there remained a strong tradition of thought that the country's independence was 'fundamentally dependent upon a strong Germany being able to contain the traditional enemy, Russia'.[33] As a result, both the SIS station in the British passport control office in Stockholm and the service attachés in the legation suffered from the uncomfortably close attention of the Swedish security police throughout the war.[34] This was not all. 'The only outspoken pro-British Swedish naval officer had been removed from Stockholm and forbidden by the Head of the Navy to meet me', the British naval attaché complains in his memoirs, adding that the captains of Swedish merchant ships were also legally prohibited from giving him information.[35]

For Allied intelligence officers in Switzerland, the vital task of communicating securely with their headquarters was perhaps the most serious obstacle they faced. After the Germans occupied Vichy France in November 1942, their own bag services ceased, and SIS, for example, was forced to rely on bribing South American diplomats in order to get documents carried out. Furthermore, the Swiss did not permit foreign missions to use wireless sets for sending messages and required all coded messages sent out by foreign missions to be routed through their post office; to make matters worse, SIS found it increasingly difficult in isolated Switzerland to get hold of the one-time pads needed for this purpose. 'These communications meant that often only messages of the highest importance could be sent by cable,' writes the official historian of SIS, 'and that much intelligence collected in Switzerland reached London only after a considerable delay.'[36] Matters were not so bad in Stockholm, where intelligence officers

32 Reid, *Winged Diplomat*, p. 164.

33 Denham, *Inside the Nazi Ring*, pp. 53–4.

34 Denham, *Inside the Nazi Ring*, pp. 44–5, 67–8, 99, 140–59; Jeffery, *MI6*, pp. 376–8.

35 Denham, *Inside the Nazi Ring*, p. 27.

36 Jefferey, *MI6*, p. 380.

at the British legation were able to send ciphered telegrams to London via Gothenburg Radio.[37]

The situation in Switzerland contrasted markedly with that in Argentina, where intelligence officers operating from all of the belligerent missions had few problems of this sort. These included those of the Axis powers, whose position so far from home and in the heart of the Americas might at first glance be supposed to have been roughly analogous to that of the Allied missions in Switzerland. In Buenos Aires, telecommunications were in the hands of foreign and domestic private interests, which provided ample opportunities for the coded transmission of intelligence either by radio or cable. Despite intense efforts on the part of the US State Department, the Argentine government refused to fall into line with the recommendations of the Rio Conference of January 1942 that all unofficial telecommunication circuits between the American republics and the Axis powers be broken or effectively controlled, and all clandestine stations sought out and closed down. As a result, the German and Japanese embassies were able to continue sending out coded intelligence – not least on shipping movements – until they were finally closed, in June 1944 and April 1945 respectively.[38] In Spain, Axis intelligence seems to have had no communications problems at all.[39] Intelligence operations based on the German consulate at Tangier were notorious in the eyes of the Allies, and Sir Samuel Hoare, the British ambassador, believed that the Japanese legation in Madrid was 'the European centre of the Japanese secret service'.[40]

[37] Denham, *Inside the Nazi Ring*, p. 38.

[38] 'Efforts to prevent communication with the Axis countries through commercial wireless companies', *FRUS, 1942*. Vol. V, pp. 108–85 *passim*. The kind of harmful intelligence being acquired by the Argentine networks of German intelligence officers, notably the one run by the naval attaché at the German embassy, was detailed at some length in memoranda presented to the Argentine government by the US embassy in Buenos Aires not long after the US entry into the war, Armour (B.A.) to SoS, 22 Oct. 1942, *FRUS, 1942*. Vol. V, p. 217ff.

[39] Hoare, *Ambassador on Special Mission*, pp. 199–200.

[40] Hoare, *Ambassador on Special Mission*, pp. 127, 255, 263–8.

Counter-intelligence in neutral capitals also has its problems, especially if this is attempted via exposure of enemy agents to the local authorities because of the obvious risk that this will backfire. For example, in early November 1942, the US embassy in Buenos Aires provided the Argentine authorities with detailed lists of German agents operating in Argentina – the main group of which was directed by Captain Dietrich Niebuhr, naval attaché at the German embassy – and urged their arrest and trial. However, when news of this inevitably leaked out, the nationalist press charged that the mere fact that the Americans were able to expose this scale of German espionage activities was proof that they had an 'even larger and more dangerous organization in Argentina'. The Germans were also rumoured to be preparing a 'counter memorandum' about this US organization.[41] This led to some nervousness in the State Department, which cautioned the Buenos Aires embassy against making any statements which might lead to 'undignified open controversy with the German Embassy or to any protracted airing of charges and counter-charges for the edification of the Argentine Foreign Office and public press.'[42] Although Niebuhr was later recalled, no fatal damage was done to German intelligence-gathering in Argentina by this means on that occasion.

The presence in the neutral capital of diplomatic missions of all belligerents also makes such cities perfect theatres for strategic deception. Thus the British legation in Stockholm played a key role in 'Operation Graffham', which was designed to deceive the Germans into believing that steps were being taken to enlist the cooperation of Sweden in an attack on northern Norway in the spring of 1944.[43] Meanwhile, in Berne, one of the British minister's main activities, he later wrote, was 'the sifting of the mass of information which poured in upon us, of which a great deal was deliberately put out by the German Legation with the object

[41] Armour to SoS, 28 Nov. 1942, *FRUS, 1942*. Vol. V, pp. 254–5.
[42] SoS to Armour, 4 Dec. 1942, *FRUS, 1942*. Vol. V, p. 256.
[43] Howard, *British Intelligence in the Second World War*, pp. 117–18.

of confusing us.'[44] Dublin and Istanbul were other neutral cities regarded as ideal centres for whispering campaigns in the Second World War.[45]

It remains to note here the activities of saboteurs and practitioners of other forms of covert action, who frequently shelter in the diplomatic and consular missions of belligerent powers in neutral states. Their purposes, depending on local circumstances and whether or not an enemy advance into the neutral is believed to be a real threat, usually embrace one or more of the following: first, blocking or at least disrupting essential supplies to the enemy which either originate in or must needs pass through or close by the neutral state; second, manipulating its politics by any means necessary, including bribery and black propaganda; third, using the neutral state as a secure base from which to run operations into adjacent territories occupied by the enemy; and fourth, preparing 'stay-behind' groups and making arrangements – with or without the knowledge and cooperation of the neutral government – to destroy key facilities such as fuel storage depots, power stations, bridges and tunnels. In the Second World War, such tasks were allocated by the British government to the officers of SOE, who – with few prospects in occupied Europe – saw the neutral states as a primary field of operation, especially in the first year and a half of fighting.[46]

In Turkey, for example, most of the officers of the large SOE station based in the British consulate-general in Istanbul were concerned with running sabotage operations in the German-occupied Balkans, but a small section also evolved with a view to operations inside Turkey itself.[47] To the latter end, dumps of explosives were established at various consular posts across the country, and work was done on a skeletal organization for post-occupation resistance. With a view to reducing the supply to

[44] Kelly, *The Ruling Few*, p. 275.

[45] O'Halpin, *Spying on Ireland*, pp. 144–9, 209–13; Berridge, *British Diplomacy in Turkey*, pp. 181, 188.

[46] Wylie, 'SOE and the neutrals', p. 158.

[47] The following paragraphs on Turkey are based on my *British Diplomacy in Turkey*, pp. 183–93.

Germany of Turkish chrome badly needed for Hitler's war effort, in the later stages of the war increasing pressure was also exerted on the ambassador, Sir Hughe Knatchbull-Hugessen, to permit attacks on Axis shipping in Turkish waters and Axis rolling stock on Turkish territory.

In a pattern repeated in the relations between SOE and the diplomats in other neutral states, notably Portugal and Sweden,[48] inevitably there was serious tension between SOE and the ambassador and his diplomatic staff at the British embassy in Ankara. Knatchbull-Hugessen was desperate to maintain good relations with the Turks so as to obtain their benevolent neutrality and nudge them into co-belligerency at the right time. In consequence, he was firmly of the opinion that SOE's Turkish operation – as opposed to the activities of its Istanbul-based Balkan section, towards which he was more indulgent – was doomed to do more harm than good, and he had tolerated it only as a result of high-level pressure from London and under vigorous protest. The other secret agencies, notably SIS, which operated more by stealth than by making 'bangs' and – unlike SOE – answered directly to the Foreign Office, also disliked the attention-drawing activities of some of the men engaged in special operations. The feelings were mutual. Some of SOE's activities, notably post-occupation planning, also overlapped with the responsibilities of the military attaché in Ankara. In the event, SOE's Turkish operation never amounted to much, although the Balkan section, which benefited greatly from consular cover, was a different matter.

In the decade after 1945, the lines of the new Cold War were established but many newly independent states refused to be drawn into it. Some of the capitals of these 'neutralist' or 'non-aligned' states, therefore, became important listening

[48] In Switzerland, the plan to sabotage the trans–Alpine railway carrying German coal to Italy was wisely abandoned, and efficient police surveillance appears to have been sufficient to prevent the SOE station in Berne from attempting anything inside Switzerland that would have really alarmed the British embassy. Like the Istanbul station, its main importance lay in the support it provided to networks in adjacent territories occupied by the enemy, as well as in Italy, Wylie, 'SOE and the neutrals', p. 170.

posts. An early one was Rangoon, the capital of Burma, a weak state anxious to preserve its independence by keeping on good terms with its more powerful neighbours, notably India and the PRC, which, following the Communist victory in 1949, it swiftly recognized. SIS established a new station in Rangoon late in 1947, shortly before Burma gained independence. Headed by the experienced and ruthless Edward ('Jimmy') James, who had cover as a second secretary in the British embassy until moving to Hong Kong in 1951, this had the chief objective of penetrating the Communist organizations active in the country – an objective which it successfully attained.[49] Rangoon was also one of the posts on the periphery of China at which the US State Department placed Chinese language officers after it decided to close its missions on the mainland at the beginning of 1950. Indeed, watching the long China–Burma border was for some time the chief task of the US mission in Rangoon.[50]

In the Vietnam War, the neutral state of most strategic significance in south-east Asia until the beginning of the 1970s was Cambodia, led by Prince Norodom Sihanouk, which had a long frontier with Vietnam.[51] However, with its huge military operation based in Saigon, the United States clearly felt it had little use for a listening post in Phnom Penh. This was just as well because, angered at CIA meddling in his country, Sihanouk had broken diplomatic relations with Washington in 1965, and it was July 1969 before they were restored. Until the seizure of power by Lon Nol in the following spring, the re-opened US embassy had no proper building, a miniscule diplomatic staff, no service attachés and – in view of Sihanouk's sensitivities on the point – *no CIA station;* it also had no direct communication with Washington, having to rely on the post office, which was always closed overnight.[52] There

49 Jefferey, *MI6*, p. 705; *Diplomatic Service List 1969*; 'Jimmy James' [obit.], *The Scotsman*, 9 Feb. 2002.

50 Martin interview.

51 In March 1970, Sihanouk was deposed in favour of the more US-leaning general, Lon Nol, who thereupon threw his own forces into the fight against the North Vietnamese and the Vietcong.

52 Rives and Antippas interviews.

were, however, other Western embassies in Phnom Penh, notably a well-established and cooperative French embassy. There were also North Vietnamese and Vietcong embassies, although these were sacked and looted of large sums of US dollars in early March 1970 during the demonstrations accompanying the fall of Prince Sihanouk.[53]

Prior to and during the invasion of Iraq by the US-led coalition in March 2003, Britain and the United States – no longer having the advantage of missions in Baghdad – found their embassies in neighbouring Jordan particularly important for gathering intelligence on Iraq. In the earlier Gulf conflict, Jordan had adopted a policy of benevolent neutrality towards Saddam Hussein's government, but on this occasion its neutrality favoured his Western enemies.[54] This no doubt made intelligence work for the embassies in Amman easier.[55] Edward Chaplin, British ambassador at Amman for two years up to April 2002, told the Chilcot Inquiry on the Iraq war that his embassy had a 'watching brief' on Iraq, which included sending members of his diplomatic staff into the country when circumstances permitted. It was 'not a bad watching post for that', he added, 'a lot of Iraqi exiles there and a lot of trade with the country'.[56]

Helping evaders and escapers

Under what used to be known as the laws of war but is now known as international humanitarian law, members of belligerent armed forces entering neutral territory for reasons of operational

[53] Some members of the North Vietnamese mission were reported to have defended their residence near the embassy by threatening the demonstrators with hand grenades, *The Times*, 12 Mar. 1970. Shortly after these events, these missions were closed and diplomatic relations severed.

[54] Hinnebusch and Quilliam, 'Contrary siblings', pp. 518–19.

[55] Jordan had its own embassy in Baghdad, which was hit by a car bomb after the invasion, on 7 August 2003.

[56] The Iraq Inquiry, Written Evidence, 1 Dec. 2009. However, the significance of the 'snapshots' of Iraq obtained by the Amman embassy was played down by Chaplin's successor, Christopher Prentice, Written Evidence, 6 Jan. 2010.

expediency or in order to *evade* capture by their enemy must – if possible – be interned by the neutral government for the duration of the hostilities. Neutrals are also required to impound any military equipment (including aircraft) which they bring with them.[57] These provisions are designed to ensure that military units do not use neutral territory in order to recuperate, reorganize and then return to the fray. Only on the understanding that this would not be permitted could an enemy be expected to halt any pursuit at the borders of the neutral state. By contrast, those who *escape* from captivity and find their way to a neutral state are permitted their freedom.[58] This rule honours the bravery and resourcefulness of escapers and was easy enough for governments to swallow because the numbers involved were never likely to be large. The distinction between 'evaders' and 'escapers' is conceptually neat, but in practice has always been problematical: in the Second World War most evaders represented themselves as escapers in order to avoid internment[59] and it was not always easy to disprove their claims.

The traditional response of diplomatic missions to members of their armed forces finding themselves in these situations occasions no surprise. It is to press, at the minimum, for treatment consistent with the laws of war for those interned, as expressed since 1929 in the Geneva Convention on the treatment of prisoners of war (revised in the third Geneva Convention, 1949); to make contact with them as soon as possible in order to obtain any intelligence they may have acquired while in captivity and then on the run; and to get escapers home as quickly as possible – and even persuade the neutral government discreetly to release interned evaders, especially if they are officers or have skills valuable to the war effort. This work has fallen usually on the service attachés, some having the advantage of assistance from

[57] Convention (V) respecting the Rights and Duties of Neutral Powers and Persons in case of War on Land. The Hague, 18 Oct. 1907, Arts. 11 and 12; ICRC, *The Law of Armed Conflict*, Lesson 8: Neutrality.
[58] Convention (V) respecting the Rights and Duties of Neutral Powers and Persons in case of War on Land. The Hague, 18 Oct. 1907, Art. 13.
[59] Foot and Langley, *MI9*, p. 19.

intelligence agencies dedicated to it.[60] In the Second World War, it was a major task, particularly for those in the diplomatic missions of the belligerent powers in Axis-surrounded Switzerland.

In Berne, the British legation alone had dealt with almost 5,000 escapers and evaders by the end of the war, and this was another reason why it was so large. A few of these service personnel consisted of air crew who had been shot down over France or Germany but managed to evade capture and make it on foot to Switzerland, but most were prisoners of war who had escaped from camps in Germany and Italy. David Kelly, the head of the British mission, had to take no special pains to ensure the proper treatment of British evaders and escapers by the Swiss authorities.[61] Indeed, the authoritative history of MI9 says that while in Spain it could take 'weeks or even months' for the police to permit an escaper to make contact with his own diplomatic mission, in Switzerland the process took only minutes.[62] Arriving from the Axis countries or from occupied France, the escapers also brought valuable intelligence: 'their observations were like missing pieces of a jigsaw puzzle', remarked Air Commodore Freddie West, the air attaché at the legation. As a former escaper himself, the military attaché, Colonel Henry Cartwright, was particularly well qualified to 'draw information' from these arrivals.[63]

Getting the escapers and internees home, however, was a more difficult matter. Even escapers – legally free men – usually had to wait their turn in the queue,[64] while 'ways and means' had to be employed in order to extricate internees from the clutches of the properly rule-conscious Swiss, who had a Commissariat for Interned Soldiers.[65] Arrangements then had to be made, with

[60] In the Second World War these were agents of MI9 in the case of Britain, MIS-X in that of the US.

[61] Kelly, *The Ruling Few*, p. 271. It was publicly admitted by the Swiss government after the war that many Russian escapers fared much worse, *The Times*, 1 Oct. 1945.

[62] Foot and Langley, *MI9*, p. 19; cf Reid, *Winged Diplomat*, p. 167.

[63] Foot and Langley, *MI9*, p. 40.

[64] Reid, *Winged Diplomat*, pp. 186–7.

[65] Kelly, *The Ruling Few*, p. 271.

the assistance of the French Resistance, to spirit them through France into the other adjacent neutral country, Spain, 'where they were duly arrested by the Spanish authorities and rescued and eventually sent home by the British Embassy in Madrid'.[66] This process – in which a key role was played by Victor Farrell, the SIS agent acting under cover as a vice-consul at Geneva – became even more difficult after Germany occupied the whole of France in November 1942.[67]

Sometimes, however, the repatriation of escapers and internees was simplified. In February 1943, for example, two 'valuable and specially trained' air crew returning to England from a photo-reconnaissance mission over North Africa had to make a forced landing at Berne Aerodrome and were duly interned. At the suggestion of the British air attaché, who was under orders from London urgently to secure their release and knew that the Germans also had badly needed air crew interned in Switzerland, the Swiss brokered a successful exchange with the German air attaché: three German airmen for the two British, plus their safe escort across France to Spain.[68] In late 1944, the Swiss themselves, who were anxious to reduce the numbers of internees on their territory swollen by the influx of escapers and refugees from Italy following the Italian surrender, proposed Allied exchanges with the Germans involving much larger numbers. As it turned out, the British were not interested, but an exchange which saw the release from Swiss internment of 1,503 Americans (790 of them airmen) eventually went through.[69] In any event, following the surrender of Italy, the Swiss were under no obligation to hold the few Allied evaders who had arrived from that country, while the more or less

[66] Kelly, *The Ruling Few*, p. 271.

[67] Reid, *Winged Diplomat*, pp. 166, 186–7; Jefferey, *MI6*, pp. 409–10, 507–8.

[68] Reid, *Winged Diplomat*, pp. 183–4.

[69] A major role in arranging this was played by Brigadier General Barney Legge, who was much experienced in this business and had long collaborated with the service attachés in the British legation, Foot and Langley, *MI9*, pp. 243–4. As the air war against Germany intensified, many more crippled US planes sought safety in Switzerland, while some were forced down by Swiss fighters for breaching Swiss neutrality, Helmreich, 'The Diplomacy of Apology'.

simultaneous re-opening of their frontier with France at Geneva following the Allied advance made the repatriation of the many more numerous escapers via Marseilles comparatively easy. The service attachés at the British legation in Berne, in concert with their colleagues at the Allied legations, had been preparing for this for some time and were heavily involved in the execution of the 'great exodus' in September 1944, as they were also in a big exchange of totally disabled prisoners of war in Switzerland in January 1945.[70]

In Sweden, where almost one thousand badly needed US air crew were interned by September 1944 (and being exceptionally well treated – better than in Switzerland), the US legation in Stockholm was under heavy pressure from Washington to get them home. As a result, it was actively involved in negotiating exchanges, not only against German internees, but also trapped German aircraft – with the offer of the sale to Sweden of US military aircraft thrown in as well. However, the Swedes were loathe to 'bargain' with the Americans and so in the end began to release large numbers of airmen 'on account' – that is, in anticipation of being able to release German servicemen who had not yet arrived! By the beginning of 1945, they had almost all been released.[71]

In Spain, predictably enough, the Allied missions had a much more difficult time than the Germans in getting home their service personnel who, for one reason or another, found themselves in the country. Axis air crew who had made forced-landings, for example, were repatriated immediately, while British air crew were interned.[72] As to British escapers, the Spanish first denied any knowledge of them and then demanded that the British embassy prove that they were escapers rather than evaders, which was no easy task. According to the British ambassador, the embassy managed to get them all out – 'and many thousands of

[70] Reid, *Winged Diplomat*, pp. 196, 206; Foot and Langley, *MI9*, p. 243.

[71] 'Negotiations with the Swedish government for release of United States airmen interned in Sweden', *FRUS, 1944*. Vol. IV, pp. 689–705.

[72] Hoare, *Ambassador on Special Mission*, pp. 198–9.

Allied personnel besides' – but the negotiations over the matter were 'almost endless'.[73]

Placating the neutral

The important task frequently falls to a belligerent embassy of placating a neutral government angered by a breach of its neutrality for which its own government is held responsible. Embassy apologies need to be the more fulsome, or explanations the more ingenious, if serious damage and casualties are inflicted in the process. For example, in the first years of the Second World War, David Kelly, the British minister in Berne, was repeatedly summoned to the Swiss foreign ministry to hear complaints about RAF planes flying over Switzerland to bomb industrial targets in northern Italy, and occasionally adding injury to insult by accidentally dropping bombs and causing casualties in Switzerland itself. Until the Air Ministry in London admitted its crews were at fault and offered to pay compensation, Kelly claimed that the English bombs responsible had probably been captured by the Germans in France, and actually dropped by them rather than the RAF in order to cause trouble between Britain and Switzerland.[74]

The accidental bombing of Swiss targets by the US Air Force in the Second World War occurred on a much larger scale, causing great damage and significant loss of life. Despite instructions to pilots not to bomb within 50 miles of the Swiss frontier without positive identification, it also increased greatly as the front moved closer to Germany in 1944 and 1945. On 4 March 1945, even Basel and Zurich were bombed.[75] This caused acute embarrassment at the higher levels of the US military and in the Department of State,

[73] Hoare, *Ambassador on Special Mission*, pp. 77–9, 132.

[74] Kelly, *The Ruling Few*, pp. 278–9.

[75] Following these incidents, the Americans agreed to extend and considerably tighten the restrictions on bombing close to the Swiss frontier. On this subject generally, see the exhaustive account in Helmreich, 'The Diplomacy of Apology'; and 'Accidental bombing of Swiss city of Schaffhausen by American planes', *FRUS, 1944*. Vol. IV, pp. 792–800.

both aware that Swiss outrage at these persistent occurrences was likely to rebound against OSS activities in Switzerland, and also make the Swiss more reluctant to release the growing number of interned US airmen. As a result, the US minister, Leland Harrison, and his military attaché, Brigadier-General Barnwell Legge, had a great deal of work to do over quite a long period – the former with the Swiss foreign minister, the latter with the Swiss commander in chief – in promptly expressing sympathy and offering apologies. (Later on they had to be assisted by high-level special emissaries.) This was the more necessary because the bombings were given wide coverage in the Swiss press, while 'the Berlin press had a field day decrying the terroristic actions of the U.S. gangsters'.[76] The American legation was also charged with making the substantial reparation payments swiftly offered to the Swiss authorities for benefit of the victims; reporting independently on the major incidents; and – via the military attaché – liaising with the Swiss military on technical procedures designed to prevent future incidents. The legation also strongly supported the eventual Swiss request to be allowed to attach observers to the Allied Expeditionary Force in Europe in order to improve military relations between them, despite the fears of some US commanders that this would present a serious security risk.

On the occasion of the next spectacular bombing of a neutral country by the US Air Force, that of Cambodia, which began deliberately in March 1969 and lasted for a full 14 months, the American embassy on the spot had less reason to worry about the need for apologising and handing over reparations. This was partly because the targets of the American bombs were the vital North Vietnamese and Vietcong sanctuaries established on the Cambodian side of the border with Vietnam, and to which the Cambodians were turning a blind eye; and partly because – provided the Americans kept quiet about it, which they did – the government of Prince Sihanouk seems to have been happy to see its unwelcome guests given a battering.[77] On the other

[76] Helmreich, 'The Diplomacy of Apology'.
[77] Isaacson, *Kissinger*, pp. 177–8.

hand, the US chief of mission did have to bear the brunt of Sihanouk's anger when one of his own outposts in the north of the country was destroyed.[78] Presumably, too, he had to listen to many Cambodian complaints about relatively minor border incidents for which US ground forces were responsible, because he complained repeatedly to Saigon about these himself.[79]

Handling peace feelers

A belligerent state with an inclination to put out a peace feeler to its enemy can do this directly by a secret message sent electronically, by sending out a special envoy, by a discreet encounter at an international body or ad hoc conference at which they both have representation – or even by a veiled hint in a public statement; it can also do it indirectly via a third party. However, each of these methods carries significant risks. Is it likely that putting out a peace feeler via a message from one belligerent embassy to another in a neutral state will be any more attractive?

Some of the risks attaching to various of the other methods apply equally to this one. To begin with, the prohibition on contact between enemy missions is a firm norm of the diplomatic corps and, as a result, diplomats who break it – even when their action is officially approved – have been known to suffer the charge of 'consorting with the enemy' and pay a heavy career price.[80] There is also the same risk that, unless concerted with allies, any such move by a belligerent may be regarded by these allies with intense suspicion – regarded, that is, as a move suggesting a disposition to desert their friends and make a separate peace with the enemy. In any case, even if there were not a 'no-contact' prohibition, in major conflicts the opportunities for the members of belligerent missions to 'bump into' each other in neutral states are limited because there is usually a severe reduction in the number of social

[78] Rives interview.

[79] Antippas interview.

[80] Murphy, *Diplomat Among Warriors*, p. 23.

events attended by the diplomatic corps, such engagements being thought unseemly in the circumstances.[81] In this connection, it is striking – although unusual – that Denham, the highly effective British naval attaché in Stockholm throughout the Second World War already mentioned in this chapter, did not even know by sight any member of the German legation.[82]

On the other hand, neutral states are often the only settings in which belligerent missions find themselves in close physical if not social proximity, the more so because embassies and legations have traditionally tended to be located in the same quarter of capital cities. In Switzerland, in the Second World War the Axis and Allied missions 'were practically within a stone's throw of each other', while in Spain the British and German ambassadors were next-door neighbours.[83] Even if elsewhere belligerent missions have a similar proximity, for example at the headquarters of an international body, neutral capitals are likely to be more removed from the public gaze. Furthermore, these capitals will probably have missions from other neutrals as well, which might be willing to serve as intermediaries. Finally, belligerent embassies in these capitals are – for reasons already noted – invariably strongly staffed, not least with intelligence officers, individuals professionally adept either at conducting or arranging secret meetings. In the circumstances, therefore, it is not surprising that these embassies have indeed often been thought to be a particularly attractive prospect to deliver or receive a peace feeler.

Switzerland was the setting for a number of peace feelers put out to Britain by Germany in the middle of 1940. Hitler's envoy, Prince Hohenlohe, met the British minister, David Kelly, on three occasions, twice at the house of the former Swiss minister in London and once at the Spanish legation.[84] In 1941, the German embassy in Madrid made numerous attempts – directly as well as via Spanish intermediaries – to entice the British ambassador to

[81] Howard, *Theatre of Life*, p. 208; Murphy, *Diplomat Among Warriors*, p. 23.

[82] Denham, *Inside the Nazi Ring*, p. 44.

[83] Reid, *Winged Diplomat*, pp. 170–1; Hoare, *Ambassador on Special Mission*, pp. 22–3.

[84] Kelly, *The Ruling Few*, pp. 271–4.

respond to peace overtures.[85] In late 1942, the British also received peace feelers from the Italians, through intermediaries from the Italian legation in Lisbon, and directly from the Italian consul-general in Geneva.[86]

In March 1943, following an increase in the number of peace feelers made by individuals from the minor German satellites in Europe to both American and British representatives in the neutrals, the US State Department sent a circular message to its missions in Ankara, Stockholm, Madrid and Lisbon. This reaffirmed the policy that missions themselves could have no truck with such approaches. It also informed them that it had warned the Office of War Information and the various intelligence services, to whom the peace feelers had usually been diverted, that – bearing in mind the need to preserve the alliance with Britain and the Soviet Union – 'no action or utterance should occur which might be misconstrued as being contrary to the spirit of our common effort'.[87] To guard further against this – somewhat later, it seems – the wise procedure was agreed between the three main allied powers that any peace overture received by one would be communicated to the other two.[88]

These were stiff constraints. Nevertheless, the State Department – with which on this the British Foreign Office was anxious to keep in line – also made clear that it had no objections to the other agencies receiving peace feelers, which could be useful sources of intelligence; and it informed missions that the agencies had been instructed to report to them any approaches received and thereafter follow the guidance of the diplomats in the country in question. In line with this approach, in April 1943, when approaches to the British from the Hungarians were anticipated in Switzerland and Turkey, the heads of mission were instructed to remain aloof while 'other channels' – obviously intelligence officers – were to be used to listen to what the Hungarians had to

85 Hoare, *Ambassador on Special Mission*, p. 105.
86 Winant (London) to SoS, 18 Dec. 1942. *FRUS, 1943*. Vol. II, pp. 315–16.
87 SoS to Steinhardt (Ankara), 13 Mar. 1943. *FRUS, 1943*. Vol. I, pp. 484–5.
88 Dept. of State to British Embassy. Aide-Mémoire, 18 Nov. 1943, *FRUS, 1943*. Vol. I, pp. 503–4.

say.[89] Later in the year, Allen Dulles in Berne was informed that the Joint Chiefs of Staff had instructed the OSS to do what it could to detach Bulgaria, Hungary and Romania 'immediately from the Axis'.[90]

It should not be forgotten, however, that the intelligence agencies to which peace feelers were put were themselves largely based in the belligerent diplomatic missions. There were also occasions on which these missions – with the connivance of their political masters – deviated from the agreed convention of official aloofness. For example, in March 1943, the US ambassador in Madrid received via the Argentine ambassador a peace feeler from the Romanian minister.[91] In September, the military attaché at the US legation in Lisbon met directly the counsellor of the Hungarian legation, an action sanctioned by George Kennan, then counsellor at the US legation.[92] While in November 1943, the US ambassador in Madrid received a further peace feeler from the Romanian legation, this time directly from its first secretary.[93]

In the end, nothing much came of this prolonged flurry of inter-belligerent diplomatic activity in the neutral capitals. But this was partly because of the discouraging US requirement of 'unconditional surrender', partly because of the intense suspicion between the Soviet Union on the one hand and the British and Americans on the other, and partly because of German actions to keep its satellites tight.

In the years following the end of the Second World War, there seem to have been fewer occasions when belligerent embassies in

89 British Embassy to Dept. of State. Aide-Mémoire, 20 Apr. 1943, *FRUS, 1943.* Vol. I, pp. 490–1. Equally, in April 1944, the British legation in Stockholm was told by the FO that a recent German peace feeler put to it indirectly, and any similar, was 'most appropriately handled by SIS', Denham, *Inside the Nazi Ring*, p. 160.

90 Wilson (OSS) to Berle (State), 10 Dec. 1943, *FRUS, 1943.* Vol. I, pp. 510–11.

91 Hayes to SoS, 21 and 23 Mar. 1943, *FRUS, 1943.* Vol. I, p. 485; see also SoS to Hayes, 26 Mar. 1943, p. 486.

92 Solborg (Lisbon) to Kroner (Military Intel., G2), 14 Sept. 1943, *FRUS, 1943.* Vol. I, p. 498.

93 Dept. of State to the British Embassy. Aide-Mémoire, 18 Nov. 1943. *FRUS, 1943.* Vol. I, pp. 503–4.

neutral states have been an important source of peace feelers. This is no doubt chiefly because there has been no similar conflict and, as a result, all of the major powers – with the exception of the PRC until October 1971 – have had large permanent missions at the UN in New York which could be used for this purpose.[94] Faster and safer air transport has also made it easier to employ special envoys, while telecommunications have improved even more dramatically. Nevertheless, it is not difficult to find post-1945 examples where the embassies of hostile if not necessarily belligerent states in neutral capitals were conduits for peace feelers.[95] The talks on nuclear matters in Beijing between the political counsellors of the US and North Korean embassies, which started at the end of 1988 and concluded with a modest success in 1994, also provide an authentic case. This is because, in the Korean War in the early 1950s, the Americans had been the standard bearers for the United Nations against the North, and there was in 1988 – as indeed there still is today – no peace settlement to bring this war formally to an end, only a ceasefire. Beijing was chosen for these talks not just because both parties had large missions there, but because the Americans regarded it as a neutral setting, while the North Koreans were highly dependent on the PRC. It also guaranteed the secrecy of the talks (except to the Chinese themselves) better than anywhere else and was a venue well calculated to maximize Chinese support for progress on the important issues under discussion.[96]

Conclusion

The belligerent embassy in a neutral state does not usually find its work radically skewed from the normal unless its host is close to the front line or is, for some other reason, of strategic importance;

[94] Berridge, 'Old diplomacy in New York'.
[95] I discussed this question at some length in ch. 5 of my *Talking to the Enemy*.
[96] This case is discussed at length in Berridge and Gallo, 'The role of the diplomatic corps: The US–North Korea talks in Beijing, 1988–94'.

but in a general war, such a neutral is not rare. If instructed to secure its benevolent neutrality, history suggests that the belligerent embassy should be neither too gentle with it, nor too heavy-handed. Propaganda has long been an embassy duty given more importance in these circumstances and, as well as requiring direct participation, usually means sending home advice on how to adjust general propaganda themes to local circumstances and reporting on their effects.

Belligerent embassies in important neutrals also become major bases for intelligence gathering, strategic deception, and special operations targeting the supply of strategic materials to an enemy, maintaining bases for incursions into neighbouring territories and so on. If the neutral is well disposed, belligerent intelligence officers usually find it relatively easy – since both are accustomed to working in secret – to enlist the assistance of local security services in activities such as these. In the Second World War, assisting escapers and evaders also became an important and time-consuming duty, especially for the belligerent missions in Berne, Stockholm and Madrid; as did placating the neutral government following any egregious breach of its neutrality. Finally, since they are in close physical proximity in capitals relatively removed from the public gaze, and stiff with intelligence officers professionally adept either at conducting or arranging secret meetings, belligerent embassies in neutral states have traditionally been attractive prospects for delivering or receiving peace feelers. As the experience of the Second World War demonstrates, however, such conditions are not sufficient for their success.

5 Embassies to Frontline Allies

Chapter Overview

The experience of the embassy of a belligerent accredited to the government of a frontline ally depends on many things, not least the strength and defensive capabilities of its ally. But two other variables are also prominent among them. The first is the nature of the military conflict in which they are engaged. Is the warfare conventional, with an identifiable if moving front line? Or is it unconventional, with no identifiable front line at all? The second is the size and nature of the military contribution being made by the embassy's own government.

In conventional warfare

Focused and stripped for action

Conventional wars such as the Korean War at the beginning of the 1950s, the India–Pakistan wars, the numerous Arab–Israeli Wars and the Gulf Wars in 1991 and 2003, are wars of movement in which the belligerents tend to commit their heaviest weapons, take large risks and look for early victory – even if their objectives are limited. In such conditions, the work and procedures of a belligerent embassy in the capital of a frontline allied state tend to change dramatically. Some routine functions – certain kinds of economic, commercial and cultural work, for example – are relegated to the sidelines or fall away altogether, and non-essential staff and dependants are sent home. These developments are the more complete if the embassy needs to follow a retreating government. In short, it is stripped for action and focused intensely on supporting immediate military priorities.

A task of the first order for an embassy in this situation is to preserve close, high-level personal contact with the allied host government in order to ensure that they keep in step on policy; this is usually as important in the weeks prior to the launch of war as in those following it. For example, as the UN-imposed deadline of 15 January 1991 approached for the *unconditional* withdrawal of Iraqi forces from Kuwait, there was a swirl of diplomatic initiatives which promised to avoid a military outcome by offering Saddam Hussein some form of compensation for pulling back. The Americans and the British were in the vanguard of those determined to avoid this, as was their key ally, King Fahd's Saudi kingdom, but all were under great pressure:

> With all these hares running loose [writes Alan Munro, the British ambassador in Riyadh] it was of the first importance for us to keep in close contact with the Saudis for the sake of mutual reassurance and to harmonise our responses … Scarcely a day passed during this tense period of waiting when we did not need to make contact over some development that might generate misunderstanding between us or obscure the objectives of our alliance.[1]

However, the *centrality* in this role of the embassy attached to the frontline ally depends, among other things, on the influence of the allied government's own embassy at the other end of the bilateral

[1] Munro, *An Embassy at War*, pp. 209–10. See also Freeman interview.

relationship. Thus, while Munro's embassy in Riyadh appears to have suffered little competition from the Saudi embassy in London, the same cannot be said for the US embassy relative to the kingdom's mission in Washington. Here, the ambassador was Prince Bandar, who was extremely close to King Fahd, and Chas Freeman, the US ambassador in Riyadh, himself acknowledges that it was Bandar who played 'the major role' in concerting policy.[2]

The task of preserving an agreed line in the same conflict also fell with particular heaviness upon the American embassy in Tel Aviv. In April 1990, in a threatening allusion to Israel, Saddam Hussein had boasted of his chemical weapons, and after the Iraqi invasion of Kuwait in early August, and what the Israelis regarded as increasingly close military cooperation between Iraq and Jordan, an attack by Israeli jets (via Jordanian airspace) on Iraqi missile bases and airfields was increasingly likely. Once Iraqi Scud missiles started landing in Israel after the war broke out in January, such an attack seemed to be approaching a certainty.[3] But the visible presence of Israel in the front rank of the anti-Saddam coalition that Washington was then putting together – especially if this brought it into conflict with Jordan as well – would have been bound to discourage participation in it of the Arab states which it was so anxious to include. The trouble was that America's relations with the Likud-led coalition government in Jerusalem had been poor for some time, and intense pressure was needed to keep it 'on the reservation'. A special radio telephone link was installed in 'great secrecy' between the US secretary of defense, Richard Cheney, and the hard-line Israeli defense minister, Moshe Arens;[4] high-level envoys were twice sent to Israel;[5] and President George Bush personally intervened with the Israeli prime minister, Yitzhak Shamir, on a number of occasions.

[2] Freeman interview. See also Berridge, *The Counter-Revolution in Diplomacy*, ch. 6

[3] Arens, *Broken Covenant*, ch. 7.

[4] Arens, *Broken Covenant*, p. 169.

[5] These were Paul Wolfowitz and Lawrence Eagleburger, Arens, *Broken Covenant*, p. 186.

But the day-by-day contribution to the restraint of the Israelis by the American ambassador in Tel Aviv, Bill Brown – especially that which he exercised on Moshe Arens, who was angrily straining at the leash but regarded Brown as a 'good friend' – was also important.[6] 'I had my role and I had my scripts', says Brown, who on one occasion divulged an item of highly important intelligence to the defense minister about the range of the SCUDS after repeatedly failing to obtain clearance from Washington for his action. 'I just felt', he remarks, 'that this had to be done if we were going to maintain a semblance of confidence and trust in achieving our main objective which ... was to keep the Israelis away from launching a pre-emptive strike at Iraq.'[7] In the event, the Israelis held back.

If the war is going badly for the allied government to which the belligerent embassy is accredited, close personal relations of the sort just mentioned always need to be exploited in order to sustain its morale. In the Korean War, for example, Harold J. Noble, who was first secretary at the US embassy in Seoul, believes that it was the embassy's 'most outstanding contribution to the war effort' to sustain not only Korean but also American morale, following the disastrous initial defeats at the hands of the North Koreans.[8]

It is also when the war is going badly that the embassy's local propaganda effort is especially valuable, since public morale – among both civilians and the military – is usually as important as that of the government itself.[9] It is also a business that cannot be ignored if there is popular suspicion in the allied state of the motives of the embassy's own government, as there was in Saudi Arabia during the Gulf War in 1991. On this occasion, both the British and American ambassadors spoke to the Saudi media in an attempt to scotch the belief in some quarters that the whole Iraq/Kuwait affair was part of a subtle infidel plan to strengthen the position of Israel and give the West a freer hand in the Gulf.[10]

[6] Arens, *Broken Covenant*, p. 62.
[7] Brown, William Andreas, interview. See also Arens, *Broken Covenant*, p. 167.
[8] Noble, *Embassy at War*, pp. 215–16.
[9] Noble, *Embassy at War*, p. 216.
[10] Munro, *An Embassy at War*, pp. 229–30, 303; Freeman interview.

When belligerent embassies have major military forces of their own on the territory of their frontline ally, the work of diplomatic and consular officers is heavily affected. This is readily seen in the case of the US embassies in Seoul during the Korean War and Saigon during the conflict in Vietnam, and also in that of the Coalition embassies in Saudi Arabia during the Gulf War in 1990–1.

In the first place, important negotiations with the host government are urgently required. These are characteristically aimed at agreement on points of military entry, location of bases, and – perhaps most importantly of all – the legal and operational status of their forces. The status of forces agreement (SOFA) signed between Britain and Saudi Arabia in the run-up to the Gulf War, which took the form of a memorandum of understanding, required lengthy negotiation. The British side consisted of an embassy team stiffened by specialists from the Ministry of Defence in London and was led by Derek Plumbly, the deputy head of mission, whose fluency in Arabic fortunately extended to technical and legal terms;[11] however, according to General Peter de la Billière, commander-in-chief of British forces in the Middle East, it was he, together with the ambassador, Alan Munro, who finally got the Saudi defence minister, Prince Sultan, to authorize its signature.[12] Like all SOFAs, the UK-Saudi agreement dealt with the question of who should have responsibility for criminal jurisdiction over members of the visiting armed forces, and in this case it was provided that British forces would remain under British military law.[13] But it also defined the role of those forces in the kingdom, required Saudi consent to their use in an offensive action and made clear that they would be promptly withdrawn once the crisis was over.[14] As it happened, in the negotiation of the US–Saudi SOFA, the American embassy in Riyadh played second fiddle to the Saudi embassy in Washington, but the agreement

[11] Munro, *An Embassy at War*, p. 173.

[12] Billière, *Storm Command*, pp. 49–50.

[13] On SOFAs generally, see Mason, 'Status of Forces Agreement (SOFA)'.

[14] Munro, *An Embassy at War*, p. 172.

is worth mentioning nonetheless since it provided that all US military personnel in the kingdom would be assigned as 'technical staff of the embassy'. Since their total came to reach over half a million, there is no reason to doubt the claim of Chas Freeman, the American ambassador, that this made the US embassy in Riyadh the largest embassy in history.[15] Perhaps it was this which assisted Freeman himself to arrange one particularly important 'understanding' with King Fahd, namely, that US troops – whose numbers included many Jews as well as Christians – would have the right to practice their own religions, provided this was done in private.[16] After all, the *droit de chapelle* is a long-established right of embassies.

When the belligerent embassy finds combat forces from its own country alongside it, another significant task usually imposed upon it – and for which it is well suited – is that of 'chief political adviser in theatre' to the senior officers commanding them.[17] Among other things, this means advice on how to integrate command of their forces with those of any other ally present in the country, how states adjacent to the theatre of war and even further afield are likely to react to significant military moves, and, above all, on how the military should conduct themselves with the host government. The last is particularly important if there are marked cultural differences between them and a lack of experience – or lack of learning from experience – in cooperation. In the Korean War, for example, when initially many American officers were 'hostile to the Korean government and even the Korean people', the US embassy had to work hard to convince commanders to take South Korea's generals seriously by inviting them to briefings, although in the end it did.[18] It also claimed credit for persuading the US army to enlist the help of Korean

[15] Freeman interview.

[16] Freeman interview.

[17] Munro, *An Embassy at War*, p. 170. In the Gulf War, the British MoD initially wanted the commander of the British forces to have his own political adviser, but he wished for this no more than the ambassador and the idea was 'quietly dropped', Munro, *An Embassy at War*, pp. 102–3.

[18] Noble, *Embassy at War*, pp. 142–4.

police battalions in detecting infiltrators, fighting as light infantry and even filling up its own ranks with Korean soldiers, 'a program which proved to be tremendously successful'.[19]

Similarly, in Saudi Arabia during the Gulf War, Chas Freeman regarded his role as local political adviser to the commander-in-chief of US Central Command (CentCom), General Norman Schwarzkopf, as vital.[20] The US military, he said afterwards, had not developed 'an adequate military-political function' and, 'given the nature of Saudi society, we could anticipate a huge amount of friction between American forces and Saudi forces unless certain things were made clear' – for example, that use of alcohol would need to be banned and that women drivers would always have to wear camouflage uniform so that they could be treated as men.[21] There was a lot of resentment about this sort of thing among the military, but CentCom's acceptance of it – greatly assisted by the fact that Schwarzkopf had political antennae of his own, was co-located with the ambassador and got on well with him – duly helped to minimize the number of incidents.[22] When they occurred nevertheless, the embassy and its consulates,

[19] Noble, *Embassy at War*, p. 216.

[20] Schwarzkopf also had his own political adviser, Gordon S. Brown, but Brown had a general remit for CentCom's area of responsibility – which extended beyond the Middle East to South Asia and the horn of Africa – and was initially much taken up with such matters as arranging the overflying rights needed to expedite the major airlift of troops and equipment from Europe to the Gulf. Besides, while he was an Arabist and, prior to his appointment to CentCom in 1989, had been responsible for Arab Peninsula Affairs in the State Department, it was over 20 years since Brown had himself been posted to Saudi Arabia. Freeman was the man on the spot and 'his relationship with Schwarzkopf was so good', says Brown, 'that he put me out of a job', Brown, Gordon S., interview.

[21] Dunford interview.

[22] Schwarzkopf had been at the helm of CentCom since July 1988. According to his own account, he attached great importance to the 'diplomatic' side of his role: 'solidifying relations with rulers and generals' throughout his area of responsibility, which fortunately for his relations with the Arab states did not include Israel. In the autumn of 1988, he had taken the intensive, pre-posting course on the Middle East provided by the US Foreign Service Institute, Schwarzkopf, *The Autobiography*, pp. 270–82, 302, 354–5. See also Brown, Gordon S., interview.

especially the one in Dhahran, had the task of resolving them or, failing that, keeping them out of the press.[23]

If they are prudent, these missions will also want to gather their own intelligence on the progress of the fighting and not rely for this entirely on the military – unless, as in the case just mentioned, relations with them are unusually good and there is great mutual confidence. Military developments have political implications and there are, in any case, 'borderline areas between military reporting and political reporting'.[24] Besides, military or paramilitary intelligence may already have proved unreliable. For example, at the major US consulate-general at Can Tho in the Mekong Delta military region of South Vietnam in 1974–5, Terry McNamara, the principal officer, had little faith in the views on Viet Cong activity of the local CIA station – almost none of whose officers had 'significant Vietnamese experience' – and nurtured his own 'excellent sources'. These seem to have proved better. There is in any case, as he says, always advantage in a second opinion.[25]

Whether the belligerent embassy is accompanied by a major military force or not, it has numerous other duties to perform once fighting has started. A particularly high priority here is advancing plans for the evacuation of any expatriates from areas seriously threatened by military action and, in the meantime, offering advice on how they might protect themselves. This task falls chiefly on consular staff, and needs to be accomplished without stimulating panic and while simultaneously trying to keep in step with allied embassies. The latter is necessary in order to avoid the discord which can result if some take early protective steps for the benefit of their expatriates that put pressure on other embassies to follow suit when, for good or bad reasons, they may have to delay. Dealing with the expatriate community is a task which is the more

[23] Freeman interview; Brown, Gordon S., interview. On the similar role of the British embassy in the Gulf War, which was also co-located with the British forces commander, see Munro, *An Embassy at War*, pp. 95–100, 170; Billière, *Storm Command*, pp. 38, 78.

[24] Noble, *Embassy at War*, p. 92; see also pp. 165–6.

[25] McNamara, *Escape with Honor*, pp. 7–8, 12–13, 49–50.

difficult to handle if it is large and spread over the country, if it is popularly feared that weapons of nightmarish effect might well be used by the enemy, and if the ally's war effort is dependent on this community for key workers. All of these circumstances existed in Saudi Arabia in the Gulf War, where many states – especially in Asia – had enormous expatriate communities.[26] In seeking to balance 'solidarity with Saudi Arabia' against its duty of protection to its own citizens – who still numbered about 19,000 on the eve of the fighting – the British embassy in Riyadh set its face firmly against early evacuation, resisting even the idea of an immediate exodus in the event of chemical attack on the additional grounds that this would be a 'logistical nightmare'.[27] Instead, while making urgent arrangements for a full evacuation as a last resort, it placed emphasis on the graduated 'thinning out' of dependants and providing guidance through the warden system on physical protection for those who stayed behind; gas masks were not issued until early January 1991, just before the outbreak of fighting was anticipated, for fear of spreading alarm, although in fact it had a quietening effect.[28] The American embassy adopted essentially the same line, although Freeman had a far less happy relationship with Washington in handling the matter, and the British and American ambassadors were unable to keep in step.[29] Fortunately, neither gas marks nor evacuation were needed.

If matters look to be going badly at the front, it will also be necessary to make or update plans to evacuate the staff of the mission itself and any outlying posts. In such circumstances, the danger of stimulating panic and public disorder by ill-chosen timing and points and modes of departure needs to be borne in mind. If defeat seems imminent, there is even the risk that allied military units will turn on the embassy if they feel that they are being betrayed, the more so if the mission is resolved to evacuate with it locally engaged staff of military age. The last risk was

[26] Munro, *An Embassy at War*, p. 236; see also Freeman interview. The situation was much the same in the smaller Gulf states.

[27] Munro, *An Embassy at War*, pp. 242–3.

[28] Munro, *An Embassy at War*, pp. 239–40.

[29] Freeman interview; Munro, *An Embassy at War*, pp. 237–42 *passim*.

seen as very real by McNamara in Can Tho in April 1975, and one which he only managed to avoid by taking the precaution of arranging the evacuation of the family of a key South Vietnamese officer prior to the flight of his own mission.[30]

The high risks, high costs and high drama of conventional wars tend to dominate the political agenda of belligerent states in a way that no other kind of military engagement can match. As a result, important visitors from home – civil and military – tend to descend on their frontline embassies in droves, as do war correspondents, and managing them is another time-consuming task. This did not begin with the arrival of the aeroplane. For example, on the outbreak of the Russo–Japanese War in 1904, in which Britain was an important but as yet uncommitted ally of Japan, even the British legation in remote Tokyo became a victim of this phenomenon.[31]

Partly because of its size and the many and varied power centres in the United States, American embassies at war tend to attract an unusually high number of visitors from home, and the complaints about this from their chiefs of mission are legendary. Ten days after the outbreak of the Sino–Indian conflict in October 1962, J. K. Galbraith, the acerbic American ambassador in India who was trying to orchestrate a policy of quiet support for its government, noted in his journal that:

> From all around the world, people seem to be converging on New Delhi and I foresee that I will spend considerable time in the next few days standing off help that I do not need. Today's offering included a Marine Corps specialist on guerrilla warfare and a deluge of Congressional delegations … .[32]

Six years later, Ellsworth Bunker, the US ambassador in Saigon during the worst period for the administration in the Vietnam

[30] McNamara, *Escape with Honor*, pp. 152–6.

[31] Nish, 'British legations in Tokyo and Beijing during the Russo-Japanese War, 1904–1905', p. 30. See also Galbraith, *Ambassador's Journal*, pp. 397, 399, 429–31; and Munro, *An Embassy at War*, pp. 61, 100, 178, 190, 325.

[32] Galbraith, *Ambassador's Journal*, p. 390; see also p. 399.

War, became so exasperated when told to expect 138 visitors in a three-week period in January 1968 that he called for the creation in Washington of a 'State/Defense Visitors Bureau' to regulate the flow of arrivals. Inevitably, no action was taken.[33] This is why matters were no different for Chas Freeman at the US embassy in Riyadh during the Gulf War. Describing his own problem of 'visitor overload' as an 'avalanche of bright lights and dim bulbs' – over 2,000 of them wanting their photograph taken with troops in the run-up to the fighting – both he and General Schwarzkopf protested about it vigorously:

> So visitor management became a major obsession very early on. As the war proceeded, I began to make requests, in cooperation with Norm Schwarzkopf, that Washington cease treating Saudi Arabia like a military theme park, with an ambassador and a general as the park rangers, and remember that we had things to do. … and were really less able to do so because we were spending all our time meeting VIPs.[34]

The protests met with little success. It was only when Iraqi Scud missiles started landing on Dhahran and Riyadh that visitor numbers dropped off. This was the 'one benefit' of these attacks, according to Freeman's deputy chief of mission, David Dunford.[35]

Large numbers of self-invited high-level visitors not only consume a great deal of the time and energy of an already stretched embassy at war, but can weaken the authority of the ambassador in the eyes of the receiving state. Nevertheless, it should not be forgotten that some have compensating advantages. For example, a visit by an able and influential defence minister, such as the British minister, Tom King, to Saudi Arabia during the Gulf War,[36] or by anyone with influence over the flow of military and other forms of assistance, will even be encouraged

[33] Schaffer, *Ellsworth Bunker*, pp. 179–80.
[34] Freeman interview. See also Schwarzkopf, *The Autobiography*, pp. 363, 393–4.
[35] Dunford interview.
[36] Munro, *An Embassy at War*, p. 161.

by an embassy. Such visits provide an opportunity to educate them on what needs to be done, and – because of the norm that ambassadors accompany high-level visitors in their calls on senior government figures – multiply the occasions on which the embassy has top-level access.[37] Since visits of this sort usually flatter the receiving state, they also add to the warmth of the relationship – thereby bringing indirect advantage to the embassy. A visit by a new head of government can also serve to underline continuity of policy and so reinforce strongly the embassy's task of reassurance on this point, as well as raise its own morale and that of any troops stationed in the country. These were certainly the reasons why the British embassy in Riyadh welcomed the arrival of John Major, who had unexpectedly replaced Margaret Thatcher as prime minister, just a week before the expiry of the 15 January 1991 deadline for Iraq to get out of Kuwait.[38]

Journalists present a special problem for belligerent embassies on the front line. In their relentless attempts to steal a march on their rivals there is a constant risk that their reports will be damaging to the war effort. These might reveal too much about allied plans and capabilities to the enemy,[39] stoke up the inevitable differences within an alliance into open controversies, encourage defeatism at home and panic in an expatriate community – or all of them at the same time. Journalists might also unwittingly allow themselves to be manipulated by enemy propagandists.[40] There were 1,600 members of the American press in Saudi Arabia during the Gulf War, all of whom were regarded by the US ambassador as 'antagonists', although he had to admit that there was not a single leak from the more than 700 backgrounders that he gave them. It

[37] Billière, *Storm Command*, p. 105.

[38] Munro, *An Embassy at War*, pp. 221, 247.

[39] Schwarzkopf reports in his account of the Gulf War his conviction 'that our own newspaper and TV reports had become Iraq's best source of military intelligence', *The Autobiography*, p. 381.

[40] It is evidence of the importance attached to 'the fourth estate' by Alan Munro, the British ambassador in Saudi Arabia during the first Gulf War, that he devotes a whole chapter to it in his memoir of the period, *An Embassy at War*; see also Schaffer, *Ellsworth Bunker*, pp. 185–7, 196–7.

did not help, he believed, that they were 'illiterate' about both the military and Saudi Arabia.[41]

The risk of antagonising the government of the frontline ally is a particularly high one – and so a formidable problem for the embassy – when the journalists are used to operating freely and find themselves in societies suspicious of, if not completely hostile to, such behaviour. Even in India, where there was a 'big press invasion' from the United States during the Sino–Indian war, Galbraith had to urge the government to be more forthcoming to the newsmen about the extent of US material support, which Delhi wished to play down. The American press, he told them, was a fact of life: 'It can be managed or mismanaged but has to be accepted.' For his own part, he sought to 'calm' the journalists by 'providing billets, communication facilities, briefings and other help'.[42] (Enlightened self-interest in this shape is generally good practice for an embassy in such a situation, if it can afford it.) In far less liberal states – for example, Japan during the Russo–Japanese War in 1904–5, and Saudi Arabia during the Gulf War – the problems presented to Western embassies by the arrival of hordes of journalists are so much the greater.[43]

If the senior staff of the embassy at war has any time left over, its members are usually inclined – and are certainly well advised – to give thought to post-war affairs, especially if war aims and a war-termination strategy have not been clearly formulated by politicians, as is too often the case. During the Second World War, as early as February 1942, Lord Halifax, British ambassador in Washington, 'realised it was the peace that was the prize and that setting the context for that time was his main effort'.[44] In the Gulf War, where little beyond the liberation of Kuwait had been agreed because of the fear in Washington that any discussion of other war aims would leak and jeopardize the fragile anti-Saddam coalition, both the US and British ambassadors brooded

[41] Freeman interview.
[42] Galbraith, *Ambassador's Journal*, pp. 401–3.
[43] Nish, 'British legations in Tokyo and Beijing during the Russo-Japanese War, 1904–1905', pp. 30, 32–5; Munro, *An Embassy at War*, pp. 84, 85–6.
[44] Kennedy, 'Lord Halifax', p. 117.

on post-war matters and sent their thoughts home. On some points the need for this was urgent because it soon became clear that the fighting would be over quickly. Apart from the question of a war-termination strategy, which particularly exercised Chas Freeman as local political adviser to General Schwarzkopf,[45] the matter demanding most immediate attention was how much money the Saudis and the Kuwaitis could be expected to pay for the war and how it was to be extracted. In the event, an important role in 'shaking down' the Saudis fell to Freeman and it was one about which he had mixed feelings because he thought the State Department radically under-estimated the financial difficulties into which the conflict had forced them.[46] Another question was how to line up lucrative contracts for companies from home in reconstruction activity in Kuwait and military force expansion in Saudi Arabia, which was urgent because there was intense competition between Coalition governments for this business. Improved regional security arrangements (including the pre-positioning of US military equipment) and a fresh start in attempts to settle the Arab–Israeli conflict, were other matters to which the embassies were able to give thought while still 'at war'.[47]

The peripatetic embassy

What is the fate of the embassy following the retreat of the government of its frontline ally when there is a threat that the latter's capital will be overrun? This depends chiefly on the speed of the enemy advance, the attitude of the sending state, and whether or not the allied government simply disintegrates or is able to retreat in reasonably good order. As a result, experience varies, although one general rule applies to all: peripatetic embassies are the leanest of all embassies at war.

[45] Freeman is vitriolic in his condemnation of Washington's failure to give Schwarzkopf any instructions at all for his historic meeting with the Iraqi generals at the Safwan airfield on 3 March, although the general himself is more restrained in *The Autobiography*, pp. 479–80.

[46] Freeman interview.

[47] Freeman interview; Munro, *An Embassy at War*, pp. 255–98 *passim*.

In April 1975, in the last days of the Vietnam War, the massive US embassy in Saigon was simply withdrawn – albeit in dangerous and humiliating circumstances – because the South Vietnamese government did not so much retreat as formally capitulate to that of the North and then dissolve. According to the deputy chief of mission at the time, the embassy withdrawal was a particularly delicate operation: huge numbers needed to be evacuated, so the consequences of panic could have been catastrophic; there was a fear that some elements in the South Vietnamese army, bitter at the prospect of being 'deserted', would attempt to obstruct the operation; and the possibility also had to be considered that a core element of the embassy should remain after the fall of the capital.[48]

The case of the embassies in Kuwait following the rapid Iraqi invasion and swift annexation of the country in early August 1990 was somewhat different. The Amir of Kuwait, together with senior members of his government, managed to escape and establish a government-in-exile at Taif near the western edge of Saudi Arabia, which was safe from Saddam's rockets but still in the region. It was also pretty soon clear that the Amir did not represent a lost cause. In principle, therefore, the embassies of the emerging UN Coalition governments might have followed him.[49] However, apart from practical and other considerations, they were ordered to stay put in order to signify the Coalition's refusal to accept Iraq's actions (see p. 28 above).

When an allied government retreats from its capital in relatively good order, however, the embassies friendly to it (and their governments) usually have a real choice about their future, although an invidious one: stay put and not only lose contact with the government to which the embassy is accredited, but also risk capture and internment by the enemy; or leave with it and encourage defeatism, invite the charge of abandoning

[48] Lehmann interview.

[49] Some governments did appoint a representative to liaise with the Amir. The British appointed Ian Blackley, deputy head of mission in Kuwait, who happened to have been on home leave at the time of the invasion. He was installed at the British consulate-general in Jedda, which was not far from Taif, Munro, *An Embassy at War*, p. 69.

the mission's consular responsibilities to any nationals unable to escape the capital, and probably have to subsist in primitive conditions with poor communications, particularly if it has to move more than once.[50] As a rule, though, it is the latter risks which are accepted: in these circumstances, it is the peripatetic life which is preferred.

Thus in the space of only a few months after the outbreak of the First World War, the British embassy in Paris followed the French government to Bordeaux and then back again to Paris; in the Second World War, it followed it first to Tours and then once more – briefly – to Bordeaux.[51] On the capitulation of France on 21 June 1940, the British embassy declined to follow the new government of Marshall Pétain to Vichy, where it finally settled, although diplomatic relations were not severed – at Vichy's instigation – until the destruction of the French fleet at Oran on 13 July in order to prevent it falling into German hands. The embassy of the United States, which at this stage was still neutral, initially remained in Paris, although an 'advance embassy group' headed by an 'interim ambassador' was sent after the retreating government. Following the armistice, the US embassy – along with many others – removed to Vichy.[52]

The peripatetic embassy was also much in evidence in the Korean War, which commenced with the North Korean attack on South Korea in June 1950. The US embassy in Seoul (close to the frontier) retreated by stages with the government to Pusan on the south-eastern corner of the peninsula; returned to Seoul after MacArthur's successful counter-attack in late September; and then – following the Chinese entry into the war – went back to Pusan in January 1951, where it remained until well after the ceasefire was finally agreed in 1953.[53] The Chinese followed the Americans. However, the staff of the French and British legations – both of whose heads had consular as well as diplomatic responsibilities

[50] Noble, *Embassy at War*, pp. 32–3, 169–73.

[51] Hamilton, *Bertie of Thame*, ch. 13; Harvey (ed.), *Diplomatic Diaries*, pp. 384–5, 388–9.

[52] Murphy, *Diplomat Among Warriors*, pp. 61, 90.

[53] Noble, *Embassy at War*.

– both stayed in Seoul, where they were captured by the North Koreans and interned for three years near Pyongyang.[54] Among those interned with them were George Blake, head of the SIS station in the British legation, and his assistant.[55]

In low-intensity warfare

Low-intensity wars themselves vary greatly, but in most of them the role of belligerent embassies in allied frontline states will be similar to that of those adjacent to a theatre of open, conventional war[56] – but it will often include other tasks as well. This is in large part because low intensity conflicts are not so disruptive of normal life, while it is important to the prestige of all belligerents to demonstrate their capacity to provide such a life for all of the citizens on their side. Instructive examples are provided by the American embassy in Zaire in the 1970s, and the British embassies which re-opened in Afghanistan in 2001 and Iraq in 2003.

The US embassy in Zaire and the Angola operation, 1975–6

In the second half of 1975 and early 1976, the United States was heavily involved in the succession struggle in Angola that followed the announcement of the departure of Portugal, its former colonial ruler. In this conflict the Soviet- and Cuban-backed MPLA – which soon established its power in the capital, Luanda,

[54] However, the British minister, Captain Vyvyan Holt, ordered his first secretary, Sydney Faithful, to leave.

[55] Confirmation that the party was safe and well was not received for over a year, and its members were not released until March 1953. It was during his internment that Blake decided to transfer his loyalties to the Soviet Union while remaining in SIS, and so became one of the most notorious double agents to come to light during the Cold War, Blake, *No Other Choice*, pp. 111–52; Hoare, *Embassies in the East*, pp. 197–200; *The Times*, 10 Sept. 1951 and 30 July 1960 (Holt obit.); Noble, *Embassy at War*, pp. 39–40.

[56] For example, the embassies in Baghdad of Britain and the US had the task of negotiating SOFAs with the Iraqi government after UNSCR authorization for their troops expired at the end of 2008, Prentice Ev to Chilcot, p. 39ff; Watkins Ev to Chilcot, pp. 16, 17, 36, 41 and 42.

on the Atlantic seaboard – was ranged against Holden Roberto's FNLA in the north and Jonas Savimbi's UNITA in the south. Lending its own support to the last two groups, as well as to its chief regional client, Joseph Mobutu of Zaire (who had reasons of his own to fear a hostile Angola and was himself backing the FNLA[57]), the Ford administration in Washington aimed to demonstrate to Moscow that Vietnam had not undermined either its will or its ability to hold its own in the Cold War. However, because of intense congressional hostility to direct involvement in any more foreign wars, America's chosen mode of intervention in Angola was covert paramilitary action by the CIA, although this was complicated by the fact that in 1975 the agency itself was under intense congressional scrutiny following dramatic revelations of its own misdeeds. This meant that the official line had to be that all that Washington was doing was supplying arms to Zaire in order to make good those that Mobutu was providing to the anti-Communist forces in Angola.

The United States had a consulate in Luanda and this housed a CIA station. However, Luanda was useless as a base for special operations because it was in effect in enemy territory and the consulate was closed down shortly before the Portuguese departed in November 1975.[58] In the new, deadly sideshow in Angola, it was, therefore, the role of the US embassy in Kinshasa, capital of neighbouring Zaire, to provide the base – official cover – for the CIA's paramilitary activities.[59] Notwithstanding its cover story, these included supervising the delivery to the FNLA and UNITA of arms flown into Kinshasa, providing them with 'advisors' on

[57] Katangese rebels who had fled to Angola posed a continuing threat to Mobutu's copper-rich Shaba province.

[58] Besides, the station chief had come to agree with the principal officer at the consulate that the MPLA was the best qualified of the contending groups to run Angola, and that the United States should come to terms with it, Stockwell, *In Search of Enemies*, p. 213.

[59] The embassy also supervised consulates at Kisingani, Bukavu and Lubumbashi (formerly Elisabethville). The last was the most important and was not far from Angola's eastern border. It had no resident CIA officers in the 1975–6 period, although there had been a large station there in the 1960s, and it re-opened following the Shaba invasions in the later 1970s, Marks interview.

their military operations within Angola and running a propaganda drive against Soviet arms shipments.[60]

Kinshasa is very close to Angola's north-western border, so the embassy was ideally located from the CIA's point of view. The embassy itself was also suitable to its cover purpose because it was huge and – removed from the fighting and conducting a large range of activities – not obviously on a war footing. According to Michael Newlin, DCM from 1972 to 1975, the post was 'Very big. I guess, in total', he says, 'we had some 400 employees when you consider all the contracts that we had.'[61] It had first class housing and recreational facilities, its own commissary, and a large Marine security guard contingent. The defense attaché's office had an aircraft which could be used for travel between the embassy and the remote consular posts. In addition to the usual sections, the embassy also had big AID and USIS missions in separate buildings, and many Peace Corps volunteers and missionaries scattered across the country to worry about as well. Dependants had not been sent away. There was also a sizeable US military mission in Zaire.[62] All of this allowed the embassy to swallow up and mask the CIA's operations targeting Angola.

The CIA occupied offices on the second floor of the embassy, while the chief of station, Victor St. Martin, enjoyed a car and driver and a 'huge villa' located 20 minutes away.[63] Already a large station, at the time of the Angola operation its numbers increased dramatically, with the addition of about 50 'temporary duty' personnel.[64] This certainly caused managerial problems for the embassy, but was a source of glee to the president of Zaire,

[60] Stockwell, *In Search of Enemies*, pp. 201, 216–17.

[61] Newlin interview. Only a small proportion of these were diplomats. The Zaire diplomatic list for September 1977 recorded 41 members at the US embassy, including a three-strong defense section and the chief and deputy chief of the military mission. The number is unlikely to have been much different in 1975–6. The Soviet Union and some of its Warsaw Pact allies also had (much smaller) embassies in Kinshasa, as did the Cubans and Vietnamese, Box 217, FCO Diplomatic Lists Archive, Univ. of Leicester Library.

[62] The US Military Mission, Congo (COMISH), was established in 1963.

[63] Stockwell, *In Search of Enemies*, p. 115; Boorstein interview.

[64] Boorstein interview; see also Stockwell, *In Search of Enemies*, p. 166.

who had come to power in 1965 with the assistance of the CIA and maintained an intimate relationship with it. It was from this base in the embassy that the agency ran its operations into Angola. Inevitably, the direct role of the CIA in the fighting in Angola came to light after a few months and, in December, Congress blocked all further funding for it.[65] In the end, therefore, the operation came to nothing. Nevertheless, it provided a salutary example of the way in which a large embassy in a friendly frontline state can provide a first-class base for the conduct of paramilitary operations in a neighbouring state, while serving to mask them for a limited period from opponents of this sort of activity at home.

The British embassies in Afghanistan and Iraq

British forces entered Afghanistan in late 2001 as part of the successful US-led operation to remove the Taliban regime which had been providing a safe haven for Al-Qaeda. In March 2003, they played an important role in another US-led invasion, the decisive attack on Iraq which toppled Saddam Hussein. British missions were swiftly re-established in both countries, but in neither was this straightforward. Their work also had an intensely political emphasis and exceptional measures were necessary in order to make possible their continued operation.

The British embassy building in Kabul had been erected in the 1920s at the expense of the Indian government and – following a legal tussle after the partition of India in 1947 – eventually transferred to Pakistan ownership. It had then been promptly leased back by the British but closed in 1989 following the outbreak of civil war. Subsequently occupied by the Pakistanis themselves, it was burned by a mob in 1995. When, therefore, the British returned in mid-November 2001, their mission had to reopen in a surviving outbuilding, although shortly afterwards it moved to a converted block of flats leased from the Bulgarian embassy.[66]

[65] Stockwell, *In Search of Enemies*, ch. 14.

[66] Having outgrown the Bulgarian property and various other buildings leased later (many staff were condemned to living in sea transport containers known as 'pods'), in 2007 or thereabouts the FO tried hard but failed to

Another difficulty was that there remained no government in Kabul that Britain was willing to recognize, so Stephen Evans, the Foreign Office's specialist on Afghanistan who was sent out to effect the reopening, had to be given the anodyne title of 'representative' rather than 'ambassador'. Only when the Afghan interim authority led by Hamid Karzai was established on 22 December did Britain's representative office become an embassy, whereupon a more senior British diplomat, Andrew Tesoriere, took over from Evans, albeit only as chargé d'affaires until an ambassador was appointed in the following May (see Appendix 1). In Iraq, a similar sequence took place, although it was more innovative, complex and protracted.

In Iraq, the former British embassy building had been abandoned on the eve of the Gulf War in January 1991 (which did not help intelligence collection prior to the invasion in 2003) and then occupied and looted by Iraqi soldiers. As in Kabul, therefore, the embassy in Baghdad was in no fit condition for immediate occupation following the invasion, while the absence of an interim government made it equally necessary to establish an 'office' rather than an 'embassy'.[67] But here the parallels ceased. Already at the beginning of the year it had been revealed that, with the difficulties experienced in Afghanistan and elsewhere in mind, the Foreign Office had decided that it needed to be able to assemble 'instant embassies', and so was inviting tenders for their supply. Such embassies would include flat-pack buildings, furniture, communications equipment and more or less edible 'rations'.[68] It was in Baghdad, in the former embassy grounds, that the first building of this sort was assembled, although – production of the kit still being in its early stages – not before a month or so had elapsed following the invasion; meanwhile, Christopher Segar, the head of the 'British Office in Baghdad', accompanied by

persuade Pakistan to sell back the original compound with a view to building on it a new British embassy, Cowper-Coles, *Cables from Kabul*, pp. 72, 101–2; *The Times*, 19 July 1960; *The Independent*, 7 Sept. 1995 and 22 Aug. 2007; and guardian.co.uk, 17 May 2009.

[67] *The Independent*, 6 May 2003; Talmon, 'Diplomacy under occupation'.

[68] BBC News Online, 4 Jan. 2003.

just three officials, had to make do with working in five 40-foot steel containers.[69] Fortunately, perhaps, Segar's new 'flat-pack embassy' was destined to have a short life. It was outside the heavily fortified Green Zone, where the Coalition Provisional Authority (CPA) was headquartered, and it was soon feared to be unsafe.[70] Following the truck bomb attack on the UN mission on 19 August, in which the UN special envoy and many others were killed, it was hastily evacuated and its staff transferred to the Green Zone.[71]

As it happened, the troubles of the flat-pack British office were not so consequential for the overall British mission in Iraq at this stage because the mission had another and more important component which was already inside the Green Zone. Led by a 'special representative for Iraq', this was the much larger and more high-powered British team installed in the CPA, which was itself headed by the all-powerful American diplomat, Paul Bremer. For the first three months, the British special representative was John Sawers, a Foreign Office heavyweight who earlier had been foreign policy adviser to the prime minister, Tony Blair. (At the time of his appointment to Iraq, Sawers was ambassador to Egypt and six years afterwards was chief of MI6.) In his evidence to the Chilcot Inquiry, Sawers implicitly represented his team on the CPA as the *de facto* British embassy in Iraq since Bremer was at that stage actually running the country – even if he was prominent among those making a hash of it. By contrast, the flat-pack embassy was not just in the wrong place, he said, but a 'pretty modest affair, and ... disconnected from the decision-making' of Bremer's proconsular administration.[72] Sawers was replaced in August 2003 by another senior diplomat, Sir Jeremy

[69] *The Independent*, 6 May 2003. See also 'British diplomats return to Baghdad'. Statement by Jack Straw, UK Foreign Secretary, FCO, 1 May 2003, posted on 'Iraq Watch', http://www.iraqwatch.org/government/UK/FCO/uk-mfa-050103.html; BBC News Online, 5 May 2003; and Sawers Ev to Chilcot, pp. 60–1.

[70] Sawers Ev to Chilcot, pp. 60–1.

[71] *Evening Chronicle*, 23 Aug. 2003.

[72] Sawers Ev to Chilcot, pp. 55–6, 60, 87.

Greenstock (previously permanent representative at the UN in New York), during whose time the British team in the CPA stood at about 100 UK-based staff.[73] This awkward division within the British mission in Iraq – a huge team in the CPA and a much smaller 'British Office' on its fringes – had to be maintained until sovereignty was nominally returned to Iraq with the dissolution of the CPA and formation of the 'Iraq Interim Government' at the end of June 2004. At this point the two components were merged into an acknowledged embassy and an ambassador, Edward Chaplin, took over.

It was with these posts (and their out-stations) that British diplomats in Afghanistan and Iraq had to attempt, while keeping in step with the military, to dovetail British aid and technical assistance with the 'stabilization' and 'reconstruction' projects of other countries, especially the United States.[74] They also had to gather their own intelligence on the character and strength of the insurgencies that were being faced because – at least in Afghanistan – there was a fear that military intelligence was congenitally over-optimistic. (The British embassy in Kabul had a 'team' of SIS officers, and there is no reason to suppose that the same was not true of the embassy in Baghdad.)[75] In addition, dealing with visitors was as much a burden for these missions as for those discussed earlier in this chapter.[76] In Iraq, diplomatic duties also involved not only talking up opportunities for private investment to visiting businessmen, but also – in the case of Shell and BP – giving them office space at the consulate-general in Basra, which was as neat an example as one could find of trade following the flag.[77] But what is particularly striking about the work of both

[73] Greenstock Ev to Chilcot, p. 75.

[74] On the strengths and weaknesses of these programmes in Iraq, see especially Stephenson, *Losing the Golden Hour*, and in Afghanistan, Cowper-Coles, *Cables from Kabul*.

[75] Cowper-Coles, *Cables from Kabul*, pp. 15, 54, 99.

[76] Cowper-Coles, *Cables from Kabul*, pp. 24, 168–70.

[77] Jenkins and Baker Ev to Chilcot, p. 49. For a very full description of the work of the British consulate-general at Basra, see Haywood and MacKiggan Ev to Chilcot.

missions during this period was their intense and sometimes open involvement in politics and, indeed, in government. In the process, they played a very important role in *creating* the frontline allies with which they had to work so closely in combating the insurgencies which had developed in both countries. This kind of activity was particularly evident in Iraq, where there were such deep divisions between Sunnis, Shias and Kurds, and governing them was thrown into chaos by the failure to make speedy provision for filling the massive gaps created in state structures and the professions by 'de-Baathification' and the disbanding of the Iraqi army. Consequently, Britain, like the United States, first as an occupying power and then on UN Security Council authority, had administrative responsibilities for much longer than it had in Afghanistan.[78] In practice, these amounted to an obligation to promote as quickly as possible the emergence of a stable, democratic and unified state, hopefully on good terms with the West.

When Sawers was instructed by the Foreign Office on his posting to the struggling CPA, he was told that his priority was political: 'the need to get an Iraqi political process going so that we could hand over authority progressively to a representative Iraqi body';[79] and exactly the same instructions were given to his successor, Sir Jeremy Greenstock.[80] Initially, this meant helping the Americans and the UN to decide on the title, membership and powers of the Iraqi governing council – a body appointed in July 2003 with both advisory and administrative functions – and then in participating in its deliberations. Paul Bremer, says Sawers, 'was happy for me to take a leading role on this'.[81] As for Greenstock, he even chaired the governing council in Bremer's absence.[82] Thereafter, the British mission continued to

[78] Wood, Second statement. The high commissions of the occupying powers in Turkey had similar responsibilities for some years after the end of the First World War.

[79] Sawers Ev to Chilcot, p. 54.

[80] Greenstock Ev to Chilcot, p. 79.

[81] Sawers Ev to Chilcot, p. 95.

[82] Sawers Ev to Chilcot, pp. 88–96; Greenstock Ev to Chilcot, p. 79.

make it an 'overwhelming priority' to actively promote national reconciliation, and support Iraq's transition through predetermined stages to 'full sovereignty' after the national elections for a new government and assembly in December 2005; it worked particularly hard to bring the Sunnis in.[83] In addition to this priority political work, the British ambassador, like his American counterpart, was a formal member of the Iraqi National Security Council, which was established in 2004 and met weekly to coordinate the operations of Iraqi and Coalition forces.[84] They remained members of this important body until well after Iraq regained its sovereignty and was, remarked Christopher Prentice, British ambassador at Baghdad from 2007–9, 'another most extraordinary aspect of serving in Iraq'.[85]

In Afghanistan, where the United States and its allies – ultimately organized into the NATO-led International Security Assistance Force (ISAF) – were equally anxious to see a stable state created, the strengthening of national and local institutions were also major priorities for the British embassy.[86] Unfortunately, the Taliban had been scattered rather than destroyed, and – with discreet support from elements in Pakistan – was able to regroup and periodically launch suicide bomb attacks on government and NATO targets even in the centre of the capital, Kabul, and much bigger attacks in the south and east. Against this background, the prudent urgings of the British ambassador appointed in 2007, Sir Sherard Cowper-Coles, that any 'reconstruction' was bound to unravel as soon as ISAF's battalions departed if the need for a political settlement embracing the neighbouring states as well as the Taliban itself was ignored, were generally not well

[83] Chaplin Ev to Chilcot, pp. 4–6; Patey Ev to Chilcot, pp. 5–7.

[84] They were the only two Coalition ambassadors on this body, Chaplin Ev to Chilcot, pp. 4–6, 20, 28, 34; Patey Ev to Chilcot, p. 36. The nearest parallel to this in Kabul was what was informally known by the NATO powers as the 'war cabinet'. This also met weekly, in the presidential palace, and consisted of the American and British ambassadors, the commander of ISAF and President Karzai with various of his ministers, Cowper-Coles, *Cables from Kabul*, p. 90.

[85] Prentice Ev to Chilcot, p. 25.

[86] HCPP (HC 302), 2 Aug. 2009, para. 219.

received, especially in Washington. Nevertheless, it is clear that his campaign made headway with some influential individuals (among them the British foreign secretary, David Miliband), and showed what impact can be had on policy by an outstanding diplomat on the spot in a thoroughly wired up world.[87]

Like the embassies of other states in Afghanistan and Iraq, Britain's missions in these countries were not destined to be able to tackle their political and other tasks without fear of attacks on their buildings, or personnel when travelling outside. In the Afghan capital, attacks from the resurgent Taliban were relatively infrequent but always likely to cause havoc when they did occur because the approaches to the embassies, which were scattered over the city, were not easy to guard.[88] At the end of 2007, the British embassy was rocked by a massive explosion caused by an attack on an unmarked American military convoy passing behind the mission;[89] in the following year, the offices of the German embassy, which was adjacent to the British mission, were wrecked in a similar incident.[90] The embassy of India – a strong supporter of the anti-Taliban government of Afghanistan – was deliberately attacked twice, once in July 2008 and again in October 2009. By contrast, in Baghdad – where the Coalition powers daily confronted the greater and more complex threat of a hydra-headed insurgency, as well as the backwash of extreme sectarian violence – the embassies were progressively concentrated inside the heavily defended Green Zone. But even this did not prevent them from coming under intense rocket and mortar attack, which could sometimes last for weeks.

[87] In early 2009 Cowper-Coles was taken away from Kabul to be the foreign secretary's London-based special representative for Afghanistan and Pakistan, a position that enabled him to shadow and bend the ear of the State Department's Richard Holbrooke, who had been given the same remit. He continued to have this role while at the same time once more running the huge embassy in Kabul in the first half of 2010 during the interregnum between the departure of his successor and the arrival of the new ambassador, Cowper-Coles, *Cables from Kabul*, pp. 204–6, 250–1.

[88] guardian.co.uk 17 May 2009.

[89] Cowper-Coles, *Cables from Kabul*, p. 112.

[90] Cowper-Coles, *Cables from Kabul*, pp. 201–2.

At the British embassies in both capitals, therefore, as well as at their provincial outposts, exceptional measures such as the building of higher walls and installation of bomb-proof armoured windows had to be taken in order to protect their facilities and numerous staff.[91] The British embassy in Kabul had also been spared a visa section, which would certainly have greatly increased its workload but also been a security nightmare.[92] Travel outside mission compounds was particularly difficult. Cowper-Coles was given a full week of 'Hostile Environment Training' by ex-Special Forces instructors before leaving for Kabul, which included how to 'cross-deck' from a disabled to a rescue vehicle; the need for this training was underlined by the 'huge leap' in his life insurance premium prompted by the appointment.[93] Even inside Baghdad's Green Zone, movement had to take place in protected vehicles, while outside it – in the 'Red Zone' – embassy staff had to travel in 'fully planned and protected convoys under personal protection'.[94] Most of this protection in both countries was provided by private security companies, a development which brought complications of its own because they were not well regulated.[95]

As a result of the dangerous conditions, all staff were volunteers and were unaccompanied by family. They worked flat out for six to eight weeks and then had one to two weeks off – 'decompression-' or 'breather-breaks'. Individual tours were also kept extremely short. In Baghdad, staff were only committed for six months, and only exceptionally allowed to stay beyond a year. (This intense rotation of personnel was itself seriously complicated by the closure of road access to the airport from the embassy because of the security situation.)[96] Ambassadors themselves only stayed for a year in Baghdad, and if they volunteered to stay for

[91] Cowper-Coles, *Cables from Kabul*, pp. 113, 202.

[92] Cowper-Coles, *Cables from Kabul*, p. 182.

[93] Cowper-Coles, *Cables from Kabul*, pp. 10, 12.

[94] Prentice Ev to Chilcot, p. 76.

[95] HCPP (HC 441-I), 29 July 2004, paras. 27–31.

[96] Chaplin Ev to Chilcot, pp. 36, 57; Prentice Ev to Chilcot, p. 76. There is a vivid description of the perils of this road – 'the most dangerous road in the

two were pulled out anyway on the grounds that an offer of this sort revealed them to be 'obviously mad'.[97] In Afghanistan, the rules on length of tours were more or less the same: six weeks on and two weeks off, with a standard tour length of 18 months.[98] As a rule, ambassadors themselves stayed in Kabul for about two years (see Appendix 1). As in Iraq, however, logistical and other problems could easily upset the normal pattern of rotation and lead to more pressures on staff.[99] With his staff constantly coming and going, Cowper-Coles thought that being head of mission in Kabul was more like 'running a railway station' than an embassy.[100]

As at the Djakarta embassy during the 'Confrontation' with Indonesia in the mid-1960s, the constant turnover of UK-based staff was an obvious threat to the build-up in these missions of knowledge about local conditions and experience in handling difficult situations; in short, a threat to continuity.[101] Coupled with the serious limitations on their movement, this made posts even more dependent on locally engaged staff – for economy reasons, a growing trend in all British missions anyway. Unfortunately, this was by no means a perfect solution because, living with their families outside the compounds, local staff are peculiarly vulnerable and cannot generally be allowed, especially in this sort of situation, to handle the most confidential work.[102] Therefore, all that the FCO could do in addition to tackle the continuity problem was to give careful attention to succession planning and pre-posting preparation, while trying to ensure sufficient overlap between arrivals and departures to provide for a useful handover.

world' or 'the road of death' – in Stephenson, *Losing the Golden Hour*, pp. 13, 121, 127.

[97] Patey Ev to Chilcot, p. 57. It is probably safe to conclude that Sir William Patey, British ambassador at Baghdad from June 2005 to July 2006, was joking.

[98] Cowper-Coles, *Cables from Kabul*, pp. 38–9.

[99] HCPP (HC 302), 2 Aug. 2009, para. 251; HCPP (Cm 7702), Oct. 2009, p. 22.

[100] Cowper-Coles, *Cables from Kabul*, p. 16.

[101] HCPP (HC 302), 2 Aug. 2009, paras. 251–2. The Chilcot Inquiry heard many complaints on this score.

[102] In Iraq, special provision had to be made for their eventual resettlement elsewhere in the country or abroad.

Whenever possible it could – and did – send out people, especially at head of mission level, who already had knowledge of the country or the region (in regard to Afghanistan, see Appendix 1).[103] The expense involved in these exceptional measures was staggering.[104]

As already mentioned, Britain also had provincial outposts in both countries. The shape of these was increasingly influenced by two factors: first, American thinking on civil–military relations in operations designed to rebuild communities in the face of well-armed insurgents; and second, the multinational character of the operations in Afghanistan and Iraq.

The essence of American military thinking, which represented a revival of the ideas which gave birth to the CORDS programme in the Vietnam War,[105] was that diplomatic, aid and military bureaucracies should aim higher than mere *coordination* of their activities; this was held to leave incompatible departmental cultures intact, make overall strategy difficult to agree, and fudge the issue of leadership in post-conflict stabilization and reconstruction. Instead, they should seek the *integration* of their activities – in the field, as well as in the bureaucracy at home.[106] In the field, the idea of such a 'comprehensive' approach to post-conflict rebuilding gave birth to the 'provincial reconstruction team' (PRT), a body which contained diplomats and superficially resembled a consular post but had a unitary rather than a federal structure, with all staff reporting to the same special department at home.

Accordingly, in Afghanistan, Britain established a PRT at Mazar-e-Sharif in the north in May 2003, and later a much smaller one was set up at Meymaneh, also in the north. In September

[103] HCPP (Cm 7702), Oct. 2009, p. 23.

[104] The cost of running the British posts in Iraq was about £57m a year (or between £0.5m and £1.0m per head of UK-based staff), which was more than the cost of Britain's entire diplomatic and consular network in North America, Prentice Ev to Chilcot, pp. 51, 74.

[105] 'CORDS' stands for Civil Operations and Revolutionary Development Support. I am grateful to Laurence E. Pope for reminding me of this precedent. See also Passage, 'Caution'.

[106] For a sympathetic analysis of this thinking, together with an historical account of its evolution, see Korski, 'British civil-military integration'.

2005, Meymaneh was transferred to Norwegian control, and in March 2006 Mazar was handed over to the Swedes. Thereafter, Britain assumed the lead in the hitherto small, US-led PRT at Lashkar Gah, the provincial capital of Helmand province in the south. This coincided with the major British troop build-up that was designed to contribute to ISAF's ambitious plan to drive the Taliban from their redoubts in this part of the country. In due course, the Lashkar Gah PRT evolved into a headquarters post for Helmand, with many civilian staff and numerous district outposts across the province; these 'forward operating bases' – where conditions were usually primitive – also containing diplomats.[107] In Iraq, Britain had more conventional-looking provincial outposts: a massive consulate on the Basra Palace site on the outskirts of the city, and a very much smaller one at Kirkuk.[108] Nevertheless, in May 2006 a PRT was also established at Basra.[109]

Although, under American pressure, the PRT concept shaped British provincial representation in both Afghanistan and Iraq from 2006 onwards, it was adopted without enthusiasm and less than completely – and appears to have contributed merely to confusion. In Afghanistan, there was no strong British tradition of conventional consular representation that might have impeded its deployment, but even here the PRT scheme did not have plain sailing. At the Lashkar Gar PRT, which – unlike those earlier established in the north – was the product of 'a genuine

[107] HCPP (HC 302), 2 Aug. 2009, para. 213.

[108] Latterly described as 'Offices of the British Embassy' or 'regional embassy offices'. In January 2007, the post at Kirkuk was shifted to nearby Erbil, seat of the Kurdistan Regional Government, HCPP (HC 50), 19 Nov. 2007, Ricketts to FAC Ch'man, 28 Mar. 2007, Ev 53.

[109] The Basra Palace site had begun to suffer serious rocket and mortar attack in October 2006, and in November the PRT was temporarily relocated to Kuwait. In the course of 2007 – together with the British forces' contingent, which was 'drawing down' – both consulate and PRT were transferred to the headquarters base of the south-eastern division of the multinational force at Basra International Airport, HCPP (Cm 6905), Sept. 2006, para. 75; HCPP (HC 50), 19 Nov. 2007, Ricketts to FAC Ch'man, 28 Mar. 2007, Ev 53; Korski, 'British civil-military integration'.

cross-departmental plan',[110] in June 2008 the commander of Task Force Helmand was for the first time made subordinate to a civilian head, a diplomat who – in the manner of the head of a consular post – answered to the embassy in Kabul.[111] To be sure, it followed that in 'mounting military operations' the task force commander was required to consult and seek guidance from him. The problem was, however, that the brigadier commanding continued to take 'military direction' from the commander of ISAF.[112] Not surprisingly, the military feared a divided chain of command[113] – and they were probably not alone. Although poor communications at the time gave him more excuse, Lord Stratford de Redcliffe, the nineteenth-century British ambassador to the sickly Ottoman Empire and head of an embassy which might not entirely facetiously be described as an 'imperial reconstruction team', would not have tolerated such a state of affairs for a moment.

In Iraq, the PRT concept fared even worse at British hands. A massive consulate was already well entrenched at Basra before the PRT was squeezed into its compound, while, only two months after the unwanted orphan appeared, a senior diplomat, Dr Rosalind Marsden, previously ambassador in Kabul, was appointed consul-general. It was therefore predictable that the Foreign Office (and DfID) only accepted the Basra PRT reluctantly and 'endowed it with few of the resources and little of the political support necessary to work'.[114] To no one's surprise, the line manager of the PRT's head was the consul-general[115] and, to make matters worse, he was not co-located with the military

[110] Korski, 'British civil-military integration', p. 18.

[111] This was Hugh Powell, member of a powerful political family. To promote continuity, he was supposed to stay for two years but in fact was replaced by a DfID officer, Lindy Cameron, in October 2009, who was in turn replaced by another FCO diplomat, Michael O'Neill, in October 2010.

[112] FCO Memorandum, in Written Evidence, HCPP (HC 302), 2 Aug. 2009, Ev 82.

[113] War and Peace. Mark Urban's Blog, 19 June 2008.

[114] Korski, 'British civil-military integration', p. 19. See also Etherington Ev to Chilcot, pp. 3–5.

[115] Etherington Ev to Chilcot, p. 7.

headquarters, which had recently withdrawn from the Basra Palace compound to the airport, and travel between the two – separated by 15 miles – was by then dangerous and difficult to arrange. Confronted by people who thought they had already got reasonable structures and programmes in place, and were coordinating as well as could be expected in the circumstances, and finding himself leading a largely presentational exercise, Mark Etherington, the first head of the Basra PRT, told the Chilcot Inquiry that 'where we were designed to simplify, we actually complicated'.[116]

Militarization and its consequences

In the Western diplomatic tradition, there is a strong norm that heads of mission should have the last word – or at least be fully consulted – on any military operation, like any other operation, in their bailiwick. In the US Foreign Service, for example, the importance of the ambassador's leadership of the 'country team' was first made explicit at the embassy in Seoul and developed as managerial doctrine thereafter.[117] In 2006, it was reaffirmed in a report to the Senate Committee on Foreign Relations.[118] The theory of ambassadorial supremacy needs a regular airing of this sort because, especially in the embassies of states allied to frontline belligerents, it is regularly under more or less subtle challenge from the military. This is particularly true of US embassies because of the growing preponderance of the military within them stimulated by the 'War on Terror', and because behind this enlarged military component will stand one of the

[116] Etherington Ev to Chilcot, p. 17. See also Etherington's declassified report on his experience at the Basra PRT, submitted to Chilcot, which in addition provides a damning indictment of the absence of any overall strategy and firm leadership in existing arrangements at Basra, 'The establishment and operation of the Basra PRT'.

[117] Noble, *Embassy at War*, p. 8; Blancké, *The Foreign Service of the United States*, pp. 137–40.

[118] 'Embassies as Command Posts in the Anti-Terror Campaign'.

five combatant commanders who rule over the unified, regional military commands (for example, CentCom, see p. 140 above) created by the Goldwater–Nicholls Act of 1985, with their vast budgets, huge staffs, personal long-distance aircraft and fleets of helicopters – and increasingly quasi-diplomatic responsibilities.[119] If the military challenge is successful and militarization of the embassy – adoption of a military outlook and style – ensues, the consequences can be serious.

When the military, with their massive resources, have a large presence on or near an embassy compound, their influence is bound to be felt in the counsels of the ambassador, whether military officers are present in numbers at daily meetings of senior embassy staff or not. On rare occasions, a commanding officer might even be double-hatted as chief of mission, as in the example of General Maxwell Taylor, who was made US ambassador at Saigon in 1964.[120] On others, a military or paramilitary figure might be the de facto chief of mission, having a closer relationship with, and more influence over, the leadership of the allied state than the ambassador. John Stockwell, chief of the CIA's Angola Task Force, wrote in his memoir that:

> Generally the CIA station chief is the second or third secretary of the embassy, but he always has considerably more free funds to spend than the ambassador and all of the legitimate State Department officers together. ... The extra money translates into greater social and operational activity, making the CIA man more visible and seemingly more important than the State Department officers. Often the CIA man will even

[119] Priest, *The Mission*, especially ch. 3.

[120] Chairman of the Joint Chiefs of Staff at the time of his appointment, the general's instructions, written by his own hand, stated that he had 'broad' responsibility for all American activity in South Vietnam. In an attempt to ensure the continuing influence of the diplomatic element at the top, America's most senior diplomat, U. Alexis Johnson, was made his number two (with the unusual rank of 'deputy ambassador'), but he was chosen by Taylor himself and believed by some to be too inclined to defer to the military, Taylor, Burke and Burnet interviews; Schaffer, *Ellsworth Bunker*, pp. 164–5, 177.

> establish a direct contact with the chief of state, leading him to believe that through the CIA he has the more authentic contact with the American government.[121]

This was without doubt the case in Kinshasa, where President Mobutu – the CIA's key ally in the fight in Angola – had even more reasons for preferring to deal with the agency rather than the embassy. Mobutu was not only the beneficiary of its largesse, but was in debt to the agency for having helped install him in the first place, and he did not – in contrast to his experience at the hands of the diplomats – have to listen to lectures from it on the corruption of his government and its abuse of human rights, or receive from it threats that aid would dry up if he did not mend his ways. The influence of CIA station chiefs in Zaire, and therefore in the Kinshasa embassy, was legendary: Zaire was regarded in the US Foreign Service as a 'CIA country'.[122]

But the military viewpoint does not only command attention because of numbers and resources. When they are working so closely with military officers, whose men and women are enduring great hardship and personal danger and need to be sanguine, it is difficult for diplomats to be downbeat about their achievements and critical of the policies which are the corollary of their optimism; it is especially hard for them to suggest that perhaps the time has come to explore a political rather than a military solution to the conflict in which they are engaged, since this implies that their blood and treasure is being wasted.[123]

The feeling that diplomats and soldiers are all in an essentially military conflict where, therefore, the military view should prevail, is likely to be further enhanced if the embassy compound resembles a largely self-sufficient military base isolated from the local population – even more so if it resembles a fortress, as so many US embassies do in conflict zones today. In these circumstances, where diplomats and soldiers are rubbing shoulders all

[121] Stockwell, *In Search of Enemies*, p. 63.
[122] Boorstein, Davis, and Blake interviews.
[123] This point comes out very strongly in Cowper-Coles, *Cables from Kabul*.

of the time, the whole atmosphere in which the diplomats operate is a military one. The extent and dangers of 'PX culture' – one in which it is taken for granted that all of the needs of daily living should be provided within the compound – was pointed out 40 years ago by the US diplomat, John Franklin Campbell.[124] However, it is not a uniquely American phenomenon; nor is it of recent origin. An early and famous variation on this theme was the Legation Quarter in Peking, fortified after the quelling of the Boxer uprising in 1900, which had led to the quarter's prolonged siege. This featured new walls around the legation compounds and three sides of the quarter as a whole, glacis on the same sides to deny cover to attackers and give the defenders a free field of fire, and much larger garrisons of soldiers. Inside were shops, hospitals, a railway station and so on.

The risk of embassy militarization is also likely to be the greater if the *sending* state is a military regime, because the corollary of this is that the military component will have greater prestige and probably more influence at home. In the mid-1950s, for example, it was widely believed that the military attachés in Egypt's embassies abroad were all the 'personal agents' of the charismatic Egyptian president, Gamal Abdul Nasser, a colonel and controlling force in the Society of Free Officers which overthrew King Farouk in a coup d'état in 1952. The influence of these attachés obviously far exceeded their relatively low status in these posts.[125] Moreover, if the *receiving* state is a military regime, or one in which the military has strong and rising influence, there might even be a temptation to promote a service attaché to head of mission. This happened three times in pre-Second World War Japan.[126]

When there is the potential for a military challenge to the authority of chiefs of mission or principal officers, whether through numerical preponderance or some special circumstance,

[124] Campbell, *The Foreign Affairs Fudge Factory*, pp. 137–8, 192–4.

[125] Trevelyan, *The Middle East in Revolution*, p. 62.

[126] The Dutch, Germans and Romanians each promoted a military attaché to be their head of mission in Tokyo, Piggott, *Broken Thread*, pp. 198, 279–80.

it takes a strong and highly respected individual with powerful support at home to resist it. Such a man was Ellsworth Bunker, who achieved 'unquestioned command' of the US embassy in Saigon during critical years of the Vietnam War, despite the fact that the weekly meetings of his 'Mission Council' included two four-star generals. It helped, it is true, that he was a hawk on Vietnam himself.[127] If, however, the military – or the paramilitary wing of a body such as the CIA – insists on getting its own way, the results are sometimes serious.

Short of complete militarization, and perhaps the worst situation of all, is an embassy divided between its diplomatic and military components. This is a standing invitation to the local government to maximize the favours granted to it by playing one off against the other; and is why General Maxwell Taylor emphasized the breadth of his own responsibility at the US embassy in Saigon. Costly mistakes can also occur when teamwork breaks down in a crisis. This was seen at the major US consulate-general at Can Tho in the Mekong Delta military region of South Vietnam in April 1975, when Saigon was on the point of capitulating to the Communists and the embassy ordered the mission to evacuate (by this time Bunker was no longer ambassador). The chief of the large CIA station in the consulate-general reluctantly agreed to obey the order of the principal officer, Terry McNamara, to join the rest of the mission in evacuating by river in order that the most vulnerable members of its Vietnamese staff could also escape. In the event, however, the 'perfidious spooks' fled precipitately by air, as they had clearly planned to do all along. This could have provoked panic, almost cost the mission its coding machines and remaining classified documents, squandered evacuation spaces and denied McNamara's small convoy the promised protection of the CIA's paramilitary arm.[128]

[127] The 'Mission Council' consisted of 'a group of a dozen or so civilian and military agency heads and embassy section chiefs'. The use of this grand title rather than the more usual and ordinary term, 'country team', 'mirrored the importance and scope of the Saigon mission and the professional standing of the council's members', Schaffer, *Ellsworth Bunker*, pp. 174–7.

[128] McNamara, *Escape with Honor*, *passim*. This is one of the major themes of

What if an embassy to a frontline ally is effectively captured by the military? The first and most obvious consequence of complete militarization has already been hinted at. It is the triumph over the policy of the embassy of the military approach to the conflict. In other words, the nature of the political advice sent home by the embassy, and the way in which it interprets its instructions to its hosts, are both shaped chiefly by the views of the military. This is unfortunate because, while not all generals are politically unsophisticated, by any means, the military have their own reflexes, one of the most common – and most consequential – of which is the repeated demand for more troops and better equipment if things are not going well on the battlefield.[129] For soldiers, political solutions are usually a last resort. From a policy point of view, a militarized embassy is no embassy at all.

A militarized embassy also produces a greater risk that insensitive behaviour by military personnel will alienate local political leaders, key officials and even important sections of public opinion. As Gordon S. Brown, General Schwarzkopf's political adviser at the time of the Gulf War, remarks:

> [O]ne thing we don't quite appreciate in the State Department is the degree to which Defense people are objective-driven. I mean, give them an objective and they will run over their mother to reach it if they want to make a star, or another star.[130]

The risk of insensitive behaviour is particularly high where bilateral relations are fragile and there are significant cultural differences between the allies. Rough and high-handed behaviour is likely to originate not so much with the attachés in the defence section (who in at least the better-run governments are selected with a view to their adaptability to the diplomatic environment)

McNamara's memoir.

[129] Cowper-Coles, *Cables from Kabul, passim*; Campbell, *The Foreign Affairs Fudge Factory*, pp. 195–6.

[130] Brown, Gordon S., interview.

as with the other military elements that gravitate to the wartime embassy, even at the highest levels. For instance, Maxwell Taylor was not well known for his delicate diplomacy:

> He got very frustrated with the internal political revolving door governments [says Robert Miller, deputy chief of his political section] and was very imperious with the Vietnamese generals. They resented that and at one point tried to get him recalled. I suppose the role of any US ambassador at that point would have been a very tough one. I think that Taylor had a military rather than diplomatic approach in terms of getting the Vietnamese to do things that we wanted to see them do.[131]

Finally, a militarized embassy – even an embassy in which a large military component remains under firm diplomatic control – has the serious disadvantage that it is likely to raise local suspicions and thus make life more difficult for the embassy in all sorts of ways. If there is a history of intervention by the sending state in the frontline ally's domestic affairs, it is a certainty that such suspicions will be aroused, even if the embassy's instructions are entirely benign.[132]

Conclusion

The experience of the embassy of a belligerent accredited to the government of a frontline ally depends chiefly on the nature of the military conflict in which they are engaged. In a conventional war, some routine functions are relegated to the sidelines or fall away altogether and non-essential staff and dependants are usually sent home, especially if the embassy needs to follow a retreating government. A first priority is to preserve close, high-level personal contact with the allied host government in order to

[131] Miller interview; see also Jones interview.
[132] 'Embassies as Command Posts in the Anti-Terror Campaign'.

concert policy and preserve morale. When belligerent embassies have major military forces of their own on the territory of their frontline ally, they also have to assist in the negotiation of such sensitive matters as a status of forces agreement, serve as political adviser to the commander-in-chief, and gather their own intelligence as a check on that presented by the military. Whether the belligerent embassy is accompanied by a major military force or not, it has numerous other duties to perform once fighting has started, among them: advancing plans for the evacuation of any remaining expatriates and, in the meantime, offering advice on how they might protect themselves; handling hordes of VIP visitors and journalists; and, if they have any time left, offering advice on post-war affairs, including a war-termination strategy. In a low-intensity conflict, the role of the belligerent embassy to an allied frontline state is normally similar but, in addition, often includes attention to at least some routine tasks in order to pretend that things are going on much as normal. When large forces of the embassy's country are committed to fighting a domestic insurgency against a new, weak client regime, as recently in Iraq and Afghanistan, what is also different is the intense and sometimes open involvement of the embassy in politics and, indeed, in government; as also in promoting reconstruction.

In the embassies of states allied to frontline belligerents, the supremacy of the ambassador is regularly under more or less subtle challenge from the military. If this challenge is successful and militarization of the embassy – adoption of a military outlook and style – ensues, the consequences can be serious. Insensitive behaviour might cause local alienation and, in some circumstances, a militarized embassy might arouse strong local suspicions about its intentions even if they are in fact benign. Worst of all, if the fighting is going badly, the embassy will be more likely to attach priority to the demand for more troops and equipment than to the search for a political solution.

Conclusion

All embassies shaped in significant degree by international armed conflict, irrespective of the different situations in which they can find themselves, have certain things in common, and to this extent it is reasonable to talk of a wartime embassy. What are the common features of such a mission? To begin with, military and related political questions inevitably assume much greater importance for this sort of embassy, and this does not exclude the mission of a neutral in a belligerent state. This usually means that they all acquire a much larger defence section, although it is true that, where they are accompanied by a major military mission, a whole clutch of service attachés with a typically large supporting staff can sometimes be seen as an irrelevance. Intelligence gathering is also a much higher priority than in peacetime, even in the case of those embassies to frontline allies accompanied by large armies, the need to check military intelligence being so widely recognized. The corollary of this is that they all contain more intelligence officers under diplomatic or consular cover. Belligerents need to know what the other side is up to, while neutrals need to know, among other things, which of them is most likely to win. There are few wartime embassies, too, which do not attach special importance to their consular work, even if – in the case of belligerent embassies to neutrals – historically this has chiefly taken the special form of assisting their evaders and escapers. In other respects, however, wartime embassies vary considerably, this depending mainly on the status relative to the conflict of both sending and receiving states.

A working (as opposed to an interned) embassy condemned to remain on enemy territory following the outbreak of armed conflict is in one sense the paradigm case of the wartime embassy, because it is the only one which is face to face with the 'enemy' and, in consequence, always at risk of paying the heaviest price, as when the British embassy in Djakarta was destroyed and its staff terrorized by a mob at the start of 'Confrontation' with Indonesia in September 1963. In another sense, however, it is the one furthest removed from the ideal type because, although it remains in principle a working embassy, its ability to function at all is seriously impaired and sometimes almost completely neutralized by the very sea of hostility in which it finds itself. But, even in the latter case, its formal existence is of great importance because this signifies the desire on the part of both parties to play down the fighting between them and their intention to avoid all-out war, as also in the case of India's China war in 1962 and the Indo–Pakistan War three years later. Furthermore, in more favourable circumstances, these embassies can even do some valuable work, notably in the consular field, and in intelligence-gathering and advising on (if not delivering) propaganda. The reluctance to break diplomatic relations on the outbreak of international armed conflict and keep working embassies in place is an encouraging development of recent times, but still rare.

As for the neutral embassy to a belligerent state, this usually has two and sometimes three distinctive features compared to other wartime embassies. The first of the usual ones is the exceptional priority attached to commercial questions. The neutral is, after all, trying to get on with its normal business, while belligerents commonly attempt to encroach on neutral rights to trade with 'enemy' states; there is also a general tendency of the state in wartime to seek greater control of commerce and this, too, invites embassy intervention. The second usual feature of the neutral embassy is a very low public profile: preferring to pretend that it is not really there at all, it has little in the way of a propaganda arm. Its third feature, which is less frequent but by no means rare, is the adoption by the neutral embassy of the role of protecting power for the interests of a belligerent which has been forced to close its own embassy. Assumption of this responsibility, which is unique to the neutral wartime embassy, means not only shouldering a heavy burden, but risking its reputation for impartiality. When neutrals agree to it nevertheless, it is chiefly because the protecting power is seen as an institution which one day they might need themselves, because it is a way of earning gratitude in powerful quarters, and because when – as gradually became more common during the twentieth century – an interests section staffed by officers of the protected power is permitted, the burden of the responsibility is much reduced. It is true that, since 1945, neutral states have been called on far less frequently to become protecting powers, but they have not escaped the duty altogether. As recently as 2011, a (relatively) neutral embassy – that of Turkey – was seen taking it on in Tripoli. Among the numerous responsibilities of the neutral protecting power's embassy, the most important is usually the protection of detained enemy civilians and prisoners of war.

The belligerent embassy in a neutral state which is close to the front line, or for some other reason of strategic importance, inevitably finds itself in a tussle with hostile embassies for the favours of the neutral government and its public opinion. As a result, this embassy is distinctive among wartime embassies by virtue of the great energy it must devote to propaganda. The intelligence war is also fought hotly by this kind of embassy, sometimes, too, by means of strategic deception and special operations targeting the supply of strategic materials to an enemy, maintaining bases for incursions into neighbouring territories and so on. It is also particularly well placed to deliver and receive peace feelers, although the embassy to a frontline ally might also find itself alongside hostile embassies (and thus with the same opportunities) if the conflict is one of low intensity, as in Kinshasa during the Angola fighting in the mid-1970s

The unique experience of the embassy of a belligerent accredited to the government of a frontline ally depends chiefly on the nature of the military conflict in which they are engaged. In a conventional war, some routine functions are relegated to the sidelines or fall away altogether and non-essential staff and dependants are usually sent home. This is especially true if the embassy faces the real threat of deliberate attack or if it needs to follow a retreating government – or both. With the decks cleared, this is perhaps the classic wartime embassy. Its first priority is to preserve close, high-level personal contact with the allied host government in order to concert policy and preserve morale. When belligerent embassies are accompanied by major military forces of their own, they also have to assist in the negotiation of such sensitive matters as a status of forces agreement and serve as political adviser to the commander-in-chief. It is also this embassy which is the one deluged by VIP visitors and journalists, although it can extract much value from both categories as well as need to expend much energy on them. In a low-intensity conflict, the role of the belligerent embassy to an allied frontline state is normally similar but, in addition, often includes attention to at least some routine tasks in order to pretend that things are going on much as normal. When large forces of the embassy's country are committed to fighting a domestic insurgency against a new, weak client regime, as recently in Iraq and Afghanistan, what is also different about the embassy is its intense and sometimes open involvement in politics and, indeed, in government; as also in promoting reconstruction.

The supremacy of the ambassador is sometimes under challenge in belligerent embassies to neutral states, but it is those with frontline allies where it is normally more serious – unless, accompanied by large military forces, the mission's defence section is wisely made redundant. If this challenge is successful and militarization of the embassy – adoption of a military outlook and style – ensues, the consequences can be serious. Insensitive behaviour might cause local alienation. In some circumstances, a militarized embassy might also arouse strong local suspicions about its intentions even if they are, in fact, benign. Worst of all, if the fighting is going badly, the embassy will be more likely to attach priority to the demand for more troops and equipment than to the search for a political solution.

What of the consular outstations of the wartime embassy? In enemy states, they have traditionally been more vulnerable to poor treatment and even attack because consular privileges and immunities are weaker than diplomatic privileges and immunities (this remains true today even though the gap has closed somewhat in recent decades); because consulates have a reputation equal to that of the embassy for sheltering 'spies'; because they tend to be smaller, more isolated and less well protected; and perhaps because of the presumption that their maltreatment is likely to be seen by sending states as less provocative than abuse of their embassies. On the other hand, precisely because they are located outside the capital and have less symbolic significance than the embassy, they are less likely to attract great hostility. For the same reason of geographical location, other wartime consulates, for example those of neutrals to belligerents, are also safer from accidental aerial attack – unless located at ports or adjacent to other points of great strategic significance. Wherever they are and in whatever relationship they stand to their hosts, consulates tend to become much more important instruments of their embassies in wartime, not least for purposes of intelligence-gathering.

It is an old saw that diplomacy does not stop when war begins, although the traditional narrative has been one of embassies closing their doors and the dialogue of states being replaced by furtive emissaries, sanctimonious intermediaries and high-level conferences of camera-seeking allied leaders. This being the case, it is as well to remember that there are also wartime embassies, that these are found in a variety of situations, and that each has valuable work of different sorts to do, often in dangerous conditions. In fact, it is probably true that embassies are never so important as in war, which is another strong argument for keeping them in good shape in peace.

Appendix 1 Heads of British mission at Kabul, 2001–10

Name	*Title*	*Start date*
Evans, Stephen[1]	Representative	19 November 2001
Tesoriere, Andrew[2]	Chargé d'affaires	22 December 2001
Nash, Ronald[3]	Ambassador	May 2002
Marsden, Dr Rosalind[4]	Ambassador	January 2004
Evans, Stephen	Ambassador	May 2006
Cowper-Coles, Sir Sherard[5]	Ambassador	May 2007
Sedwill, Mark[6]	Ambassador	April 2009
Cowper-Coles, Sir Sherard	Minister and Chargé d'Affaires	February 2010
Patey, Sir William[7]	Ambassador	May 2010

NB: the notes below mention only previous posts of direct relevance to the Kabul post, while dates are those of appointment.

[1] Counsellor (Economic, Commercial and Aid), Islamabad, 1993; secondment to UN Special Mission to Afghanistan, 1996; head of South Asian Department [which included Afghanistan], FCO, 1999.

[2] Oriental secretary, Kabul, 1976; on secondment as head of field operations, UN Office for the Co-ordination of Humanitarian Affairs (Afghanistan), 1994; acting head of mission and senior political adviser UN Special Mission to Afghanistan, 1998.

[3] Ambassador at Kathmandu, 1999.

[4] Director (Asia Pacific), FCO, 1999. Left Kabul to be consul-general in Basra.

[5] Previously ambassador to Israel and Saudi Arabia, the 'heavy hitter' brought in as part of the British government's determination to upgrade the civilian effort in Afghanistan in line with the major increase in its military commitment in this period. From February 2009 to September 2010, also Special Representative to Afghanistan and Pakistan.

[6] Deputy High Commissioner in Pakistan, 2003; subsequently NATO Senior Civilian Representative in Afghanistan.

[7] Ambassador to Iraq, June 2005; and to Saudi Arabia, 2007–10.

Appendix 2 Appointment of Protecting Powers and of their Substitute: Article 5 of the Protocol Additional to the Geneva Conventions of 12 August 1949, and relating to the Protection of Victims of International Armed Conflicts, 8 June 1977.[1]

1. It is the duty of the Parties to a conflict from the beginning of that conflict to secure the supervision and implementation of the Conventions and of this Protocol by the application of the system of Protecting Powers, including inter alia the designation and acceptance of those Powers, in accordance with the following paragraphs. Protecting Powers shall have the duty of safeguarding the interests of the Parties to the conflict.

2. From the beginning of a situation referred to in Article 1, each Party to the conflict shall without delay designate a Protecting Power for the purpose of applying the Conventions and this Protocol and shall, likewise without delay and for the same purpose, permit the activities of a Protecting Power which has been accepted by it as such after designation by the adverse Party.

3. If a Protecting Power has not been designated or accepted from the beginning of a situation referred to in Article 1, the

[1] Adopted at the Diplomatic Conference on the Reaffirmation and Development of International Humanitarian Law applicable in Armed Conflicts, Geneva, 1974–7. State parties 170; state signatories, 5. Entered into force 7 December 1978.

International Committee of the Red Cross, without prejudice to the right of any other impartial humanitarian organization to do likewise, shall offer its good offices to the Parties to the conflict with a view to the designation without delay of a Protecting Power to which the Parties to the conflict consent. For that purpose it may, inter alia, ask each Party to provide it with a list of at least five States which that Party considers acceptable to act as Protecting Power on its behalf in relation to an adverse Party, and ask each adverse Party to provide a list of at least five States which it would accept as the Protecting Power of the first Party; these lists shall be communicated to the Committee within two weeks after the receipt of the request; it shall compare them and seek the agreement of any proposed State named on both lists.

4. If despite the foregoing, there is no Protecting Power, the Parties to the conflict shall accept without delay an offer which may be made by the International Committee of the Red Cross or by any other organization which offers all guarantees of impartiality and efficacy, after due consultations with the said Parties and taking into account the result of these consultations, to act as a substitute. The functioning of such a substitute is subject to the consent of the Parties to the conflict; every effort shall be made by the Parties to the conflict to facilitate the operations of the substitute in the performance of its tasks under the Conventions and this Protocol.

5. In accordance with Article 4, the designation and acceptance of Protecting Powers for the purpose of applying the Conventions and this Protocol shall not affect the legal status of the Parties to the conflict or of any territory, including occupied territory.

6. The maintenance of diplomatic relations between Parties to the conflict or the entrusting of the protection of a Party's interests and those of its nationals to a third State in accordance with the rules of international law relating to diplomatic relations is no obstacle to the designation of Protecting Powers for the purpose of applying the Conventions and this Protocol.

7. Any subsequent mention in this Protocol of a Protecting Power includes also a substitute.

Source: UN Treaty Series, no. 17512, vol. 1125-I-17.

References

Abbreviations used in this list:
BDOHP: *British Diplomatic Oral History Programme* [www]
CAC Cam.: Churchill Archives Centre, University of Cambridge
DGFP: Documents on German Foreign Policy, 1918–1945, Series D (1937–1945)
FAC: Foreign Affairs Committee [British House of Commons]
FRUS: Foreign Relations of the United States
FAOHC: *The Foreign Affairs Oral History Collection of the* [US] *Association for Diplomatic Studies and Training*, http://memory.loc.gov/ammem/collections/diplomacy/
GPO: [US] Government Printing Office
HCPP: House of Commons Parliamentary Papers
ICRC: International Committee of the Red Cross

Atherton, Alfred Leroy, Jr. [Assistant Secretary, Near East Affairs (1974–8); Ambassador-at-Large, Middle East Negotiations (1978–9); Ambassador to Egypt (1979–83)], interview, 1990, *FAOHC*

Andrew, Christopher, *Secret Service: The making of the British intelligence Community*, London: Heinemann, 1985

Antippas, Andrew F. [political officer, US embassy, Phnom Penh, 1970–2], interview, 19 July, 1994, *FAOHC*

Arens, Moshe, *Broken Covenant: American foreign policy and the crisis between the U.S. and Israel*, New York: Simon & Schuster, 1995

Atkin, Nicholas, *The Forgotten French: Exiles in the British Isles, 1940–44*, Manchester and New York: Manchester University Press, 2003

Bailey, Thomas A., *The Art of Diplomacy: The American experience*, New York: Appleton-Century-Crofts, 1968

Banerjee, P. K., *My Peking Memoirs of the Chinese Invasion of India*, Delhi: Clarion Books, 1990

Bernstorff, Count, *My Three Years in America*, London: Skeffington, 1920

Berridge, G. R., 'Old diplomacy in New York', in G. R. Berridge and A. Jennings (eds), *Diplomacy at the UN*, Basingstoke: Macmillan 1985

—*Talking to the Enemy: How states without 'diplomatic relations' communicate*, Basingstoke: Macmillan, 1994

—*Diplomatic Classics: Selected texts from Commynes to Vattel*, Basingstoke: Palgrave Macmillan, 2004

—*Gerald Fitzmaurice (1865–1939), Chief Dragoman of the British Embassy in Turkey*, Leiden and Boston: Martinus Nijhoff, 2007

—*British Diplomacy in Turkey, 1583 to the Present: A study in the evolution of the resident embassy*, Leiden and Boston: Martinus Nijhoff, 2009

—*Diplomacy: Theory and practice*, 4th ed. Basingstoke: Palgrave Macmillan, 2010

—*The Counter-Revolution in Diplomacy and Other Essays*, London and Basingstoke: Palgrave Macmillan, 2011

—Maurice Keens-Soper, and T. G. Otte, *Diplomatic Theory from Machiavelli to Kissinger*, Basingstoke: Palgrave-Macmillan, 2001

—and Nadia Gallo, 'The role of the diplomatic corps: the US-North Korea talks in Beijing, 1988–94', in Jan Melissen ed. *Innovation in Diplomatic Practice*, Basingstoke: Macmillan, 1999

—and Alan James, *A Dictionary of Diplomacy*, 2nd ed. Basingstoke: Palgrave-Macmillan, 2003

Best, Antony, 'Sir Robert Craigie as Ambassador to Japan, 1937–1941', in Ian Nish ed. *Britain and Japan: Biographical portraits*, Folkestone: Japan Library, 1994

—'Shigemitsu Mamoru and Anglo-Japanese relations', in Ian Nish ed. *Britain and Japan: Biographical portraits*, Vol. 2, Richmond, Surrey: Curzon Press, 1997

Bhutani, Sudarshan, *Clash of Political Cultures: Sino-Indian relations (1957–62)*, New Delhi: Roli, 2004

Billière, General Sir Peter de la, *Storm Command: A personal account of the Gulf War*, London: HarperCollins, 1992

Blacker, Carmen, 'Two Piggotts', in Sir Hugh Cortazzi and Gordon Daniels (eds), *Britain and Japan: Themes and personalities, 1859–1991*, London: Routledge, 1991

Blake, George, *No Other Choice: An autobiography*, London: Jonathan Cape, 1990

Blake, Robert O. [DCM, US embassy in Brazzaville, 1964–6], interview, 29 December 1988, *FAOHC*

Bodine, Barbara K., 'Saddam's siege of Embassy Kuwait: A personal journal, 1990', in Joseph G. Sullivan ed. *Embassies under Siege: Personal accounts by diplomats on the front line*, Washington, DC and London: Brassey's, 1995

Bohlen, Charles E., *Witness to History, 1929–1969*, New York: Norton, 1973

Boorstein, Michael [Personnel Officer, US embassy, Kinshasa, 1974–6], interview, 13 September 2005, *FAOHC*

Brown, Frederick Z. [US consul-general, Da Nang, South Vietnam, 1971–3], interview, 1990, *FAOHC*

Brown, Gordon S. [Political Advisor, CENTCOM, 1989–91], interview, 11 December 1996, *FAOHC*

Brown, William Andreas [US ambassador to Israel, 1988–92], interview, 3 November 1998, *FAOHC*

Burke, John R. [political officer, Saigon], interview, 1989, *U.S. Foreign Affairs Oral History Collection on CD-ROM*, Arlington, VA: ADST, 2000

Burnet, Frank N. [political adviser to C-in-C Pacific Command], interview, 1990, *FAOHC*

CAC Cam., The Papers of Sir Andrew Graham Gilchrist, GILC

Campbell, John Franklin, *The Foreign Affairs Fudge Factory*, New York: Basic Books, 1971

Cecil, Lamar, *The German Diplomatic Service, 1871–1914*, Princeton, NJ: Princeton University Press, 1976

Chaplin, Edward [British Ambassador to Iraq, 2004–5], Evidence of to the Chilcot Inquiry, 7 December 2009, available at: http://www.iraqinquiry.org.uk/media/40471/20091207amchaplin-final.pdf

Churchill, Winston S., *The Second World War, Vol. I: The Gathering Storm*, London: Cassell, 1948

('Church Committee Report') *Foreign and Military Intelligence. Book I. Final Report of the Select Committee to Study Governmental Operations with respect to Intelligence Activities, United States Senate, together with Additional, Supplemental, and Separate Views*, 26 April 1976, Washington, DC: US Government Printing Office, 1976

Ciano, G., *Ciano's Diary, 1939–1943*, ed. with an introduction by Malcolm Muggeridge, Heinemann: London, 1947

Clark, William Jr. [US ambassador to India, 1989–92], interview, 1994, *FAOHC*

Cole, Robert, *Britain and the War of Words in Neutral Europe, 1939–45*, Basingstoke: Macmillan, 1990

Cortazzi, Sir Hugh, 'Sir Vere Redman, 1901–1975', in I. Nish ed., *Britain and Japan: Biographical portraits*, Vol. 2, Richmond, Surrey: Japan Library, 1997

Cowper-Coles, Sir Sherard, *Cables from Kabul: The inside story of the West's Afghanistan campaign*, London: Harper Press, 2011

—Sir Sherard, *FCO Bloggers: Global conversations*, available at: http://blogs.fco.gov.uk/roller/cowpercoles/

Craig, Gordon A. and Francis L. Loewenheim (eds), *The Diplomats, 1939–1979*, Princeton, NJ: Princeton University Press, 1994

Craigie, Sir Robert, *Behind the Japanese Mask*, London: Hutchinson, c.1945

Crosby, Sir Josiah, *Siam: The crossroads*, London: Hollis and Carter, 1945

Damodaran, A. K., 'Diary of an old China hand', in Tan Chung ed. *Across the Himalayan Gap: An Indian quest for understanding China*, New Delhi: Gyan, 1998

Davis, Allen C. [DCM, US embassy, Kinshasa, 1977–80], interview, 26 June 1998, *FAOHC*

de la Mare, Sir Arthur, *Perverse and Foolish: A Jersey farmer's son in the British Diplomatic Service*, Jersey: La Haule Books, 1994

Dembinski, Ludwik, *The Modern Law of Diplomacy*, Dordrecht and Boston: Martinus Nijhoff, 1988

Denham, Henry, *Inside the Nazi Ring: A naval attaché in Sweden, 1940–1945*, London: John Murray, 1984

Denza, Eileen, *Diplomatic Law: Commentary on the Vienna Convention on Diplomatic Relations*, 3rd ed. Oxford: Oxford University Press, 2008

de Reynoso, Don Francisco (recorded by A. P. Kleeman), *The Reminiscences of a Spanish Diplomat*, London: Hutchinson, 1933

DGFP, Vol. XIII. The War Years. June 23–December 11, 1941, Washington, DC: US Government Printing Office, 1954

Dreyfuss, Robert, 'The CIA crosses over', *Mother Jones*, Jan./Feb. 1995

Duggan, John P., *Herr Hempel at the German Legation in Dublin, 1937–1945*, Dublin and Portland, OR: Irish Academic Press, 2003

Dulles, Allen, *The Craft of Intelligence*, New York: Signet, 1965

Dunlop, Thomas P. H. [Political Officer, Saigon, 1972–4], interview, 1996, *FAOHC*

Dunford, David J. [DCM, US embassy Riyadh, 1988–92], interview, 30 March 2006, *FAOHC*

Easter, David, *Britain and the Confrontation with Indonesia, 1960–1966*, London and New York: Tauris Academic Studies, 2004

'Embassies as Command Posts in the Anti-Terror Campaign', *A Report to Members of the Senate Committee on Foreign Relations, December 15, 2006*, Washington, DC: US Government Printing Office, 2006

Ericson, Richard A. Jr. [Political Officer, US Embassy London, 1963–5], interview, 19 April 1995, *FAOHC*

Etherington, Mark [Head of the Basra PRT, April 2006–January 2007], Evidence of to the Chilcot Inquiry, 9 July 2010

—'The establishment and operation of the Basra PRT, April 2006–January 2007: lessons identified, Declassified Document handed to the Chilcot Inquiry, 9 July 2010

Fischer, Thomas, 'Switzerland's good offices: a changing concept, 1945–2002', Centre for International Studies: Zurich. Beiträge Nr. 37, December 2002, available at: http://e-collection.library.ethz.ch/eserv/eth:25944/eth-25944-01.pdf

Flott, Frederick W. [Special Assistant to Ambassador Henry Cabot Lodge, Saigon, 1963], interview, 1992, *FAOHC*

Foot, M. R. D. and J. M. Langley, *MI9: The British secret service that fostered escape and evasion 1939–45 and its American counterpart*, London: Futura, 1980

Forsythe, David P., 'Who guards the guardians? Third parties and the law of armed conflict', *American Journal of International Law*, vol. 70, (1), Jan. 1976

Franklin, William McHenry, *Protection of Foreign Interests: A study in diplomatic and consular practice*, Washington, DC: US Government Printing Office, 1946

Freedman, Sir Lawrence, *The Official History of the Falklands Campaign. Vol. I: The Origins of the Falklands War*, London and New York: Routledge, 2005

Freeman, Chas W. Jr. [US Ambassador at Riyadh, 1989–92], interview, 1995, 1996, *FAOHC*

Frey, Linda S. and Marsha L., *The History of Diplomatic Immunity*, Columbus, OH: Ohio State University Press, 1999

FRUS, see 'US Dept. of State' below.

Galbraith, John Kenneth, *Ambassador's Journal: A personal account of the Kennedy years*, Boston, MA: Houghton Mifflin, 1969

Gerard, James W., *My Four Years in Germany*, London and New York: Hodder and Stoughton, 1917

Gilbert, Felix, 'Ciano and his ambassadors', in Gordon A. Craig and Felix Gilbert (eds), *The Diplomats, 1919–1939*, Princeton, NJ: Princeton University Press, 1953

Gore-Booth, Lord ed. *Satow's Guide to Diplomatic Practice*, 5th ed. London and New York: Longman, 1975

Gorodetsky, Gabriel, *Grand Delusion: Stalin and the German invasion of Russia*, New Haven and London: Yale University Press, 1999

Greenstock, Sir Jeremy [Special Envoy for Iraq, 2003–4], Evidence of to the Chilcot Inquiry, 15 December 2009

Grew, Joseph C., *Ten Years in Japan: A contemporary record drawn from the diaries and private and official papers of Joseph C. Grew, United States Ambassador to Japan, 1932–1942*, New York: Simon and Schuster, 1944

Guinn, Gilbert, *The Arnold Scheme: British pilots, the American South and the Allies daring plan*, Charleston, SC: The History Press, 2007

Hägglöf, Gunnar, *Diplomat: Memoirs of a Swedish envoy in London, Paris, Berlin, Moscow and Washington*, London: Bodley Head, 1972

Hamilton, Keith, *Bertie of Thame: Edwardian ambassador*, Woodbridge, Suffolk: Boydell Press for the Royal Historical Society, 1990

Hamilton, Keith and Richard Langhorne, *The Practice of Diplomacy: Its evolution, theory and administration*, 2nd ed. London and New York: Routledge, 2011

Hare, Raymond A. [US ambassador at Cairo, 1956–9], interview, 22 July 1987, *FAOHC*

Harrison, E. D. R, 'On secret service for the Duce: Umberto Cammini in Portuguese East Africa, 1941–1943', *English Historical Review*, 2007, vol. CXXII, no. 499

Hart, Jane Smiley, interview, 30 March 1988, *FAOHC*

Hart, Parker T. [DCM, US embassy, Cairo, 1955–8; US Ambassador to Saudi Arabia, 1961–5], interview, 1989, *FAOHC*

Hartman, Arthur A. [US Ambassador at Moscow, 1981–4], interview, 1989, *FAOHC*

Harvey, John ed. *The Diplomatic Diaries of Oliver Harvey, 1937–1940*, New York: St. Martin's Press, 1970

Hayes, Carlton J. H., *Wartime Mission in Spain, 1942–1945*, New York: Macmillan, 1946

Hayter, Sir William, *A Double Life*, London: Hamish Hamilton, 1974

Haywood, Nigel, and Keith MacKiggan, Evidence of to the Chilcot Inquiry, 7 January 2010, available at: http://www.iraqinquiry.org.uk/media/41738/100107am-haywoodmackiggan.pdf

HCPP (666), 26 Oct. 1967: *Fourteenth Report from the Estimates Committee: Diplomatic Buildings Overseas*

—(Cmnd. 5000), June 1972: *Exchange of Notes between the UK and Argentina concerning Communications between the Falkland Islands and the Argentine Mainland, Buenos Aires 5 Aug. 1971 (with Joint Statement and related Notes)*

—(31–ii), 15 Nov. 1982: FAC, *Falkland Islands, Minutes of Evidence*

—(Cmnd. 8787), Jan. 1983: *Falkland Islands Review: Report of a Committee of Privy Counsellors* [The Franks Report]

—(408), 13 May 1987: Defence Committee, Session 1986–87. *Defence Commitments in the South Atlantic.*

—(143–I), 9 July 1991: FAC, *The Middle East after the Gulf War, Vol. I, Report, together with the Proceedings of the Committee: 'The Gulf Crisis (GF 79): Memorandum submitted by the FCO, 24 Oct. 1990*

—(HC 246), 20 Mar. 2001: FAC, *Government Policy towards the Federal Republic of Yugoslavia and the wider region following the fall of Milosevic*

—(Cm 5220), July 2001: FAC, *Government Policy towards the Federal Republic of Yugoslavia and the wider region following the fall of Milosevic. Response of the Secretary of State for Foreign and Commonwealth Affairs*

—(HC 922), 1 Aug. 2002: FAC, *Private Military Companies*

—(Cm 5642), Oct. 2002: FAC, *Private Military Companies. Response of the Secretary of State for Foreign and Commonwealth Affairs*

—(HC 441-I), 29 July 2004: FAC, *Foreign Policy Aspects of the War against Terrorism*

—(Cm 6905), Sept. 2006: FAC, *Foreign Policy Aspects of the War against Terrorism. Response of the Secretary of State for Foreign and Commonwealth Affairs*

—(HC 50), 19 Nov. 2007: FAC, *FCO Annual Report 2006–07. First Report of Session 2007–08. Report, together with formal minutes, oral and written evidence*

—(HC 302), 2 Aug. 2009: FAC, *Global Security: Afghanistan and Pakistan*

—(Cm 7702), Oct. 2009: *Eighth Report from the Foreign Affairs Committee, Session 2008–09. Global Security: Afghanistan and Pakistan. Response of the Secretary of State for Foreign and Commonwealth Affairs*

Healey, Denis, *The Time of my Life*, London: Penguin Books, 1990

Heikal, M., *The Road to Ramadan*, London: Collins, 1975

Heinrichs, Waldo H. Jr., *American Ambassador: Joseph C. Grew and the development of the United States diplomatic tradition*, Boston, MA: Little, Brown, 1966

Helble, John J. [Political Officer, US Embassy Saigon, 1973], interview, 1996, *FAOHC*

Helmreich, Jonathan E., 'The Diplomacy of Apology: U.S. Bombings of Switzerland during World War II', *Aerospace Power Journal*, Summer 2000, available at: http://www.

Hemingstam, Lars, 'Drottningholm and Gripsholm: The Exchange and Repatriation Voyages during WWII', available at: http://www.

Hemsing, Albert E. [Public Affairs Officer, US Embassy Bonn, 1964–7], interview, 1989, *FAOHC*

Henderson, Sir Nevile, *Failure of a Mission: Berlin, 1937–1939*, London: Hodder and Stoughton, 1940

Hinnebusch, R. and N. Quilliam, 'Contrary siblings: Syria, Jordan and the Iraq war', *Cambridge Review of International Affairs*, 19, (3), Sept. 2006

Hoare, Sir Samuel, *Ambassador on Special Mission*, London: Collins, 1946

Howard, Esme, *Theatre of Life, 1863–1905*, Boston, MA: Little, Brown, 1935

—*Theatre of Life: Life seen from the stalls, 1903–1936*, Boston, MA: Little, Brown, 1936

Howard, Michael, *British Intelligence in the Second World War*, Vol. Five: *Strategic Deception*, London: HMSO, 1990

Hoyt, Joy Wasson, *For the Love of Mike*, New York: Random House, 1966

Hoyt, Michael P. E., *Captive in the Congo: A consul's return to the heart of darkness*, Annapolis, ML: Naval Institute Press, 2000

Hull, Cordell, *The Memoirs of Cordell Hull*, Vol. 2, London: Hodder and Stoughton, 1948

Hyde, H. Montgomery, *The Quiet Canadian: The Secret Service story of Sir William Stephenson*, London: Hamish Hamilton, 1962

ICRC, Commentary on Article 8 (Protecting Powers) of Convention (III) relative to the Treatment of Prisoners of War. Geneva, 12 August 1949, available at: http://www.icrc.org/ihl.nsf/COM/375-590011?OpenDocument

—Commentary on Article 5 (Appointment of Protecting Powers and of their substitutes) of Protocol Additional to the Geneva Conventions of 12 August 1949, and relating to the Protection of Victims of International Armed Conflicts (Protocol I), 8 June 1977, available at: http://www.icrc.org/ihl.nsf/COM/470-750008?OpenDocument

Isaacson, Walter, *Kissinger: A biography*, London: Faber and Faber, 1992

Jeffery, Keith, *MI6: The history of the Secret Intelligence Service, 1909–1949*, London: Bloomsbury, 2010

Jenkins, John, and Frank Baker, Evidence of to the Chilcot Inquiry, 8 Jan 2010, available at: http://www.iraqinquiry.org.uk/media/41796/100108am-jenkins-baker.pdf

Jones, Ray E. [Embassy and Staffing Protocol Officer, Saigon, 1964–5], interview, 1994, *U.S. Foreign Affairs Oral History Collection on CD-ROM*, Arlington, VA: ADST, 2000

Keeley, Robert V. ed., *First Line of Defense: Ambassadors, embassies and American interests abroad*, Washington, DC: The American Academy of Diplomacy, 2000

Kelly, Sir David, *The Ruling Few, or The Human Background to Diplomacy*, London: Hollis & Carter, 1952

Kennan, George F., *Memoirs, 1925–1950*, London: Hutchinson, 1968

Kennedy, Greg, 'Lord Halifax: Wartime ambassador to the United States, 1941–1946', in C. Baxter and A. Stewart (eds), *Diplomats at War: British and Commonwealth diplomacy in wartime*, Leiden and Boston: Martinus Nijhoff, 2008

Kirby, Stuart, *Japan and East Asia: Documentary analyses 1921–1945*, London: Tauris, 1995

Kissinger, Henry A., *The White House Years*, London: Weidenfeld and Nicolson, 1979

Koblyakov, I., 'On the way home from Berlin', *International Affairs* [Moscow], no. 5, vol. 16, 1970

Korski, Daniel, 'British civil-military integration: the history and next steps', *The RUSI Journal*, Dec. 2009, vol. 154, no. 6, pp. 14–24

Kux, Denis [Deputy Director for Nepal and India, Washington, DC, 1972–7], interview, 13 Jan. 1995, *FAOHC*

Lehmann, Wolfgang J. [DCM, Saigon, 1974–5], interview, 1988, *FAOHC*

Lewandowski, Józef, 'Early Swedish information about the Nazis' mass murder of the Jews' (POLIN 13, 2000), available at: http://www.jozeflewandowski.se/texter/Early_Swedish_Information_about_Holocaust.htm#_ednref2

Lewis, Samuel W. [US ambassador to Israel, 1977–84], interview, 9 August 1988, *FAOHC*

Liddell Hart, B. H., *History of the First World War*, London: Pan Books, 1972

McLachlan, Donald, *Room 39: Naval Intelligence in action, 1939–45*, London: Weidenfeld and Nicolson, 1968

McNamara, Terry, with Adrian Hill, *Escape with Honor: My last hours in Vietnam*, Washington and London: Brassey's, 1997

Maley, William, 'Risk, populism and the evolution of consular responsibilities', in Ana Mar Fernández and Jan Melissen (eds), *Consular Affairs and Diplomacy*, Leiden and Boston: Martinus Nijhoff, 2011

Marks, Edward [consul at Lubumbashi, 1974–6; Zaire desk officer at State Dept., 1976–7], interview, 12 August 1996, *FAOHC*

Marks, John D., 'How to spot a spook', *Washington Monthly*, November 1974

Martin, Edwin Webb [political officer and China specialist at the US embassy, Rangoon, 1950–1], interview, 4 June 1987, *FAOHC*

Mason, R. Chuck, 'Status of Forces Agreement (SOFA): What is it, and how has it been utilized?' *CRS Report for Congress*, Congressional Research Service, 18 June 2009, available at: http://www.fas.org/sgp/crs/natsec/RL34531.pdf

Melbourne, Roy M., *Conflict and Crises: A Foreign Service Story* (University Press of America: Lanham, MD, 1993), excerpt from in American Diplomacy, vol. 2, no. 1, Mar. 1997, available at: http://www.unc.edu/depts/diplomat/AD_Issues/amdipl_3/melbourne2.html

Miller, Robert H. [Deputy Chief, Political Section, Saigon Embassy, 1962–5], interview, 1990, *FAOHC*

Muggeridge, Malcolm, *Chronicles of Wasted Time, vol. 2, The Infernal Grove*, London: Purnell, 1973

Munro, Alan, *An Embassy at War: Politics and diplomacy behind the Gulf War*, London and Washington: Brassey's, 1996

Murphy, Robert, *Diplomat Among Warriors*, London: Collins, 1964

Neilson, Keith, 'Sir Cecil Spring Rice and the United States, 1914–1917', in C. Baxter and A. Stewart (eds), *Diplomats at War: British and Commonwealth diplomacy in wartime*, Leiden and Boston: Martinus Nijhoff, 2008

Newlin, Michael [DCM at US embassy, Kinshasa, 1972–5], interview, 10 October 1997, *FAOHC*

Newsom, David D. ed. *Diplomacy under a Foreign Flag: When nations break relations*, London: Hurst; New York: St. Martin's Press, 1990

Newton, David G. [US Ambassador to Iraq, 1984–8], interview, 1 November 2005, *FAOHC*

Nish, I., 'British legations in Tokyo and Beijing during the Russo-Japanese War, 1904–1905', in C. Baxter and A. Stewart (eds), *Diplomats at War: British and Commonwealth diplomacy in wartime*, Leiden and Boston: Martinus Nijhoff, 2008

Noble, Harold Joyce, *Embassy at War: An account of the early weeks of the Korean War and U.S. relations with South Korean President Syngman Rhee*, ed. with an introduction by Frank Baldwin, Seattle and London: University of Washington Press, 1975

O'Halpin, Eunan, *Spying on Ireland: British Intelligence and Irish neutrality during the Second World War*, Oxford and New York: Oxford University Press, 2008

Oliphant, Sir Lancelot, *An Ambassador in Bonds*, London: Putnam, 1946

Papen, Franz von, *Memoirs*, trans. by Brian Connell, New York: Dutton, 1953

Passage, David, 'Caution: Iraq is not Vietnam', *Foreign Service Journal*, November 2007

Patey, Sir William [British ambassador to Iraq June 2005–July 2006], Evidence of to the Chilcot Inquiry, 5 January 2010, available at: http://www.iraqinquiry.org.uk/media/43290/20100105am-patey-final.pdf

Philby, Kim, *My Silent War*, St. Albans, England: Panther, 1969

Phillips, Horace, *Envoy Extraordinary: A most unlikely ambassador*, London and New York: Radcliffe Press, 1995

Phillips, William, *Ventures in Diplomacy*, London: John Murray, 1955, published in the USA, 1952

Piggott, Major-General F. S. G., *Broken Thread: An autobiography*, Aldershot: Gale and Polden, 1950

Pooley, A. M. ed. *The Secret Memoirs of Count Tadasu Hayashi G.C.V.O.*, New York and London: Putnam's, 1915

Prentice, Christopher [British Ambassador to Iraq Sept 2007–Nov 2009], Evidence of to the Chilcot Inquiry, 6 January 2010, available at: http://www.iraqinquiry.org.uk/media/43293/20100106-prentice-final.pdf

Priest, Dana, *The Mission: Waging war and keeping peace with America's military*, New York and London: Norton, 2004

Probst, Raymond, 'The "good offices" of Switzerland and her role as protecting power', in David D. Newsom ed., *Diplomacy under a Foreign Flag: When nations break relations*, London: Hurst; New York: St. Martin's Press, 1990

Prugh, Major General George S., *Law at War: Vietnam 1964–1973*, Washington, DC: Dept. of the Army 1975, available at: http://www.history.army.mil/books/Vietnam/Law-War/law-fm.htm

Rana, K. S., 'A young Indian diplomat in China in the 1960s and 1970s', in Tan Chung ed. *Across the Himalayan Gap: An Indian quest for understanding China*, New Delhi: Gyan, 1998

Rankin, Haywood [Chief of the Political Section, US embassy at Baghdad, 1986–8], interview, 24 July 1998, *FAOHC*

Raschen, Dan, *Diplomatic Dan: A military attaché in Sweden*, London: Buckland, 1997

Rendel, Sir George, *The Sword and the Olive: Recollections of diplomacy and the foreign service, 1913–1954*, London: John Murray, 1957

Reid, P. R., *Winged Diplomat: The life story of Air Commodore 'Freddie West' V.C., C.B.E., M.C.*, London: Chatto and Windus, 1962

Reynoso, Don Francisco de, *The Reminiscences of a Spanish Diplomat*, London: Hutchinson, 1933

Riad, M., *The Struggle for Peace in the Middle East*, London: Quartet, 1981

Rives, L. Michael [Chargé d'affaires at US embassy, Phnom Penh, 1969–70], interview, 25 July 1995, *FAOHC*

Roberts, Sir Ivor ed., *Satow's Diplomatic Practice*, 6th ed. Oxford: Oxford University Press, 2009

Robertson, S. R., *Making Friends for Britain: An incursion into diplomacy*, Buenos Aires: Guillermo Kraft, 1948

Rogerson, Sidney, *Propaganda in the Next War*, London: Geoffrey Bles, 1938

Rumbold, Sir Horace, *Recollections of a Diplomatist*, vol. I, London: Edward Arnold, 1902

Rumbold, Sir Horace, *The War Crisis in Berlin, July–August 1914*, London: Constable, 1944

Satow, Rt. Hon. Sir Ernest, *A Guide to Diplomatic Practice*, 2nd and revised ed. vol. I, London: Longmans, Green, 1922

Sawers, Sir John [Special Representative in Iraq, May–July 2003], Evidence of to the Chilcot Inquiry, 10 December 2009

Schaffer, Howard B., *Ellsworth Bunker: Global troubleshooter, Vietnam hawk*, Chapel Hill and London: University of North Carolina Press, 2003

Schwarzkopf, Gen. H. Norman, *The Autobiography: It doesn't take a hero*, London: Bantam Press, 1992

Seitz, Raymond, *Over Here*, London: Weidenfeld and Nicolson, 1998

Selby, Sir Walford, *Diplomatic Twilight, 1930–1940*, London: John Murray, 1953

Sherman, William C. [Deputy Chief of Mission, Tokyo, 1977–81], interview, 27 October 1993, *FAOHC*

Singh, K. Gajendra, 'Ambassador's Journal: Gulf crisis – Lessons from 1991', *Asia Times Online*, 13 December 2002

Smith, Colin, *England's Last War Against France: Fighting Vichy 1940–42*, London: Weidenfeld and Nicolson, 2009

Smith, Walter B., II [Bureau of Intelligence and Research, Washington, 1969–70], interview, 1988, *FAOHC*

Spear, Moncrieff J. [US Consul-General, Nha Trang, S. Vietnam, 1973–5], interview, 1993, *FAOHC*

Special Committee [of the US Congress] on Un-American Activities (1938–1944). Investigation of Un-American Propaganda Activities in the United States. Appendix – Part VII. Report on the Axis Front Movement in the United States, Washington: GPO, 1943

Srodes, James, *Allen Dulles: Master of spies*, Washington, DC: Regnery, 1999

Stephenson, James, *Losing the Golden Hour: An insider's view of Iraq's reconstruction*, Washington, DC: Potomac Books, 2007

Stern, Thomas [Administrative Counselor, US Embassy Bonn, 1965–9], interview, 1993, *FAOHC*

Stockwell, John, *In Search of Enemies: A CIA story*, London: Futura, 1979

Summerhayes, David [Consul-general, political counsellor, British embassy, Buenos Aires, 1965–70], interview, undated, *BDOHP*

Sweden and Jewish Assets [the final report of an official commission appointed by the Swedish MFA in 1997] (Swedish Ministry of Foreign Affairs: Stockholm, 3 Mar. 1999)

Talmon, Stefan, 'Diplomacy under occupation: the status of diplomatic missions in occupied Iraq', *Anuario Mexicano de Derecho Internacional*, vol. 6, 2006, pp. 461–511

Taylor, Gen. Maxwell D. [Ambassador, Saigon, 1964–5], interview, 1981, *FAOHC*

Taylor, Philip M., *War and the Media: Propaganda and persuasion in the Gulf War*, Manchester and New York: Manchester University Press, 1992

Tomseth, Victor L., 'Crisis after crisis: Embassy Tehran, 1979', in Joseph G. Sullivan ed. *Embassies under Siege: Personal accounts by diplomats on the front line*, Washington and London: Brassey's, 1995

Toon, Malcolm [Ambassador, Moscow, 1976–9], interview, 9 June 1989, *FAOHC*

Trevelyan, Humphrey, *The Middle East in Revolution*, London: Macmillan, 1970

UN Conference on Diplomatic Intercourse and Immunities, Vienna 2 March–14 April 1961. Official Records. Vol. I: Summary Records of Plenary Meetings and of Meetings of the Committee of the Whole, A/Conf.20/14 (Geneva, 1962), available at: http://untreaty.un.org/cod/diplomaticconferences/diplintercourse-1961/vol/english/vol_I_e.pdf

US Dept. of State, *FRUS, 1917*. Supplement 1, The World War, Washington, DC: GPO, 1917 http://digital.library.wisc.edu/1711.dl/FRUS.FRUS1917Supp01v01

—*FRUS, 1936*. Vol. III: The Near East and Africa, Washington, DC: GPO, 1936, available at: http://digital.library.wisc.edu/1711.dl/FRUS.FRUS1936v03

—*FRUS, 1939*. Vol. I: General, Washington, DC: GPO, 1939, available at: http://digital.library.wisc.edu/1711.dl/FRUS.FRUS1939v01

—*FRUS, 1940*. Vol. I: General, Washington, DC: GPO, 1940, available at: http://digital.library.wisc.edu/1711.dl/FRUS.FRUS1940v01

—*FRUS, 1940*. Vol. III: The British Commonwealth, the Soviet Union, the Near East and Africa, Washington, DC: GPO, 1940, available at: http://digital.library.wisc.edu/1711.dl/FRUS.FRUS1940v03

—*FRUS, 1940*. Vol. IV: The Far East, Washington, DC: GPO, 1940, available at: http://digital.library.wisc.edu/1711.dl/FRUS.FRUS1940v04

—*FRUS, 1941*. Vol. I: General, The Soviet Union, Washington, DC: GPO, 1941, available at: http://digital.library.wisc.edu/1711.dl/FRUS.FRUS1941v01

—*FRUS, 1941*. Vol. II: Europe, Washington, DC: GPO, 1941, available at: http://digital.library.wisc.edu/1711.dl/FRUS.FRUS1941v02

—*FRUS, 1942*. Vol. I: General, the British Commonwealth, the Far East, Washington, DC: GPO, 1942, available at: http://digital.library.wisc.edu/1711.dl/FRUS.FRUS1942v01

—*FRUS, 1942*. Vol. V: The American Republics, Washington, DC: GPO, 1942, available at: http://digital.library.wisc.edu/1711.dl/FRUS.FRUS1942v05

—*FRUS, 1943*. Vol. I: General, Washington, DC: GPO, 1943, available at: http://digital.library.wisc.edu/1711.dl/FRUS.FRUS1943v01

—*FRUS, 1943*. Vol. II: Europe, Washington, DC: GPO, 1943, available at: http://digital.library.wisc.edu/1711.dl/FRUS.FRUS1943v02

—*FRUS, 1944*. Vol. IV: Europe, Washington, DC: GPO, 1944, available at: http://digital.library.wisc.edu/1711.dl/FRUS.FRUS1944v04

—7 FAM [Foreign Affairs Manual] 1000: Protection of Foreign Interests and Third Country Protecting Power, available at: http://www.state.gov/m/a/dir/regs/fam/07fam/c22711.htm

Urban, Mark, *UK Eyes Alpha: Inside British Intelligence*, London and Boston: Faber and Faber, 1996

Walden, George, *Lucky George: Memoirs of an anti-politician*, London: Allen Lane, The Penguin Press, 1999

Wark, Wesley K., 'Three military attachés at Berlin in the 1930s', *The International History Review*, vol. 9, (4), November 1987

Wicquefort, Abraham de, *The Embassador and His Functions*, trans. John Digby, London: Bernard Lintott, 1716; first published, in French, in 1680–81

Williams, E. S., *Cold War, Hot Seat: A Western defence attaché in the Soviet Union*, London: Robert Hale, 2000

Wolter, Tim, *POW Baseball in World War II: The national pastime behind barbed Wire*, Jefferson, NC: McFarland, 2002

Wood, A. C., 'The English embassy at Constantinople, 1660–1762', *The English Historical Review*, vol. XL, 1925

Wood, Sir Michael, Second statement by: 'The rights and responsibilities of occupying powers', 28 January 2010, available at: http://www.iraqinquiry.org.uk/media/44055/wood-statement-occupying-powers.pdf

Wright, Peter, *Spycatcher: The candid autobiography of a senior intelligence officer*, Richmond, Victoria: William Heinemann Australia, 1987

Wylie, Neville, 'Protecting powers in a changing world', *Politorbis*, no. 40, 1/2006

—'SOE and the neutrals', in Mark Seaman ed. *Special Operations Executive: A new instrument of war*, London and New York: Routledge, 2006

Young, John W., *Twentieth-Century Diplomacy: A case study of British practice, 1963–1976*, Cambridge: Cambridge University Press, 2008

Index

www.ingramcontent.com/pod-product-compliance
Lightning Source LLC
Chambersburg PA
CBHW050434280326
41932CB00013BA/2106

* 9 7 8 1 4 4 1 1 8 0 0 7 0 *